W9-BYK-522

James Meredith

James Meredith

Warrior and the America That Created Him

Meredith Coleman McGee

Foreword by Isao Fujimoto

 PRAEGER

AN IMPRINT OF ABC-CLIO, LLC
Santa Barbara, California • Denver, Colorado • Oxford, England

Library of Congress Cataloging-in-Publication Data

McGee, Meredith Coleman.
    James Meredith : warrior and the America that created him / Meredith Coleman McGee.
        pages cm
    Includes bibliographical references and index.
    ISBN 978–0–313–39739–4 (hardback) — ISBN 978–0–313–39740–0 (ebook) 1. Meredith, James, 1933– 2. University of Mississippi—Students—Biography. 3. African American college students—Mississippi—Biography. 4. University of Mississippi—History—20th century. 5. African Americans—Civil rights—Southern States—History—20th century. 6. Civil rights movements—Southern States—History—20th century. 7. United States—Race relations. I. Title.
LD3412.9.M38   2013
378.76283—dc23   2012044719

ISBN: 978–0–313–39739–4
EISBN: 978–0–313–39740–0

17 16 15 14 13   1 2 3 4 5

This book is also available on the World Wide Web as an eBook.
Visit www.abc-clio.com for details.

Praeger
An Imprint of ABC-CLIO, LLC

ABC-CLIO, LLC
130 Cremona Drive, P.O. Box 1911
Santa Barbara, California 93116-1911

This book is printed on acid-free paper (∞)

Manufactured in the United States of America

This book is dedicated to the memory of the interview participants who have journeyed to the hereafter: Hattie Meredith Dates, Ollie Patterson, Sean Devlin, Kendrick Portis, Jimmie L. Stokes, Charles W. Tisdale, Dr. George Harmon, and Thelma Meredith Franklin. In memory of my best friend, Belinda C. L. White; her oldest sister, Sandra R. Jefferson; my oldest brother, Robert J. Coleman II; my god-sister Treda Beasley; and my cousin Dr. Joseph H. Meredith. In loving memory of Mrs. Luana Clayton, who edited the early draft of my manuscript and became my friend and advisor; she was also the former English teacher of my aunts, Miriam Meredith, Mary June Meredith, and Mary Meredith. To Walter Liddell, Thomas and Ethel Roach, Helen Gray, Willie and Mary Evelyn Scott, Ellen Means, Mary Holmes, Harrison Hilliard, Bracey Beasley Sr., Bracey Beasley Jr., Christell McGee Wilson, Odessa McGee, Fred McGee Sr., Fred McGee Jr., Granny (Susie Haywood Ephraim), Mama Tina, Mama Annie, Petrel, Sonny, and Dear (Bernice Morris).

Journey of Influence
By Meredith Coleman McGee

History precedes life's journeys.
The past is the stem of one's path.
Every individual takes his or her place in this life.
Some grab life by the throat,
and push justice into its heart,
and shoves spirit and righteousness in this world,
and shakes things up,
and moves mountains.
Stories of these movers awaken generations,
and influences the future.
The world holds many stories,
be implored to learn the great ones.

Contents

Foreword

Meredith C. McGee tells an incredible story of a remarkable American. James H. Meredith persevered to attain social justice. His goal was to end white supremacy by attacking the color barrier at the college level in his home state of Mississippi. His overall goal was not just to win the battle of gaining entrance into the University of Mississippi but to win the war against white supremacy. He persisted despite being criticized, misunderstood, and shot.

Meredith's rage against injustice came out of his family's experience of humiliation under the tentacles of white supremacy. But his rage was channeled into constructive action that was strategic, drawing on his understanding of what it took to avert the deadly reaction of bigots and the timing necessary to take advantage of the dawning possibilities opening up in America.

Others who preceded James H. Meredith's efforts to open up colleges in Mississippi encountered catastrophic results.

Clennon King who applied for entrance into Ole Miss in 1958 was labeled mentally insane and committed to a mental institution.

Clyde Kennard who in 1959 attempted entry into Mississippi Southern was sentenced on a trumped-up charge to serve seven years in the state penitentiary and died of cancer with a criminal record that he did not deserve.

In the case for a more equitable jury selection system in Mississippi, the challenger, Mack Charles Parker, was lynched before the case went to trial.

Realizing the lessons of such previous efforts to break through Jim Crow barriers, Meredith understood the realities of the risks involved and what it meant to bear the brunt of acting alone. He recognized the importance of having the support of the entire black community and timing his action when the possibilities for support appeared nationally. Thus, on the day after John F. Kennedy was inaugurated, Meredith applied for admission to attend Ole Miss.

Though this book focuses on the person and actions of James Meredith, this is more than the story of a single fighter for justice. Meredith C. McGee brings to life scores of people who inspired or supported James Meredith. These include figures like Stokely Carmichael and Martin Luther King Jr. who rallied to continue the Walk Against Fear after Meredith was shot in Hernando, Mississippi. Other personalities who appear are part of a vast network of fighters for justice and equity. These include Ralph Bunche, Unita Blackwell, Aaron Henry, Fannie Lou Hamer, Charles Sherrod, Minniejean Brown, and numerous community and grassroots organizations including the Rural Development Leadership Network of which Meredith C. McGee herself is a part.

For his actions and stands, James H. Meredith has been subjected to being misunderstood and tarnished by falsehoods. Some examples include accusations that he was against a holiday for Martin Luther King Jr. and that he opposed minimum wage laws. Meredith did not oppose a holiday for MLK. Rather, he opposed the MLK Commission promoting nonviolence as a theory for change. Regarding the minimum wage, Meredith said it was the worst thing that ever happened to poor people. Given this reality, Meredith saw low-wage jobs and a legislated federal minimum wage rate as a means of perpetuating poverty and removing moral sanctions for employers to pay a living wage. Such differences of selective misinterpretation add to the difficulty of appreciating the contributions of James H. Meredith as an advocate for social change.

What make the life and actions of James H. Meredith vibrant and controversial are his efforts for a more complete recognition and liberation of Afro Americans in this country. His goal was not just to settle for integration but to advocate for equality, and not just for equality of rights and treatment but equality in terms of being viable, economically strong,

and participating citizens. Meredith C. McGee adds greatly to our understanding of the contribution of a "warrior made by America."

Isao Fujimoto, PhD
Rural Development Leadership Network Institute
UC Davis

Acknowledgments

I thank my uncle, James H. Meredith, who envisioned a better America for all of its citizens. Much love to my mother, Hazel Meredith Hall, whose children's book *My Brother J-Boy* gave birth to this project. I would like to extend my appreciation to my fathers: Robert J. Coleman, a former Marine and the author of *TAATA: Time and After Time Ahead*; and Charlie F. Hall, a former Air Force sergeant, who is now deceased.

I must pay homage to Dorothy Mayes James, a Memphis, Tennessee, schoolteacher, who after learning that I was quite versed on the subject suggested I write a book on my uncle for an adult audience. Hats off to my grandfathers—Joseph J. Coleman, Moses A. Meredith, John Sealey, Dave Suddeth, Coleman Weathersby, and Pleasant Thomas—and to my grandmothers Beulah Mae and Roxie Mariah, whom these men loved.

Much love to the 60 people I interviewed and the dozens of others who I consulted when I was gathering research for this book. Special thanks to my cousin Ronald Patterson, who marked and read the early manuscript drafts repeatedly with all of its inconsistencies and errors; my cousins Theatrice Meredith, Sheila Griffin, and Susanne Lowe for their genealogy research assistance; and my aunts, uncles, and cousins who shared their invaluable stories, research documents, and rare family photographs. I want to thank Dr. Isao Fujimoto, my former instructor at UC Davis, for the foreword. I extend my appreciation to Kathleen Supernaw, Rural Fellow, Rural Development Leadership Network, for editing my manuscript and recommending that I add a genealogy chart as a guide to readers; many thanks to Sara Davidson and Africa Houston, who helped me contact interview participants from Oxford, Mississippi, and to the book acquisition editors who offered priceless advice, constructive criticism, and encouragement.

_____ CHAPTER 1 _____

Family Roots of a Warrior

Second Reconstruction icon, James Howard Meredith, named simply the initials J.H. at birth, was born on June 25, 1933, to Moses and Roxie Meredith in Kosciusko, Attala County, Mississippi. Mississippi was the 20th state to join the Union in 1817, and Attala County was formed in 1833 with 500 square miles of land formerly owned by the Choctaw Nation.

The Merediths were mixed with Choctaw, Scottish Irish, and African blood. The Chickasaw, Choctaw, and Natchez Indian tribes became the first settlers in the present state of Mississippi during the early 1500s.[1] The state was named for the river located on its western border. The Chippewa Indians, who live in present-day Illinois and Wisconsin, called this body of water _mici zibe_, which means "great water." The Gulf of Mexico is the ocean basin located off the shores of the Mississippi Gulf Coast in the southern region of the state.[2]

Mississippi is located in the Deep South, which was known as the Lower South (Alabama, Georgia, and Mississippi) during slavery.[3] At the onset of the American Civil War (1860–65), two-thirds of the world's cotton was produced in this region. Southern planters acquired insurmountable wealth from the production of cotton. Slaves worked in the cotton fields from sunup to sundown. While slaveholders were eating the fat of the land and living in luxurious mansions, slaves were given daily rations of food and living in shacks.

The county was named for "Atala," a fictional Native American heroine from a popular novel by French writer François-René de Chateaubriand. The evocative language and description of nature that he used in the novels *Atala* (1801) and *Rena* (1802) became a trademark of romantic fiction. He later became known as the founder of romanticism in French literature.[4]

The town of Kosciusko was named for Thaddeus Kosciusko, a Polish hero, who was a chief engineer under General Nathanael Greene during the American Revolution. Attala County was a slave-holding county, but the views of the founding fathers clashed with those of Thaddeus, who referred to slavery as the "peculiar institution" because he did not believe a civilized society should tolerate the inhumane conditions of chattel slavery.[5]

At the time of J.H.'s birth, life had only marginally improved for southern blacks, who were required to abide by Jim Crow laws, which was similar to apartheid in South Africa because it gave whites social, political, and economic control. Like colonized Africans, southern blacks were primarily uneducated, second-class citizens, earning considerably less than their white counterparts; they were social outcasts required to live under demeaning and unjust segregation laws.

The idea that whites were superior to people of color was so entrenched in society that some communities prohibited blacks from giving whites direct eye contact and required them to go to the other side of the street when whites were walking in close proximity to them. Blacks who resisted the status quo were terrorized, publicly beaten, jailed, and sometimes lynched.

Moses and Roxie were both descendants of the Choctaw Nation, which was one of the Five Civilized Tribes, considered so by white settlers because when they discovered the southeastern region of the Mississippi Territory in the late sixteenth century, Choctaws had log cabins, an established form of government, and other signs of civilization. Moses and Roxie's farm was located on land that had been ceded to white settlers from their Native ancestors, who had been in the present state of Mississippi for 2,000 years prior to the American slave trade.[6]

J.H.'s paternal great grandfather, Sam Cobb, was born in 1795, three years before the Mississippi Territory was established; he was a Choctaw chief who adopted a Western name. He served as a general for the U.S. Army under Major General Andrew Jackson during the War of 1812, which ended in 1815 when the United States defeated the British in New

Orleans, Louisiana. General Sam Cobb and his warriors had also sided with the French during the Indian wars.[7]

Indians, volunteers, and the Battalion of Free Men of Color were instrumental in helping to win the Battle of New Orleans, which was known as the Second War of Independence. It was fought to uphold America's maritime rights. Great Britain and America have never fought as enemies since that war. General Jackson was said to have publicly thanked the men of color for their help, but none of them received full citizenship or the land that the government had promised them. Similar promises made by America to Native Americans would be broken in the following decades. The freemen battalions were disbanded in 1834, and organized groups of blacks did not serve in the U.S. Army again until the Civil War.[8]

According to Native legend, the Choctaws and the Chickasaws were a remnant group of the Aztec empire who migrated to the American South in the sixteenth century from Mexico after the Spanish Empire collapsed. The Choctaws, Seminoles, Chickasaw, and the other tribes in the present southern U.S. region fought off white settlement during the era of Hernando de Soto. De Soto lost the battle with Chief Tascalusa, the leader of the Choctaw Nation in 1540.[9] However, by the middle of the century, various diseases were spread to the Natives from their contact with the Spaniards, which wiped out 70 to 90 percent of the Native population.[10]

The Choctaws signed a series of treaties with the United States from 1801 to 1830 that ceded 32 million acres of their land and relocated most of them to Indian Territory, which is present-day Oklahoma. Some 4,000 Choctaws remained in Mississippi hoping to obtain land grants from the government that had been promised by treaty terms, but only slightly over 1,000 received the grants. By 1850, many of them had been swindled out of their land, forcing them to become tenant farmers and sharecroppers of the land they had once owned.[11]

Around 1830, General Nathan Bedford Forrest, who later became the Grand Wizard of the Ku Klux Klan, took possession of Sam Cobb's cabin off the Natchez Trace Road. Cobb and thousands of Choctaw warriors hid in the woods rather than submit to the removal terms of the 1830 Treaty of Dancing Rabbit Creek, which was allegedly signed by numerous Choctaw chiefs at the Dancing Rabbit Creek site, located in present-day Macon, Noxubee County, Mississippi.[12] Treaty records reveal that a Samuel Cobb affixed his X to the document, but Cobb and many chiefs disagreed with the terms of the treaty.

In spite of Indian rebellions against the treaty, 15,000 Choctaws migrated to Indian Territory from 1831 to 1833, but Cobb and other Choctaws did not go with their relatives and died in the land of their birth. Choctaw migration continued from 1846 to 1903, and by 1930 fewer than 2,000 of them remained in Mississippi. Life was hard for them, because they had been stripped of their homes, resources, and assets, which exposed them to extreme poverty by rendering them low-wage laborers. In his book *Choctaw Nation*, James H. Meredith described this event by saying, "However, emotionally it was sad. Every material possession we had accumulated for over two thousand years was confiscated by the incoming white settlers."[13]

In the decades prior to the American Civil War, the Five Civilized Tribes became involved in Negro slavery. They were exposed to chattel slavery by white traders, many of whom married Indian women. However, without exception, most Indian slaves were held by white traders and mixed-blood chieftains. Some full-blood Indians owned slaves, but they did not aspire to have worldly riches because they were inclined to live marginally. An estimated 5,000 Negro slaves migrated to Indian Territory in the 1830s, but most of them were held by mixed-blood Indians.[14]

The family surname, Meredith, was derived from J.H.'s paternal great grandfather, Edward Meredith, a Canadian trader who married his great grandmother, a Choctaw woman whose name is unknown. It is clear that Edward benefited from the disintegration of the Choctaw Nation because he acquired 698 acres of former Choctaw land in Attala County from 1841 to 1846. Alberta Meredith was conceived by this union, and she and Sam Cobb gave birth to Ned. In the Choctaw Nation, surnames were passed through the mother. Hence, Ned became Ned Meredith. After Ned, the surname passed through the males.[15]

Ned was born in 1849. He was a Choctaw of African descent; his paternal grandmother was a Choctaw and his paternal grandfather was African. Ned was a common Native American name, which had an English origin meaning "Mine Ed." Ned married four times and fathered 14 children from 1879 to 1919. Moses's mother, Francis Brown, was born in 1865; she was a 22-year-old schoolteacher when she married Ned in 1887. Oral history reported that after their marriage, for reasons unknown, she was fired from her teaching post. However, she passed on her zeal for learning to her children, whom she taught reading, writing, and math at night and on rainy days.

According to census records, Ned's minor son J.C.—James Cleveland—who had been born in 1879 to his first wife, Ellen Franklin Meredith, was living in the household of Ned and Francis at the age of 10; Ned and J.C. were both illiterate. Though racially mixed, Ned and Ellen were classified in 1877 as white on their marriage license in Philadelphia, Neshoba

County, Mississippi, because of their Indian ancestry. After marriage, they moved to Cairo, Illinois. Ned returned to Mississippi with J.C., but his other son stayed with his mother's side of the family.

Francis Brown was the oldest child of Millie Brown, a former female slave of Josiah Abigail Patterson (JAP) Campbell, an Attala County slaveholder. JAP identified his slaves by age and gender on his 1865 contract on file with the Freedom Bureau, but he did not list their first names. Some sources list JAP as Josiah Arthur Patterson. However, family sources say he was named for his maternal grandparents, Josiah and Abigail.[16]

JAP was born on March 2, 1830, in South Carolina. He had a white family in Jackson with his wife, Eugenia Nash Campbell, where he was a lawyer. His father, Robert Bond Campbell, was a Presbyterian minister. He graduated from Princeton Theological College, now Princeton University. His mother, Mary Ada Patterson, was the daughter of Josiah Patterson, a wealthy planter from Abbeville District, South Carolina. JAP's maternal grandmother was Abigail Blair Patterson. According to family genealogy records, Abigail died in South Carolina in 1823 before JAP was born.[17]

JAP's judicial record was clearly arbitrary toward blacks, for he helped draft the Confederate Constitution and the Mississippi Code of 1890, which disenfranchised blacks by instituting voting requirements that included a poll tax and a literacy test.[18] However, he did deviate from his bigoted behavior once as a fifth circuit judge, by releasing a black child from an apprenticeship program when the child's parents proved they could take care of him. Other fifth circuit judges followed suit. Campbell was appointed by Governor John Marshall Stone to the Mississippi Supreme Court in 1876. He served as chief justice of the court from 1885 to 1894.[19]

A *New York Times* editorial referred to Campbell as one of "the ablest and most distinguished jurists in the South."[20] His early education is credited to his parents, but particularly his mother, Mary Ada, who taught all six of her children reading, writing, arithmetic, geography, and English grammar at home.[21]

Francis died around age 39, leaving Ned and 10 of the 13 children she had conceived. Ned married Julie Holton Winters in 1905; one child, Betty, was born to their union. Ned landed a railroad job possibly as a Pullman porter or a cook after moving to the Mississippi Delta in 1913, where he became a landowner and fathered his last three children—Hattie, Daniel, and John—by his fourth wife, Sarah Dodd Meredith, whom he married in 1911. Also in 1911, Moses had married Barbara Nash. Ned and Moses both fathered children in 1916 and 1917. Hattie

Meredith Dates recalled, "Popper used to sit in his chair, peel raw sweet potatoes with his pocket knife, and eat them." Ned died around age 72 in Boyle, Bolivar County, Mississippi.

J.H.'s maternal great, great grandmother, Caroline Patterson, was born in 1815 into the institution of slavery in South Carolina. According to J.H., his maternal great grandfather, Columbus, was the son of William Patterson, a founder of Attala County. Columbus was born in South Carolina in 1842; he was classified as a mulatto in 1870. His first wife, Mariah, was classified appropriately as an Indian in the 1870 census, but she was reclassified as black in 1880.

According to census records, some of Caroline's children were born in the state of Alabama to Duncan Patterson. Duncan was a native of Alabama and one of the founders of the Center community in Attala County. Duncan owned a large plantation and many slaves. He died at age 50 on March 6, 1862. Whereas Duncan and his wife, Elizabeth, were buried in the Patterson cemetery for whites in the Center community, Caroline and her family were buried in the Patterson cemetery for blacks.[22]

According to the 1880 census, by age 65 Caroline was a maid, living in a home with 20 people whose surnames were Patterson, McCoy, and Massey. J.H.'s maternal grandmother, Roxie Lee Hickman, was born on October 10, 1874; she was the illegitimate daughter of Judge Harvey Davis, an Englishman, and Arteal Hickman. She was Harvey's 12-year-old domestic servant in 1873.

Harvey had served as colonel of a Confederate militia during the Civil War. Arteal's family called her pregnancy rape; but in white society, black women and girls were fair game to white males, and the rape of a black female by a white male was not considered immoral nor illegal.[23] The 1880 census listed Arteal's name as Artilla. At that time she was living in a household with 20 people whose surnames were Beeman, Coleman, Dulin, Hollingsworth, Hickman, Kern, and Lee.

The sexual act took the one valuable possession (virginity) men sought in those days when they chose a bride, but things turned out in Arteal's favor. She later married, moved to West Helena, Arkansas, and had three children: Sambo, Will, and Kattie Hawthorne. In 1886, Arteal married Calain Winters. Marcelles was born to their union.

Oral history reported that Roxie Hickman was raised by her mother's sister, Gillie, and her uncle, Andy Lee. Roxie had a bond with her biological mother, but she adored her aunt and uncle, who raised her, and she remained close to both of them for the rest of their lives. Roxie was listed in the 1870 census as Roxiana, but everyone called her Roxie. Her children called Gillie Grandma Lee and they called her husband Uncle Andy.

Roxie Lee Hickman, 1874–1947, J.H.'s maternal grandmother. (Meredith C. McGee Collection)

Family stories revealed that Roxie grew up to be a beautiful woman with long, silky hair that stretched the length of her back. She inherited features from her white father, with whom she had no contact when she was growing up. At age 16, Roxie married 20-year-old William (Will) Patterson in December of 1890. He was remembered for turning the heads of his neighbors when he purchased the first Model T Ford in his community. Will and his 13 siblings inherited land from their father, Columbus. Will accumulated several hundred acres of land before he reached middle age but lost all but 40 acres during the Great Depression.[24]

According to oral history, when Roxie was quite young Judge Davis asked Gillie to bring Roxie to the road or porch near his office so he could see her, but walking past the window was humiliating. Roxie's children had ill feelings toward him because of the event. However, by the time Roxie reached middle age, she had a friendly relationship with her father and at least one of her white half brothers.

William "Will" Patterson, 1870–1937, J.H'.s maternal grandfather. (Meredith C. McGee Collection)

J.H.'s older first cousins shed additional light on the subject. Ollie Patterson said, "I remember Grandmama's daddy stopping by her house in 1929. I think he had a Model T Ford. For years after Gillie died Andy Lee, who lived near the Patterson School, walked to visit Ma' Roxie often. He often spent the night at their house, because, by then, he had a hard time walking." Blanch recalled that Andy Lee had a white beard and a long mustache and that Gillie Lee had gone blind before she died. Carrie remembered, "I met Ma' Roxie's half brother, who was white when we were fishing at the creek behind our house when I was a little girl." As of publication of this book, Blanch and Carrie at age 93 were Ma Roxie's oldest surviving grandchildren.

During the Jim Crow South, few whites extended general courtesies to blacks publicly. Roxie's white half brother socialized with her at her private creek, but he would not have been allowed to share a drink with her at a fountain shop in town where local customs prohibited the inter-mingling of the races and public policy discouraged racial reconciliation. Blacks and whites could not even attend church together, and they were even buried in separate cemeteries.

Four years before Roxie's birth in 1874, black males obtained the right to vote, but by the eve of her 16th birthday in 1890, the Mississippi legis-lature was revised to strip black males of their voting rights, and JAP, the grandfather of the her future son-in-law, helped draft this legislation. White supremacy and Jim Crow were powerful forces in southern soci-ety. Will became a registered voter prior to the 1920s and exercised his voting rights until he was too ill to go to the polls; but very few black males were registered voters or could even afford to pay poll taxes, while the masses simply could not read and interpret a section of the Mississippi Constitution, which was the literacy test imposed on blacks in Mississippi at that time.

Moses Arthur Meredith, who was known as "Cap" (short for "Captain"), was born on September 13, 1891, in an ugly Mississippi. According to family lore, as a boy he witnessed the sale of blacks on the auction block. Though the Thirteenth Amendment of the U.S. Constitution had abolished slavery in 1865, the Mississippi legislature had established quasi-slavery by allowing orphans to enter white-sponsored apprenticeship programs. Cap despised the demeaning treat-ment of blacks and he demanded respect. A younger white male once told Cap, "Call me Captain." Cap replied, "Why should I call you my name?"

Cap had brown skin, very light brown eyes, and was 6 feet 2 inches tall. He was darker than both of his parents, who were light skinned. His birthplace of Noxapater, Mississippi, in Winston County is home of the sacred mound site Nanih Waiya, believed to have been built 2,000 years ago by Indians. Cap grew up in a rented three-room house on a former slave plantation, where he and his family members toiled the land for nominal wages.

His first set of children was conceived with Barbara Nash Meredith, whom he married on August 19, 1911. On their wedding day, Cap was 20 years old and Barbara was 18. Cap and Barbara were blessed with five years to bond as a couple, because their firstborn, Emmett, did not arrive until 1916. According to Thelma, young Emmett, who perhaps imitated his parents, called his father Cap and his mother Bye. Although the cou-ple did not particularly love their existence in society, they were accus-tomed to southern culture, and their love and devotion to one another added balance to their lives as sharecroppers. They both grew up in rural

Attala County on the outskirts of Kosciusko, in the New Garden-Mt. Vernon Community, and attended the Mt. Vernon Episcopal Methodist Church where they obtained a formal education. He had a fifth-grade education, but it is not known how far Barbara went in school. In those days, academic activities, biblical teachings, and extracurricular programs were facilitated in the church, which was the hub of social life.

Cap was an excellent farmer who walked away from his job as a share-cropper at age 31 and paved the path of landownership for a new genera-tion to follow. According to oral history, one day while he was working he suggested to the white landowner a way to improve the crops. The land-owner replied, "Now Cap, if you want to be the boss, you need to go and buy your own land to farm." The next day, Cap looked for available land and soon secured a $1,000 note with Merchants & Farmers Bank (now known as M & F Bank) to purchase 84 acres of farm land in Kosciusko, Mississippi, which included a three-room shack on Highway 43.

Oral history noted that Cap and Barbara's baby, Thelma, was six months old when they moved to the farm in April of 1923. Cap's sixth child and third daughter, Mary, died on their farm in 1924 while an infant. Their youngest daughter, Miriam, was born on their farm in October of 1926. The family kissed the freedom of landownership, remarking, "Ain't God good!" Emmett (age seven) and Leroy (age six) attended school regularly, because they no longer had to abide by the tenant rules that kept children from attending school during planting and harvesting seasons.

Family stories reported that after becoming a landowner, Cap regis-tered to vote at the courthouse in Kosciusko. During this era, blacks but not whites were required to pay poll taxes as a voting prerequisite. At that time, fewer than 5 percent of Mississippi blacks were registered voters, and the only black elected officials lived in Bolivar County, a predo-minantly black county. Although technically speaking Cap's vote was essentially a needle in a haystack toward the betterment of his race, he exercised his voting privileges for the remainder of his life.

On December 18, 1929, Cap's sweetheart and wife of 18 years became sick. He drove Barbara to Charity Hospital in Jackson hoping to obtain better health care than the service available in Attala County; but at the onset of the Great Depression, health care had only slightly improved for southern blacks since slavery. Charity Hospital was located at the present site of University of Mississippi Medical Center on State Street.

In large sections of the state, many blacks were treated in crowded hall-ways or in basements.[25] On that gloomy day Barbara, who was only 36 years old, died while undergoing gallbladder surgery. Although Cap was deeply hurt by Barbara's passing, he was a devout Christian who accepted the will of God. He often said a simple phrase: "God don't make no mistakes."

In those days, substandard health care was a contributing factor to the short life of black women. Like her mother, Lugina, Barbara was middle-aged when she passed. Barbara's father, Ed Nash, was raising a new set of children by the time Barbara reached adulthood. Cap's mother, Francis, had not lived to be 40 years old either. She died shortly after giving birth to her last child, Clifton (called Cliff), in 1902. By the end of the Great Depression, 80 percent of black babies in Mississippi were delivered by midwives, while only 10 percent of them were delivered in a hospital. At that time, some midwives were sometimes ill-equipped to handle complications, which resulted in fatalities during the delivery process.[26]

Cap married Roxie Mariah Patterson on April 4, 1931. She was born on May 30, 1903, in Center (spelled Centre in the 1870 census), Attala County. Her parents were landowners, and she was the 9th of 14 children. Roxie was named after her mother, and her middle name, Mariah, was in honor of her father's mother, who was an Indian. Marriage gave Cap and Roxie a fresh start, introducing her to motherhood and giving him new love and his children a mother.

Roxie was the last girl and oldest of her siblings to marry. Most people in her generation married after World War I, but Roxie's father, Will, rejected all of her suitors before Cap. On her wedding day, she was 27 and Cap was 39. "I was an old maid when I got married," she complained, but Cap was a good catch, because he was a visionary, a landowner, and a man of means, who embraced opportunities; plus, he did not drink, smoke, or chase women.

Roxie gracefully assumed her responsibility on the farm and Cap supported her. His oldest daughter, Sister, said, "I was glad Miss Roxie came. She took the burden off me." At the age of nine, Sister had assumed the responsibility of cooking, cleaning, and taking care of the house after her mother, Barbara, passed, which was no small task. Water was drawn in barrels from the well outside and taken indoors; peas were shelled before they were cooked; eggs were collected from the henhouse; biscuits were made from scratch with flour, milk, and lard; and fruit and vegetables were preserved and canned for the winter.

Oral history noted that Roxie received a formal eighth-grade education at the Patterson School, which was founded by her father, relatives, and community residents. The school was located in the woods in a one-room unpainted, wooden structure off what is now called Ridge Road near Center Church of God. Roxie's older sister Caroline's daughter

Roxie Mariah Patterson, age 19, 1922, mother of J. H. Meredith. (Meredith C. McGee collection)

Carrie attended the one-room school too, and she recalled that the children walked across a log over the creek to get to school; they learned by memorizing and reciting sayings in class and on the school yard. The older children tutored the younger children and served as teaching aides. Family members recalled the following rural schoolhouse classroom/ yard saying:

Star light, star bright, first star I saw tonight, I wish I may,
I wish I might, I have a wish I wish tonight . . .
Roses are red, violets are blue, sugar sweet, just like you.
Here I stand on two little chips, please come kiss my sweet little lips.

J.H. grew up in the twentieth century in the Jim Crow South at a time when blacks were second-class citizens. His ancestors were the creators, benefactors, and victims of white supremacy. His bloodline included African, Choctaw, English, and Scottish Irish. Long before Attala County, Mississippi, was formed, those lands felt the Merediths' dancing feet, witnessed their struggles, and watched their civilization crumble. They were the heirs of oppression, yet the plight of inequality created a breed of brave souls who resisted white dominion. J.H., the son of Cap and Roxie, became known across the globe in 1962 when he became a warrior on behalf of his race in pursuit of equal citizenship rights.

CHAPTER 2

Path of a Warrior

J.H. was his father's seventh child and his mother's firstborn. Roxie called her son J-Baby, but his pet name J-Boy stuck. Everyone called Moses "Cap," so few people knew his given name. His children called their new mother "Miss Roxie." Like his older siblings, J-Boy called his mother "Miss Roxie" too.

The Meredith's home was a small wood-framed house, which had no electricity or indoor plumbing on an 84-acre farm, off Highway 43, in rural Attala County on the outskirts of Kosciusko, Mississippi. J-Boy grew up in a segregated and unequal America, during the Great Depression, which was the longest and most severe depression (1929–39) ever experienced by the industrialized Western world (North America, Europe). During this bleak period in history, the banks collapsed, placing the economy in ruins; unemployment rose from 3.2 percent in 1929 to 24.9 percent in 1933 when President Franklin D. Roosevelt took office.[1]

The Merediths were fortunate to survive off their farm crops, while Americans in urban districts were forced to live off food scrapes and water. In those days, people in urban centers in particular were dying from starvation instead of old age and chronic disease; some people were lucky if they could find food in garbage cans. Like millions of Americans,

Moses Arthur "Cap" Meredith, father of J. H. Meredith. (Meredith C. McGee collection)

the Merediths became delinquent on their farm payments, but they brought them current when the economy recovered.

American blacks were accustomed to problems that the Great Depression presented, because they were plagued by massive poverty after the Civil War, and many of their descendants have remained in this predicament. Discrimination, unfair labor practices, poor public educational systems, political disconnect, and exploitation were factors that kept them at the bottom of the economic ladder.

Cap was tall in stature, and his persona matched his height. He had a strong will and he commanded respect from others regardless of their race. His mother, Francis, named him Moses after the biblical character, who saved the Israelites from the Pharaoh of Egypt. Francis had instilled in Cap the idea that God would make life better for their race. She taught him practically every biblical story in the Bible.[2] Like Francis, Cap and Roxie taught their children biblical stories, and religion was the center of their principal beliefs.

Cap's two boys, Emmett and Leroy were 17 and 16, and his three girls, Delma, Thelma, and Miriam, were 11, 9, and 7 when J-Boy was born. From birth, J-Boy was the center of attention at home. His first steps, signs of teeth, and progress in general were celebrated by his family. Thelma fondly recalled, "J-Boy was a lap baby, meaning he bounced from one lap to another."

Roxie was slender, muscular, shapely, quite reserved, and tall. She was 13 years older than Emmett and related well with them. She was known to Cap's children prior to her marriage to their father as "Miss Roxie," because she was their first cousin's aunt and their aunt's sister. Roxie's older sister Caroline Patterson Nash was married to Barbara's oldest brother, Emmitt. Emmett was named after his uncle though a vowel distinguished the spelling of their names. The children had a long list of common ancestors because they were doubly related. While Cap's children and J-Boy called Roxie "Miss Roxie," the children from the Patterson lineage called her Aunt Sis. Similarly, Delma's nickname was Sister.

On the farm, Roxie and the boys did most of the field work and Cap worked in town at the Oil Mill earning $2 per day, but his wages dropped to 75 cents per day as a result of the staggering economy. Though small framed, Roxie was strong. She could pick 200 pounds of cotton; she was accustomed to field work for she had performed most of the gardening at home for her aging parents until she married Cap in 1931. During the early morning hours, while the children were at school, she would lay J-Boy at the end of the row in a basket and tend the crops. Their dog Spot would bark if J-Boy cried.[3]

Roxie belonged to Center Church of God, which was established in 1911. It was located across the street from her parents' home in Center, Mississippi. She traveled from their farm to Center on most Sundays to attend her home church even after she married Cap. Her father donated the land for the church site when she was 8 years old. According to church history, her mother, Roxie, and townswomen Mollie Luse, Callie Rushen, and Nealy Holden took it upon themselves to recruit a church following by walking door to door to facilitate home church services. When walking was inconvenient the women rode horses, mules, or in wagons to promote the establishment of the church.

Cap and the maternal grandparents—the Lees—of famed talk show host Oprah Winfrey belonged to Buffalo Methodist Episcopal Church. J-Boy and Oprah have several things in common—she started reading Bible verses before she was age three and he started formal school at age three when his mother enrolled him in Cook Private School, which was located near their farm on a gravel road in a one-room, unpainted, wooden schoolhouse. The Meredith children often read Bible verses at the supper table. Oprah's father, Vernon Winfrey, and J-Boy attended school together. It was none other than ironic that two Americans who never crossed paths but attended the same church on a dusty road would become Kosciusko's most famous citizens.

J-Boy walked to school every morning with his older sisters, Thelma and Miriam. "That boy was a little fellow, but he kept up with us; he was smart and he learned fast too," Thelma boasted. The teachers, Mary Carr and Luella Benjamin, loved teaching and inspired the children to learn. J-Boy excelled in all subject areas. By the age of four, he could recite his ABC's forward and backward.

Very early in life J-Boy developed a love for nature; he could identify the fowl, birds, and animals on the farm. He asked a lot of questions and had plenty of teachers. When he was two years old, his oldest brother, Emmett, graduated from high school at Central Mississippi College in Kosciusko. The following year Attala County Training School, which had previously ended at the 11th grade, added a 12th-grade curriculum, where the rest of the Meredith children graduated from. Completing high school was a great accomplishment in 1935, because there were 177,605 illiterate blacks in the state, which was very problematic because it is impossible for an illiterate person to understand a contract, a land deed, and to teach their child basic literacy.

The fall after J-Boy started school his mother gave birth to her third child—Everett Herman. Roxie's second child, Clifton, who was named after Cap's youngest brother Clifton (Cliff), died as an infant from meningitis. Everett called his mother "Mama" and his father "Daddy." The three surviving children born after him followed suit, but J-Boy and the older children called their mother "Miss Roxie" for the rest of her life. J-Boy and his siblings were raised with good old southern values. Their parents taught them moral lessons such as "Do unto others as you would have people do unto you" and "The Lord lets the rain fall and the sun shine on everyone." Cap's substitute cussing phrase was "dat blame." When he uttered those words, someone had ruffled his feathers. Though Cap and Roxie did not believe in sparing the rod, they seldom used one. However, a leather strap hung on the wall in full view, and the children had to pull their own switches from branches if Roxie got a hold of them.

Cap did not believe it suitable to strictly punish children because he thought severe discipline would destroy a child's will. He felt it was abusive to hit a child on his or her head. The couple communicated with each child concerning all family matters. Therefore, the children seldom got the opportunity to divide their parents, who made it their business to stay on the same page in the same book when it related to matters concerning their children. If one of the children went to Cap and asked for something, he would tell him or her to ask Roxie and she would tell him or her to ask Cap.

Roxie's favorite saying was "If a task is once begun, never leave it, 'til it is done, be the labor, great or small, do it well or not at all." Roxie used that saying to teach the value of work. Every child was expected to complete tasks and to do their best. She also quoted "Nothing beats failure but a try and you can't fail if you never try," meaning one should not be afraid to accept new challenges. The children contributed to the maintenance of the house and farm, and nobody sat around idle, as idleness was believed to be the devil's workshop. Cap and Roxie were conservative with money and resources, and wastefulness was unacceptable. A nail on the ground was salvaged, worn shoe soles were repaired in Cap's wood shop, and no one left a penny in the road.

Roxie often said, "Don't let your eyes get bigger than your belly." In other words, plates for breakfast, dinner (the midday meal), and supper (the evening meal) were expected to be empty when each child got up from the table. J-Boy and his mother ate quail, goat, and other meats, but the younger children were picky. If they refused to eat a particular meat dish, Roxie would not force them to eat it immediately but would sometimes cleverly recycle the meat and serve it in another dish.[4]

In spite of parent protest, during the 1939–40 school year Cook Private School was taken over by Attala County School District and renamed Marble Rock School. The school takeover was a blatant act of discrimination because a public school system took over a school which had been funded with private funds. When the school's administration changed, Cap resigned from the board of directors and withdrew his children from the school. Then J-Boy joined his brother and sisters, Leroy, Sister, Thelma, and Miriam, and walked four-and-a-half miles to attend Attala County Training School. The walk took one hour before school and one hour after school. Even though the journey to school was far, the children could not miss school unless they were sick, so they walked to school whether it was raining, sleeting, or snowing.

Cap believed in the power of an education; his mother had been a plantation schoolteacher and he personally was a math wizard. He could add the return for his cotton in his head before the employee at the cotton gin had a chance to work out the problem on a blank sheet of paper. Cap felt an education would give his children access to better job opportunities, since he once missed the opportunity to obtain a good job in Canada because he did not have a seventh-grade education. Like Cap's oldest son, Emmett, the Meredith children were expected to graduate from high school.

As Cap's oldest children were reaching adulthood, he was continuing to father children. Roxie gave birth to her fourth child and first girl, Hazel Janell ("Nell") on January 6, 1939. By then, 22-year-old Leroy was working part-time at Monford-Jones Hospital in Kosciusko in the operating room and performing janitorial services. Leroy and Sister had graduated from Attala County Training School the previous year, and she was enrolled in Rust College in Holly Springs, Mississippi, pursuing a teaching certificate. After completing her studies, she raised the standard from high school to trade school and acquired a teaching position at a one-room school near Sallis, Mississippi.

Leroy did not see a future working at the hospital, and he joined the army air corps in 1940, becoming Cap's first child to leave home. In 1947 the army corps was dissolved and the air force was created. Shortly thereafter, Emmett left home and moved to St. Petersburg, Florida, to live with his uncle Cliff. Emmett left his black Buick with his father, which J-Boy used occasionally to drive him, Everett, and Nell to school. Cliff, a security guard, was the tallest male in the family, at six feet five inches. Unlike his older siblings, Cliff was illiterate like his father and his oldest brother, James Cleveland. Cliff did not learn to read because his mother died when he was very young.

After graduating from high school, Thelma, like Sister, obtained a teaching certificate from Rust College. Then, Thelma accepted a teaching job at a rural one-room school in McAdams, a nearby town, became a boarder, and took Everett, a first grader, with her; he was recovering from a broken collarbone, which occurred when he was playing in the barn with J-Boy. On the first day of school, Thelma had repeated problems with Everett. "Every time I turned my back one of the children would say, 'Miss Thelma, your "bother" [brother] hit me,' " she recalled. When asked if he had hit a child, he would say, "I didn't hit him [or her]." Thelma concluded, "I think he just enjoyed hitting the other kids."

Thelma began to dislike her teaching position; plus, the school lacked the resources necessary to provide the children with basic instruction. "They [the school system] wanted to keep blacks dumb," Thelma complained. In those days, discrimination was one of the greatest problems with public education, for white elected officials allocated very few public funds to support black schools, and there was a prevailing attitude against the education of blacks. To make up for the school's shortcomings, Cap and Roxie encouraged their children to be the best they could be, and learning continued at home.

J-Boy's older sister, Thelma, remembered that when she and Sister started courting, Cap would play his guitar and sing a few phrases. "Our friends were entertained by Daddy's singing, but we hated to hear him sing. 'Poor gal sat on the road and cried, she didn't have no home and couldn't be satisfied,' was one of the choruses that I remember Cap singing," Thelma stated. "We would be trying to court and Theodore [Thelma's boyfriend] would say hush! we trying to hear Mr. Cap sing," she added.

At age 50, Cap became sick with sugar diabetes and stopped working at the Oil Mill. To help the family financially, Leroy started sending an allotment from his military check home, and Roxie took a job at a Laundromat in Kosciusko. While in Florida, Emmett married his high school sweetheart, Georgia, and they later moved to Detroit, Michigan, where he became a street car conductor, collecting street car tickets and selling tickets to patrons.

"Daddy and Mama's first home in Detroit was on Arndt Street. Their mortgage payment was $32 per month," Terry Meredith Street noted. Like Cap and his father, Ned, Cap and Emmett were fathering children at the same time. Emmett's oldest son, Marvin, and his younger sister, Nell, were 18 months apart, and Emmett's daughter, Barbara, and his youngest sister, Willie Lou, were close in age.

At age 18 on August 15, 1942, with her father's blessing Thelma married Theodore Franklin in Kosciusko. Sister married Henry Leake on the same day in a separate ceremony. Thelma continued to teach and Theodore joined the army. Afterward, Theodore and Thelma gave Cap money to purchase a lot in Kosciusko for them. Cap purchased the lot on their behalf, and acting as a contractor, he facilitated the construction of their new home.

As it turned out, Sister and Thelma disliked their chosen professions and like Leroy, they did not see a future in Kosciusko, so they moved to Detroit with Emmett and his wife, Georgia, while Theodore and Thelma's house was under construction. Cap completed the construction of the house, sold it and the lot, and forwarded the proceeds to the couple.

During summer breaks, J-Boy helped his father drive the family to Detroit. On some occasions, the family attended the Detroit Tigers baseball games in Tiger Stadium. Cap required all of his children to learn how to drive and obtain their driver's license when they turned 15 years old, but Roxie never learned to drive even though she did attempt to learn on a couple of occasions.

Like many blacks, Emmett, Leroy, Sister, and Thelma left Mississippi in search of the good life promised elsewhere. Black migration from the

South had begun after the Civil War and continued after the turn of the twentieth century. From 1900 to 1920, thousands of blacks moved to Chicago, New York, Philadelphia, Detroit, and other large urban cities in search of jobs and racial equality. From 1917 to 1918, 50,000 Alabama, Georgia, Louisiana, and Mississippi blacks arrived in Chicago. During World War II, black flight from the South exploded again, because President Truman lifted the discrimination ban for civil service jobs and blacks were allowed to work in defense plants.[5]

Back at home in Kosciusko, life on the farm was normal. Cap and Roxie had four children at home, Miriam, J-Boy, Everett, and Nell. In May 27, 1942, Arthur Claudell was born. When he arrived Roxie was 40, Cap was 54, Miriam was 18, J-Boy was 11, Everett was 8, and Nell was 5 years old. Every morning before school, J-Boy and Everett milked the cows and took the milk to the road where it was picked up by an employee of Luvel Dairy Products, a milk-processing plant in Kosciusko. Milk sales provided a small income to the family. However, cotton was their largest cash crop.

Sugar, salt, baking powder, and flour were a few of the commodities that the family purchased; corn meal was processed with their corn at the grist mill in Kosciusko. Roxie made some of the girls' dresses, and some clothing was acquired through a hand-me-down process where clothes were passed from one friend or relative to another when they were outgrown.

On the farm the Meredith's work load was harder, but they raised chickens and produced eggs, butter, milk, etc., while the family members in Detroit were mainly consumers. However, there were more job opportunities, lively black business districts, and far more options for entertainment in Detroit than in Kosciusko. In Detroit, Thelma recalled going to the corner store and buying live chickens which were butchered and bagged by a store clerk while she waited. Sister took a piece of home—quilting—with her. She became a master quilter, and she made perfectly square patterned quilts with coordinated color arrangements. Miss Roxie used old clothes to make her quilts, but Sister designed quilts that kept one warm and that were also very beautiful.

Though city life in Detroit had its advantages, it was not perfect. On June 20, 1943, housing and job conflicts between blacks and whites erupted into a race riot, which resulted from conflicts that began on February 28, 1942, when the first black families attempted to move into the Sojourner Truth Housing Project. According to historian Lerone Bennett Jr., 25 blacks and 9 whites were killed and 461 people were injured before federal troops restored order. "People burned down houses and businesses that year. I didn't go to work, because I was afraid," Thelma said, "Emmett did not miss a day of work during the riots; he went back and forth from work and home unharmed."

Detroit blacks had a different attitude about race in America. However, on the farm, life was pretty simple. The girls played hop scotch, ring around the roses, hide and go seek, and made dolls from corn cob and used the corn silk for doll hair. The family listened to sporting events and variety shows on the radio. The Brown Bomber was their favorite boxer and hero. Occasionally, J-Boy and Everett went to the movies in town which was segregated requiring blacks to sit in the balcony.

Like most children, they were disobedient. J-Boy said smiling, "When I could get away with it, I didn't finish my chores." The children used to burst open watermelons and sit under a tree in the grass, relaxing for a while. If they were being mischievous when they saw their parents or an adult in the distance, they would all scatter and resume their work routines. Even though they were not permitted to play with the animals, Nell recalled holding their cow's tail and being dragged by the animal for quite a distance. She was so muddy afterward she had to wash up in their pond, and fortunately for her, her clothes were dried by the sun before she returned to the house.

J-Boy and his siblings faced few racial incidents growing up; however, on a few occasions the white school bus driver intentionally splashed muddy water on them as he drove by while they were walking to school. One morning a white student stuck his head out of the window and yelled, "Niggers." J-Boy retaliated and threw a rock into the bus, which hit the student. That evening, the student's father paid Cap a visit and Cap expressed a few choice words: "Don't mess with my children." No one yelled out of the bus afterward.

In May of 1944, Miriam graduated from Attala County Training School and was honored class valedictorian; that fall she enrolled in Jackson College for Negro Teachers (now called Jackson State University) and majored in elementary education, becoming the first child to attend a four-year college; she completed several years of school, but she discontinued her studies and moved to St. Petersburg, Florida, with her uncle Cliff and obtained a job at a dry cleaners.

On October 4, 1945, Roxie gave birth to another daughter, Willie Lou, who was named after Cap's youngest sister. During this time, J-Boy, Everett, and Nell created a business enterprise selling crickets and black grasshoppers to fishermen. J-Boy listened to the fishermen and discovered what kind of insects they preferred, and insect sales increased significantly. "Mama had to make J-Boy split the proceeds with us," Nell complained. By age 14, J-Boy became a golf caddie, earning 75 cents for every 18 holes, but insect sales had triggered his drive to earn money.

J-Boy's grandmother, Roxie, died in 1947. Blanch said, "Grandma Roxie was taken to Ashford & Turner Funeral Home on Bill Street in Kosciusko." Bill Street was the location of the town's black business district. Annie Lee Patterson Dotson attended the funeral and remembered that it was a simple ceremony, which included songs, prayers, the eulogy, and the viewing of the body. After the service concluded, the funeral home attendants closed the casket and everybody followed the hearse to the Patterson Cemetery, which was about a mile away from Center Church of God. Family and friends picked flowers from their flower garden, made bouquets, and placed them on Ma' Roxie's grave. There was no repast or a written funeral program.

Many of Ma' Roxie's children migrated from the South before she passed. "Uncle Sol [Solomon] migrated to Chicago during WWII, and some of the Patterson's migrated to Chicago too," Annie Lee Patterson Dotson stated. "He was the only son drafted to serve in WWII," she added. Bennie and other family members followed Sal to Chicago. During the next decade, Sal moved to Los Angeles, California, and his younger brother Bennie and other family members moved there too. In the years that followed, Sal and Bennie returned home to visit every summer for the rest of their lives.

In the summer of 1948, 15-year-old J-Boy and 12-year-old Everett were humiliated while riding the train to Mississippi after visiting Emmett, Georgia, Sister, Thelma, and Theodore in Detroit. From Detroit to Memphis, J-Boy and Everett rode in an integrated car, but after reaching Memphis, the conductor asked them to get out of their seats. A white couple sitting across from the teens told them not to get up because they had paid the same fare as white patrons. When they took the couple's advice and remained seated, the conductor raised his voice, "You niggers better get up now!" They ended up keeping their seats because there was no room in the colored car, but the psychological damage was planted.

In 1950 Cliff drove to Kosciusko to pick up J-Boy, who had just completed the 11th grade, and moved him to St. Petersburg, Florida, for his senior year in school. Miriam was living in St. Petersburg at that time, working at a hotel. Everett, Nell, Arthur, and Willie Lou were sad to see their big brother leave, but a part of growing up is taking one's wings in flight to leave the nest.

While stationed at Forbes Air Force Base in Topeka Kansas, Leroy met and fell in love with Cora L. Harvey. Cora recalled, "Lee first saw me at the Skating Ring." Cora called Leroy "Lee" for short; the spelling of his name had been changed by the military to Lee Roy. He did not seek approval to marry as some people did in those days. Cora declared that Lee Roy said, "I got a fine woman here and I don't need no approval to marry her." Lee Roy used to tease Cora and tell her, "You married me because I have a car," but Cora admitted love brought them together. Shortly after J-Boy moved to Florida, Lee Roy took Cora and his son, Reginald, to Kosciusko to meet his family.

Cora said, "Cap and Miss Roxie called Lee 'Ned.' Occasionally she called him Lee Roy, but Cap always called Lee, 'Ned.'" Apparently, Lee Roy looked like his grandfather. When Lee Roy's parents met Cora and Reginald they embraced them. Cap took Reginald outside in the yard where the chickens were running around, and he showed Reginald the cows and other farm animals and gave him a tour. Miss Roxie and Cora sat and talked as if they had known each other for years. "Lee's parents were just beautiful people!" Cora stated.

Cora recalled that Reginald, who grew up in an urban community in Topeka, Kansas was fascinated with the farm. "Reginald got up every morning at 4 o'clock with his grandfather and helped him gather eggs. By 6 o'clock in the morning Miss Roxie had food on the table: biscuits, grits, scrambled eggs, jelly, sausage, bacon, orange juice, and milk." At that time, there were two young children, Arthur Claudell and Willie Lou in the house. "Everett, and Nell were teenagers, and J-Boy was in Florida. Everybody ate breakfast together, but we were not used to getting up that early; they enjoyed our company and each child took turns taking Reginald around with them," she added.

Cliff enrolled J-Boy in Gibbs High School for the 1950–51 school term. During the school year, J-Boy (called J.H. in school) entered the American Legion Annual Essay Contest and accepted the task of writing an essay on the topic "Why I Am Proud to Be an American." He wrote and submitted an essay, and within a couple of weeks, he received a folder back from his high school's screening committee. His original paper was not in the folder, so he went to Mrs. McLin, his English teacher, to find out what happened to it. With the cooperation of Mrs. McLin, the school's Essay Committee had rewritten his paper and changed the title of the paper to "Why J.H. Is Proud to be an American." "My theme said I was proud to be an American for what it could become rather than what it was," J-Boy stated.

His teacher asked J.H. to sign the alternate paper so that the new version could be sent to the American Legion contest officials. He was angry that his paper had been rewritten and did not sign the revised version, but instead he retyped his paper with his Uncle Cliff's blessing and sent it directly to the contest officials himself.

The school's committee was infuriated that J.H. sent an essay directly to the contest officials, so they tried to get it disqualified; however, the officials said it was within their guidelines for students to send entries in themselves. In spite of the controversy, J-Boy won the contest, and two white girls won second and third place. The award ceremony took place the following Saturday. That Sunday, J-Boy (J.H. Meredith) appeared on the front page of the *St. Petersburg Times* standing between the two girls.

J-Boy was forced to change his name in order to obtain a Florida driver's license, so he chose the name James Howard. James was a common name in his family. His cousin J.C. had named himself James Cleveland after his grandfather who was Cap's oldest brother when he joined the military. In spite of the essay incident, living with Uncle Cliff and Miriam was very enjoyable, and the school system there was much better than the one in Mississippi. In St. Petersburg, many teachers had bachelor's degrees, and some of them were pursuing master's degrees, whereas the teachers at Attala County Training School primarily had high school diplomas and teaching certificates.

Florida had other attributes: it was beautiful, the paved streets were lined with palm trees, the weather was nice year-round, and oranges and grapefruit could be picked from the trees in the yard. Uncle Cliff often took J-Boy for walks through the parks, and J-Boy could use his uncle's car to go on outings on the weekends. In May of 1951, J-Boy walked across the stage at Gibbs High School and received his high school diploma, dreaming of conquering unknown challenges.

After high school, he decided that the military would be a fine career choice, so he went to Detroit and stayed with his oldest brother Emmett and his family in order to join the air force. He would not have been able to join the air force in the segregated South, although President Truman had written an executive order in 1948 requiring the armed forces desegregate. J-Boy was accepted into the air force and assigned to Sampson Air Force Base in New York for boot camp.

J-Boy grew up in an America, which deemed the mixing of the races unpopular on a national basis. Therefore desegregation was a slow and tedious process. The air force, in 1951, was the first military branch to begin desegregation efforts. J-Boy went to a technical training school in Silver City, New Mexico, called Western College and became a clerk typist for an all-white B-52 bomber unit. By then, he was an experienced typist, for he and Miriam had taken private typing lessons while they were living at home. Being the only black in the unit was not particularly pleasant, but life was not perfect for blacks in America during the middle of the twentieth century.

J-Boy wrote home regularly and called occasionally after his parents installed a two-party telephone line, which was used by their household and one of their neighbors. In other words, if a member of one household picked up the phone and someone was on it, he or she would hang up the phone and wait until the line was free. Like other rural Americans, the Merediths were catching up with the rest of the country, and electricity was installed in their house. However at that time, 80 percent of Mississippi blacks had no indoor plumbing or electricity.

In 1952 at the age of 19, J-Boy was informed about an opportunity to purchase 40 acres of land by his father, which was selling for $10 per acre that belonged to Cap's oldest sister, Alberta; she had remarried and moved in town. The land was near Cap's old church home—Mount Vernon Methodist Church. J-Boy thought buying some land was a good idea, so he sent money home so his father could made arrangements to purchase the land. The following year, J-Boy gave Cap some more money to purchase 15 more acres, which included the old Cook Private School site. The acreage was later reduced to 12 acres when Attala County widened Highway 43. J-Boy welcomed his father's guidance and when his father suggested that he buy the farm in the mid-1950s, he starting making payments on it.

Roxie obtained a job in Attala County Training School's cafeteria for the 1953–54 school year; she was an excellent cook and became a great asset to the cafeteria staff. Everett, Nell, Arthur, and Willie Lou walked to school every morning with their mother, who was able to communicate with them and their teachers on a daily basis.

After Everett completed the 11th grade, he got permission to complete his senior year of high school in Detroit. In the summer of 1954, he moved in with Theodore and Thelma on Pasadena Street and was enrolled in Central High School. Theodore and Thelma were buying a duplex home with Sister. They lived on the left side of the duplex and Sister and her daughter, Brenda, lived on the right side.

At that time, Detroit was emerging as a metropolitan city. It became known as Motor City and was home to the legendary Motown Records, the record label that introduced Diana Ross and the Supremes, a girl group from Detroit's Brewster-Douglass public housing project, as well as Smokey Robinson, Marvin Gaye, the Temptations, the Jackson Five which featured Michael Jackson, and many other black entertainers.

Detroit blacks were better off than those in Mississippi, where white on black murder reached historic levels over racial tensions. On May 7, 1955,

Reverend George Lee, a Belzoni, Mississippi minister, was shot by Klansmen in his car minutes after dropping Reverend Alexander Conner off on Church Street and First Street where Conner's car was parked. Both men were members of the NAACP's Regional Council and had attended a local chapter meeting that night promoting voter registration. After being shot, Lee lost control of his car and it crashed into the nearby home of Katherine Blair where he died.[6] In 1953, Lee became the first black registered voter in Humphreys County. Local whites asked Lee to end his voter registration efforts, but he refused.[7]

Even though the left side of Lee's face had been torn off by shotgun blasts, Sheriff Ike J. Shelton quickly labeled Lee's death a "freak accident." No autopsy was performed, and fear silenced most of the eyewitnesses. However, over two thousand people attended Lee's funeral which was held outside. Dr. T. R. M. Howard, a wealthy Mound Bayou, Mississippi physician, who was the president and founder of the Regional Council noted during the funeral services, "We are not afraid. We are not fearful. Some of the rest of us here may join him as courageous warriors and not as cringing cowards."[8] The following excerpt from the article *Blood Flows on Streets of Belzoni* add more light to this event:

> Rev. George T. Lee, 51, was killed gangland-fashion by shotgun blasts fired through the open window of his car by the occupants of another car carrying two white men and a Negro. Called the most militant Negro minister in Mississippi, Rev. Lee was No. 1 on the Citizens Council violence list of eight, was one of the original 92 (ten withdrew) Negroes who were determined to vote in the August primary.[9]

The Council's death list included T. B. M Howard, who hired a body guard; Clinton Battle, an Indianola physician; Medgar W. Evers, the NAACP's state secretary and the youngest individual at age 30 on the list; Gus Courts, a Belzoni grocer; Emmett J. Stringer, a Columbus dentist, and A. H. McCoy, a Jackson dentist and the president of the NAACP.

Many continued to fight for social rights in the wake of the murder. Battle went on record saying, "I'm here, not backing down." While Battle and others continued to fight for equal rights, Conner recalled that entrenched fear of local whites prompted some blacks to move out of the state after the incident.[10] A few weeks later, another black male, Lamar Smith was killed in front of the courthouse in broad daylight in the presence of witnesses after casting his ballot in Brookhaven, Mississippi. Sadly, no one was ever arrested for either murder.[11]

During the post *Brown* era, Mississippi blacks were struggling to become active in the electoral process, but Detroit citizens elected 31-year-old Charles C. Diggs, Jr., as their first black congressman in 1954. Diggs was a native of Detroit whose family owned a mortuary, a funeral insurance company, and an ambulance service. His father had served as a Michigan state representative in the 1920s. Diggs was active in civil rights and had attended a Regional Council meeting in Mississippi in 1955 urging citizens to participate in a national boycott.

Mississippi whites successfully kept blacks away from the voting polls; however, the course of the American South became to change when 14-year-old Emmett Till was brutally murdered for whistling at Carolyn Bryant, an adult white store clerk, while visiting his family in Money, Tallahassee County, Mississippi. Carolyn's husband, Roy, and his half brother, J. W. Milam, admitted that they kidnapped Till from his great uncle Moses Wright's house, beat him, shot him in the head, fastened a metal fan to his neck with barbed wire, and threw his body in the Tallahatchie River.

Till's mother Mamie, who was broken hearted after losing her only child, moved his body back to their hometown of Chicago, Illinois, and authorized an open-casket funeral to expose the torture inflicted on her son, whose face was severely disfigured beyond recognition. Till's murder was personal for most blacks. Arthur Meredith recalled, "I was Emmett Till's age." Thousands of blacks waited in line to view Till's body. His story was published in newspapers and publications around the world. The sight of his mutilated face angered blacks across the country. To add tragedy to the story, Bryant and Milam were acquitted of their murder charges by an all-white jury consisting of only male jurors.

However, Till's murder ignited the seeds of the Second Reconstruction, better known as the civil rights era. A new generation of black youth were emboldened to challenge discrimination, and they yelled with all of the conviction in their being, "Jim Crow must go," as they attempted to complete the unfinished business of restoring full citizenship to colored citizens that had begun during the Reconstruction era of the nineteenth century. Black youth wanted Jim Crow to go because it endorsed white supremacy, murder, violence, and all forms of racial prejudice.

Incidentally, music and sports prompted a limited form of race mixing in America, usually consisting of an all-white audience being entertained by a black sports figure and/or entertainer. In 1956, Frankie Lymon and the Teenagers' hit song, "Why Do Fools Fall in Love," was popular among white youth. However, racial prejudice was so ugly that on April 10th three members of the North Alabama Citizen's Council attacked Nat

King Cole, a black entertainer, while he was in the middle of his third song, "Little Girl," at the Birmingham Municipal Auditorium. After being rescued by the local police, Cole stood on his feet and announced to the audience that he had to discontinue the show to go to the doctor.[12]

Everett was aware of the dreadful conditions of southern blacks but he was impressed with the social standing of Detroit blacks. By the time he graduated in May of 1955 from Central High School, segregation was still being maintained in Detroit, but blacks were fairing well economically and socially, and had also made political strides. Like J-Boy, Everett followed in the footsteps of his older brother Lee Roy and joined the air force after high school. Everett was assigned to Holloman Air Force Base in Alamogordo, New Mexico, for his basic training. By then, more blacks were serving in integrated military units, but the stench of racism was alive and well as was evident by the nasty disregard by whites of black servicemen.

While stationed at Peru Air Force Base in Peru, Indiana, J-Boy was able to fellowship with more blacks, but racial tensions remained common. During this time, he met Mary June Wiggins. His relationship with her blossomed and in December of 1956, 23-year-old J-Boy married 18-year-old Mary June Wiggins in Gary, Indiana, in a ceremony well attended by Mary June's family and friends.

Miriam returned to Mississippi from Florida to complete her degree in 1955. She obtained a BS in elementary education from Jackson State College in May of 1957, becoming Cap's first child to obtain a four-year degree. Miriam married Allen Griffin, whom she had met while living with Uncle Cliff in St. Petersburg, Florida. One by one, the Meredith children were charting their own paths.

That same month, Nell graduated as valedictorian of her class from Attala County Training School in Kosciusko. No other student from rural Kosciusko had achieved that honor since Miriam had in 1944. Cap, Roxie, Sister, Thelma, Arthur, Willie Lou, J-Boy, and his wife, Mary June, attended Nell's high school graduation. The family members smiled with pride in the audience as Nell received her awards. At the end of the ceremony, Cap told his daughter, "Well done." That fall, she enrolled in Mississippi Vocational & Technical College, now called Mississippi Valley State University, in Itta Bena, Mississippi, located in the Mississippi Delta. The school had been formed in 1950 by the Mississippi legislature. Hazel majored in clothing and textiles. By 1958, Arthur and Willie Lou were the only children left on the farm.

J-Boy completed his payments on the farm in 1959 and owned 137 acres of land. He listened to his father, made sound investments, and amassed a sizable net worth early in life. No matter how far J-Boy traveled from his home state, he always returned because he was bonded to his land. J-Boy and Mary June purchased their first home and celebrated the birth of their first child, John Howard, who was born on January 19, 1960 in Tachikawa, Japan, where J-Boy earned extra money by making loans to soldiers at inflated interest rates. Mary June was a very classy women who socialized with an esteemed group of friends who called her by her middle name "June." She was called "Aunt June" by her nieces and nephews. Tachikawa, Japan, was a great place to live in term of race relations. The Japanese considered black servicemen simply Americans and gave them more respect than their white comrades did. In America, blacks were hardly worth common decency by many whites.

In December of 1960, (Nell) completed her course work early obtaining a BS degree; afterward, she moved to Jackson with J-Boy and Mary June, who had recently moved returned to America from Japan and moved in the Maple Street Apartments down the street from Lanier High School, where the famous black writers Richard Wright and Lerone Bennett, Jr. attended.

Nell's first job after college was working for Hinds County Extension Service as a 4-H agent. While working in Jackson, she fell in love with and married a football player who was a senior at Jackson State College named Robert J. Coleman. On December 14, 1961, their first child, Robert Joseph (Bobby) Coleman II, was born. Cap and Roxie loved their family and had a heralding passion for their grandchildren.

Like his older brothers, Arthur wanted to spend his senior high school year away from the farm. So he obtained permission to go to St. Petersburg, Florida, to complete high school. Cap said, "You can go to Florida after you help finish the house for your mama." Cap had predicted correctly that his wife would outlive him, and he used the money J-Boy paid him for the farm to purchase a half-acre lot at 227 Allen Street in Kosciusko. Arthur was leaving and Willie Lou was in the ninth grade. She too would leave in a few years, and Cap and Roxie were too old to manage a farm. That summer, Cap hired some men, who framed the house and Arthur serving as a carpenter helper assisted the construction crew with the completion of his parent's new home. Then, Cap transferred ownership of the farm to J-Boy.

The house was completed in 1960; it included two bedrooms, a living room, one bathroom, a kitchen, and was equipped with indoor plumbing. The farmhouse had been remodeled over the years and included 11 rooms, but Roxie and Cap would not need a roomy house in the future. By then, eight of their children had left Mississippi. Emmett, Sister, and

Thelma were in Detroit. Lee Roy, J-Boy, and Everett were in the air force. Miriam was a Florida elementary schoolteacher and Arthur was a senior at Gibbs High School. Nell was working in Jackson, and Willie Lou was 15 years old and had matriculated to the 10th grade. Cap and Roxie ended a chapter of their lives when they left the farm and moved into town.

The Meredith family was very close, and through many struggles they maintained an undying devotion to each other. Cap had correctly envisioned that education would be a vehicle that would improve his children's standard of living. He blessed his seventh child, J-Boy with the opportunity to purchase the family farm. Cap told J-Boy, "Well done." Of Cap's 10 children, the oldest boys, Emmett and Lee Roy, completed high school. Sister and Thelma obtained teaching certificates, J-Boy and Everett were pursuing college degrees, and Miriam and Nell had obtained bachelor's degrees.

J-Boy grew up, served in the first integrated air force boot camp in 1951, broke Mississippi's integration policies, became a human rights pioneer, and earned a jurist doctorate degree. He was inspired to rise in society by his father who taught him to feel superior and his mother who fostered his dreams.

Cap and Roxie had not imagined that she had given birth to a warrior on a humid June day in 1933. James Meredith's name was recorded in history when he became the first black to attend an all-white college in the state of Mississippi. Mississippi mothers cried when they saw him on television walking through the college doorway. Humanitarians worldwide rejoiced upon hearing the news that justice had prevailed, Jim Crow had been breached, and freedom was in the air.

CHAPTER 3

Public Education in America

According to Leslie E. Laud, public education in colonial America began in 1647 to teach moral values to children. At that time, the Massachusetts Bay Colony decreed that every town of 50 or more families should have an elementary school to ensure that Puritan children could learn their religious doctrine and how to read the Bible. The Massachusetts School Act of 1647, known as the Old Deluder Satan Act, established that the colonists would provide moral and religious doctrine to the population. The act stated:

> It being one chief object of the old deluter, Satan, to keep men from the knowledge of the Scriptures, as in former times by keeping them in an unknown tongue, so in these latter times by persuading from the use of tongues, that so at least the true sense and meaning of the original might be clouded by false glosses of saint-seeming deceivers, that learning may not be buried in the grave of our fathers in the church and Commonwealth.[1]

While only the elite class in Europe had access to education, the colonists extended public education to all children living in towns with 50 or more households. This commitment to mass public education was monumental in Western society.[2] Harvard, the oldest institution of higher learning in America, was formed by a vote of the Great and General Court of Massachusetts Bay Colony in 1636.[3] The College of William and Mary was formed in 1693 under the royal charter from the English monarchs William and Mary. In 1790, the Pennsylvania state constitution established free public education for poor children.[4]

The city of Boston created the first public high school in 1820. The city of New York established the first free public school for blacks, and six other schools started receiving public funding in 1824. Local authorities in Canterbury, Connecticut, were opposed to schools for Negroes, but a local Quaker named Prudence Crandall founded a Negro girls school. Local whites unsuccessfully tried to burn the school, while politicians used a vagrancy law requiring girls to receive 10 lashes of the whip for attending school to curtail school attendance. In spite of local protest and legal ramifications, the school continued. However, in the years that followed, educating blacks remained unpopular.

In 1830, southern states enacted laws forbidding slaves from receiving an education. Some northern states adopted similar laws. In 1834, the Connecticut legislature passed a law making it illegal to provide free education to blacks. However, in spite of the law, around 5 percent of the slave population became literate. A slave named Francis Fredric, who was taught to read by her mistress, recalled a saying among slaveholders, "The bigger the fool, the better nigger."[5]

However, laws forbidding slaves and African Americans from learning were not universally accepted. Some whites went to great lengths to ensure that blacks were educated. John Chavis ran a secret school for blacks at night in Raleigh, North Carolina. Unfortunately, Margaret Douglass was caught running a school for blacks in Norfolk, Virginia, and was convicted for her crime and imprisoned.[6]

The beliefs of Thaddeus Kosciusko for whom James Meredith's hometown of Kosciusko, Mississippi, was named clashed with southern ideology. After his death in 1834, he bequeathed 500 acres of land in Ohio to be sold to free slaves.[7] However, his bequest was not honored; instead the land was used to found the Colored School of Newark, New Jersey.[8]

In 1855, the Massachusetts legislature declared that "no person shall be excluded from a public school on account of race, colour, or prejudice."[9] By the late 1800s, blacks could attend some colleges. In 1888, Alfred Hampton became the first black to graduate from Antioch College, an all-white college in Yellow Springs, Ohio.[10] While blacks were making educational progress in the North, Chinese immigrants on the West Coast faced discrimination from 1850 to 1930 by California's public school system.[11]

A 1855 school policy excluded public education to nonwhites, but in 1859 officials opened a public school for Chinese in San Francisco's Chinatown. The Chinese community felt the school was inferior, so many families refused to send their children to it. The white community blamed low attendance on a lack of student interest and demanded that the school be closed because funding it was a waste of taxpayers' money.[12]

By 1870, the California legislature revised the school code and literally prohibited Chinese Americans from attending public and separate schools from 1871 to 1885. The Chinese had helped construct the transcontinental railroads during America's western expansion. However, during the economic recession of 1870, white Americans accused the Chinese of stealing jobs. Afterward, the Chinese were stereotyped and belittled for their ethnic appearance and religion, and were socially, politically, and legally ostracized. American workers developed resentment against the Chinese, who became the target of widespread violence.[13]

In 1906, when San Francisco's school board converted the Chinese Primary School into the Oriental Public School to segregate Japanese children, Japanese Americans and Japanese in Japan united and opposed San Francisco's school policies. The Japanese press claimed American segregation had reached international proportions. In an address to Congress, President Theodore Roosevelt reacted by announcing that anti-Japanese hostility was discreditable and would not benefit our nation. Subsequently, Japanese children gained admission to integrated schools and did not remain isolated.[14]

Discriminatory laws were enacted nationally against people of color. In 1864, the U.S. Congress ruled that it was illegal for Native Americans to be taught in their native languages. When Indian children turned four years old, they were removed from their home and sent to Bureau of Indian Affairs off-reservation boarding schools. From 1865 to 1877, free public education was introduced to the South for the first time, but the quality of education was inferior for blacks and Native Americans just as it had been for the Chinese in San Francisco. In fact, up until the 1960s, Mississippi Choctaw youth barely obtained a fifth-grade education.[15]

In 1896, the U.S. Supreme Court established the "separate but equal" doctrine in the *Plessy v. Ferguson* case, which rendered separate railroad cars for blacks and whites legal. As a result of the *Plessy* case, legislators continued to rubber-stamp the legal separation and discrimination of the races, and Jim Crow was born. In 1915, the South Carolina legislature voted to appropriate 12 times more funds to educate white students than black children. During that same year, a South Carolina factory established separate work entrances, working rooms, pay windows, and water glasses for workers.

In 1922, Mississippi established Jim Crow taxicabs. Clifton L. Taulbert, who grew up in Glen Allan, Mississippi, during the Jim Crow South, could not try on clothes before his parents purchased them because he was black, while white children could try on clothes in local department stores. In addition, Taulbert had to clean the bathroom at work, but he could not use it, because it was reserved for white patrons. Blatant social isolation stigmatized minority children and gave them grave feelings of inferiority.[16]

The American Revolution had been fought over the issue of taxation without representation, yet white society forced minorities to be taxed without political representation. Many legal and social battles were won in order to help minorities obtain a better education and the civil rights that were guaranteed to them by the U.S. Constitution.

At the end of World War II, the G.I. Bill of Rights gave thousands of Americans, including minorities, scholarships. A portion of James Meredith's college education was furnished through the G.I. Bill of Rights.[17] With the assistance of the NAACP, James Meredith would fight the longest educational battle from January 21, 1961 to September 30, 1962 ever waged by a citizen against the state of Mississippi. "I never wanted to win the battle, I wanted to win the war," James Meredith said.[18] However, he ended up winning a battle and fighting the war for the rest of his life.

CHAPTER 4

Returning to Mississippi from Active Duty

The 1954 Supreme Court desegregation ruling in *Brown v. Board of Education* mandated that black students have access to the same educational opportunities as white students. The ruling gave blacks the false impression that change was within immediate reach, but by 1960 fewer than 2 percent of southern blacks attended integrated schools.[1] In fact, they were continuing to study in inferior learning environments.

National black college enrollment increased from 124,000 in 1947 to 233,000 in 1961.[2] However, black college students had limited career choices because black colleges offered arts and mechanical studies, but legal and medical fields of study were not available. In fact, Alabama, Arkansas, Georgia, Mississippi, South Carolina, and Tennessee offered no legal and medical curriculums at any of their state black colleges.

Nationally, only five black colleges—Florida Agriculture and Mechanical School of Law, established in 1949; North Carolina Central University School of Law, established in 1940; Howard University School of Law, established in 1869; Southern University Law Center, established in 1947; and Texas Southern University Thurgood Marshall School of Law, established in 1940—offered law degrees. Likewise, pharmaceutical science was offered at only five historically black colleges and universities: Florida Agriculture and Mechanical College, established 1951; Hampton

University: School of Pharmacy, established 1868; Howard University: School of Pharmacy, established 1870; Texas Southern University: College of Pharmacy, established 1951; and Xavier University of Louisiana, established 1915.[3]

James Meredith returned to Mississippi during the spring of 1960, after serving nine years in the air force. He aspired to be a lawyer like his two white great grandfathers, Justice Josiah Campbell and Judge Harvey Davis, and to eventually enter politics. The problem with Meredith's dream related to the fact that he would not be able to study law in his home state, unless Mississippi was forced to integrate its institutions of higher learning.

Meredith sought to gain victory over discrimination, oppression, the unequal application of the law, white supremacy, and all of its manifestations because he wanted fairness, justice, and plain old common decency for him and his kind. The task at hand was not going to be easy, but he felt it was his divine responsibility to make the world a better place for him and his people. "Blacks are nice folk; they want to do nice things, but I want us to control, because we are the better rulers," he stated in a personal interview in 2008.

In 1938, when James was only five years old, Lloyd Gaines, a young black male, wanted to enroll in a law school in his home state of Missouri. With the assistance of NAACP attorneys, Gaines won the right in court to attend the University of Missouri Law School. The court ruled that Missouri must provide an equal education "within the state" for all citizens. Therefore Missouri was required to admit Gaines to the white law school because the state could not provide him with an equal educational opportunity at a state black school because there were no law schools in any of the black colleges in the state.[4]

Upon hearing of the 1938 ruling, Constance Motley, a junior in high school, who previously had no goals of attending college, made up her mind that she would become a lawyer. Her parents, Willoughby and Rachel Huggins Baker, were immigrants from the British West Indies. They assumed college was impractical for women, who usually were employed as domestic servants; her mother was employed as a cook for Yale University. Motley became a full-time lawyer at the NAACP in the early 1950s upon the request of Thurgood Marshall, and eventually would head James Meredith's legal defense team.[5]

The state offered to pay Gaines's tuition to attend a law school in another state to solve the matter, but he refused to accept their offer. He wanted to change the law, but he was silenced. He disappeared one night after leaving his room in the Alpha House in Chicago, headed to the post office to purchase stamps.[6] His disappearance, which many believe was an unsolved murder, has remained a mystery for over 70 years.

The NAACP's Legal Defense Fund attorney Thurgood Marshall relied on Lloyd Gaines's case as legal precedent when he argued for the plaintiffs in the *Brown* case—one of the greatest citizenship gains for blacks in the twentieth century because the U.S. Supreme Court struck down the "separate but equal" clause, which the court established in 1896 in *Plessy v. Ferguson*, wherein the justices maintained that separate facilities for blacks and whites were equal.

Overall, white Mississippians did not want their children to have to attend school with blacks. Before the *Brown* ruling was handed down, a speaker at a school meeting in Indianola, Mississippi, told the audience that he predicted that the Supreme Court would desegregate schools in America. Most of the parents were stunned to hear the news, but one grandparent could not hold his peace and asked, "You mean I have to send my grandchildren to school with niggers after we built that good nigger high school?"[7]

In 1957, the federal courts ordered the integration of Central High School in Little Rock, Arkansas, based on the *Brown* case. Daisy Bates, who headed the Arkansas NAACP, recruited students to integrate the school. Originally, 75 black students filled out school enrollment applications; but their families were terrorized by local whites, and the number of enrollees decreased to 25, then 16, and eventually to 7: Ernest Green, Melba Pattillo, Jefferson Thomas, Elizabeth Eckford, Minniejean Brown, Carlotta Walls, and Gloria Ray.

President Dwight Eisenhower deployed 1,200 National Guard and federalized 10,000 members of the state's National Guard to the school to ensure the students' safety. For the first time since Reconstruction, the National Guard was deployed to keep white racists from interfering with the civil rights of blacks. Eisenhower ordered members of the National Guard to attend classes with the students, but white students yelled insults at the students like "Nigger, bitch, and coon," making their daily school life a living hell. The taunting was unbearable to 16-year-old Minniejean Brown, who retaliated and threw a bowl of chili on the head of a boy who repeatedly called her "Nigger."[8]

Mississippi refused to give an inch toward desegregating its public schools. James O. Eastland, a Mississippi senator, openly urged for "massive resistance to integration."[9] A decade after the *Brown* ruling, neighboring states gradually integrated their public schools, and private schools popped up rapidly in Mississippi. Among a few of the all-white private schools created in Mississippi after the *Brown* ruling to guarantee the continuation of segregation are Jackson Academy, Jackson, established 1959; Bayou Academy, Cleveland, established 1964; Indianola Academy, established 1965; Copiah Academy, Gallman, established 1967; Benton Academy, Benton, established 1969; Parklane Academy, McComb, established 1970; Jackson Preparatory School, Flowood, established 1970; Hillcrest Christian Academy, Jackson, established 1970; and Strider Academy, Charleston, established 1971.

In August of 1960, James and Mary June Meredith enrolled in Jackson State College, an all-black college. James's sister Miriam had graduated from the institution in 1957. He majored in history and political science, a new field of study, while Mary June, a freshman, majored in English. A classmate of James Meredith's named Dolores Smith recalled, "James Meredith was an exemplary student, who often wore khaki pants and military clothes. I could see greatness in him during our school years." She recalled that Meredith participated extensively in class discussions. "He could answer any question that our teacher asked and he could hold a discussion concerning any event with the teacher. I felt he was destined to be somebody in life," she added.[10]

Meredith's nine years of service in the air force had broadened his worldview. He had lived in various regions of America, as well as abroad in Japan. After age 15, when he and his brother Everett were asked to move to the colored-only section of the train in Memphis, Meredith developed a hatred of Jim Crow laws. His boot camp experience in the armed services only added fuel to the fire. The state of America and race relations were big topics on campus, and he openly expressed his inner feelings.

Meredith was involved in college life and mingled with a group of intellectuals, who wanted the world in which they lived to become an equitable world for all. As a class assignment, he was required to write a paper for his philosophy class entitled "What I Believe." The conclusion of the paper summed up his uncertainty about the direction of his race:

> I hope by the end of this study I will have confirmed, disproved, or replaced some of my beliefs. But I must add that it is going to be hard to convince me that anyone knows the exact philosophy that I should believe. Evidently no one knows the right approach for me and my people to use in our struggle, because up to this time no one has led us from our miserable position.[11]

Meredith's paper entitled "My Philosophy of Life" summarized his thoughts on the political state of America and his view of the fears exhibited by blacks:

Why are men afraid to speak in a society whose very existence is based on freedom of expression? Why are men afraid to meet when the law says that freedom of assembly is an undeniable right? Why do men call good bad and right wrong, when they know its true nature? Is this freedom? My answer is no.

Negroes in Mississippi talk about their constitutional rights ... They complain that the law failed to dispense justice in a lynching case. The fact is that every facility of law did operate to the purpose for which it was established: To protect the white man and to provide conditions under which he could control everything around him, including the black man. This white man took the facilities at his disposal and made them work for his benefit. He intends to preserve all that he has in his favor and to add more, if possible.

We have just had an election. Negroes keep talking about what President Kennedy is going to do for the Negro. We talk about the new administration that is going to give us more voting privileges. The state of Mississippi has just put into its laws new restrictions on voting. Unless we do something ourselves nothing of value will be done.[12]

Meredith had watched the debates between President Richard Nixon and Senator John Kennedy, which was the first televised presidential debate in U.S. history. Presidential debates allowed Americans to evaluate the intellectual capacity of the candidates. Meredith felt that if Senator Kennedy was elected, his views on civil rights would advance desegregation in America. Meredith was also impressed with the debate process. He felt a debate team would be of value to campus students and wrote a letter to students and faculty suggesting a debate team be formed on campus.[13]

Three weeks later, the Jackson State Debaters Club was organized and temporary officers were selected. Open debate was also used in a secret organization called MIAS (Mississippi Improvement Association of Students), which Meredith helped organize. MIAS sought to improve life for their race, without ending up in jail; therefore members did not participate in protests.[14]

Before Meredith left his hometown of Kosciusko at the age of 17, he had determined that there were three things he wanted to do in life: become a man, run for governor of the state, and obtain a degree from the University of Mississippi (Ole Miss). He had large goals, but people with vision usually accomplish unbelievable things. Though he and his kind were shackled by society, the creation of the debate team and MIAS gave Meredith and others an outlet to debate current events and the inspiration to climb the hurdles ahead.

Senator John F. Kennedy (JFK) won the 1960 presidential election. Based on the civil rights agenda that JFK incorporated into his televised speech at the Democratic convention, Meredith felt the newly elected president would support desegregation efforts. JFK was inaugurated into office on January 20, 1961, and Meredith, acting alone, made plans to pursue one of his goals. He mailed a letter on January 21, 1961, to the University of Mississippi to obtain an application for admission. The registrar sent the application forms to Meredith on January 26, 1961, and the response said:

Dear Mr. Meredith:
   We are very pleased to know of your interest in becoming a member of our student body. The enclosed forms and instructions will enable you to file a formal application for admission. A copy of our General Information Bulletin, mailed separately will provide you with detailed information.
   Should you desire additional information or if we can be of further help to you in making your enrollment plans, please let us know.
   Sincerely yours,
   Robert B. Ellis, Registrar.[15]

Meredith asked the University of Maryland, Washburn University, and the University of Kansas to send his transcripts to Ole Miss. In the meantime, one of Meredith's friends, Beverly "Doc" Gardner, introduced him to Medgar Wiley Evers, who worked in the Masonic Temple on Lynch Street not far from campus in a striving black business district. After learning of Meredith's plans to integrate Ole Miss, Evers wanted Meredith's integration efforts to succeed and initiated a friendship. Evers suggested that Meredith write a letter to the NAACP's Legal Defense Fund, which was headed by Thurgood Marshall.

Marshall was a Howard University Law School graduate. Located in Washington, DC, Howard is the oldest historical black college and law school in America; it was established in 1869. Evers knew in advance that Meredith's application to Ole Miss would be denied and that Meredith would have to win in court to obtain the right to attend Ole Miss. In fact, Evers knew a lot about Mississippi's white power machinery.

Marshall misjudged Meredith and questioned his sincerity to follow through with his plan, which caused contention, but Evers interceded and kept the situation in perspective. Evers had excellent interpersonal skills, knew how to deal with multiple personalities, and was a master negotiator. The NAACP's red tape was just a formality, for in reality Evers had enough clout in the NAACP to get Meredith's case on board.

During the early 1960s, Evers was the leading man fighting racial inequality in the state of Mississippi, and he became Meredith's most significant ally. Evers had become an activist during the 1950s, trying to buck the white supremacy machinery, which was backed by the Southern Christian faction, who had used the Bible to promote slavery and was maintaining segregation through the White Citizens' Council and state legislators. Evers maintained a rigorous schedule and traveled extensively throughout the state, participating in voter registration drives, investigating lynchings, and supporting efforts that advocated social, political, and economic advancements for blacks. Meredith's integration of Ole Miss became one of Evers's priorities.

Born on July 2, 1925, in Decatur, Mississippi, in Newton County, Evers was the son of James and Jessie Wright Evers and the third of four children. The Evers family owned their own home and property. Jessie was of Indian descent, and James's father, Mike Evers, had been a free black farmer who owned 300 acres of land. Mike Evers's land in Scott County had been illegally confiscated from him by local whites. Blacks had to deal with blatant acts of discrimination, and the unfair treatment of blacks burned a hole in Evers's heart.

He served in the military during World War II then became a soldier in the race war after returning to Mississippi where death, beatings, threats, discrimination, and terror were a part of the daily life of blacks. Evers had made an application to gain entrance to the University of Mississippi Law School shortly after the U.S. Supreme Court ruled in the *Brown* case. He had been denied entrance into the school, but his efforts were noticed by the NAACP's national office, who appointed Evers Mississippi's first field organizer, a post that intensified his status on the Klan's hit list. Fifty-year-old Rev. Charles Dubra, the black pastor of St. Mark's Episcopal Church in Gulfport, Mississippi, had applied to enter the law school previously. He had a bachelor's degree from the University of Boston, but the state's board of trustees denied his application, claiming the University of Boston was unaccredited.[16]

Evers and Meredith discussed current events and analyzed segregation policies, for the events of the past were relevant to the future of the advancement of the black cause. On June 4, 1958, Clennon W. King Jr., a former teacher of Alcorn Agricultural & Mechanical College, now called Alcorn State University, attempted to enroll at Ole Miss. Alcorn was the state's second college and the country's first land grant college for Negroes.

Alcorn had been established in 1871 with the support of John Roy Lynch, a black Reconstruction congressman in Mississippi.[17] King was the first black Ole Miss applicant to show up for registration. When he arrived on campus, Oxford police were not quite sure how to handle the situation, but they were ordered to escort him from campus. Lafayette County police charged King with disturbing the peace and resisting arrest. Before being taken into custody, King was emotional and loud and pleaded for his safety.[18]

Upon the suggestion of Gov. James P. Coleman, King was taken to Jackson, where a lunacy hearing was scheduled in Hinds County Chancery Court. King's black attorney, Sidney Tharp, asked, "Why do you think a man is crazy just because he wants to go to the University of Mississippi?"[19] Tharp's question was not desirable; therefore the white judge threw him out of the courtroom for interfering with the hearing process. Several physicians diagnosed King as mentally insane; then he was confined in Mississippi State Hospital (the state's mental institution) in Whitfield, Mississippi. R. Jess Brown, a Vicksburg, Mississippi, attorney, and C. B. King, an Albany, Georgia, attorney, unsuccessfully tried to obtain Clennon King's release. Prominent black leaders Medgar Evers, Roy Wilkins, and Martin Luther King Jr. protested King's confinement.[20]

On June 18, 1958, King was released from the mental institution. His 14-day confinement sent a strong message to the community. King was, in fact, a thinker in a realm before his time, and he was labeled an idiot by whites as well as blacks for attempting to buck Jim Crow, but not even that slowed him down. He became the first black presidential candidate in 1960, and attempted to integrate President Jimmy Carter's all-white Baptist church in Plains, Georgia, in 1976. His father was a community activist and the former chauffeur of Booker T. Washington, who had formed the Tuskegee Institute in 1881 on an abandoned farm.[21] Following in his father's footsteps, King also reached high, for he envisioned change that America was not ready to render, which is why he acquired the title the "Black Don Quixote."

Evers and Meredith had also discussed Clyde Kennard, who unsuccessfully attempted to integrate Mississippi Southern College in Hattiesburg, Mississippi, now called the University of Southern Mississippi, in 1959. Kennard made several attempts to integrate the school. Mississippi Gov. Coleman offered to pay his tuition at an out-of-town school. However, Kennard wanted to attend school near his home to help take care of his aging parents. Based on the *Brown* ruling, Kennard, a veteran, thought he had an inherent right by law to attend any school of his choosing. The whites in Forrest County, which had been named after Nathan Bedford Forrest, a former Grand Wizard of the Ku Klux Klan, were harsher on Kennard than the whites in Lafayette County had been on King.

Kennard was forcefully removed from campus during his registration interview. As he was driving from campus, he was stopped by several constables and arrested for reckless driving and illegal liquor possession, though he had been sober all of his life. In addition, he was framed and convicted of those charges and also for stealing $25 worth of chicken feed. After his conviction, Clyde Kennard, a Korean War veteran, was sentenced to serve seven years at the state penitentiary in Parchman, Mississippi.[22]

Originally, Mississippi State Penitentiary was one of two prisons designated to house young black males. It had been established in 1900 by the Mississippi legislature, which had allocated $80,000 to purchase an old slave plantation, previously owned by the Parchman family in Sunflower County. During its early years, the state operated the prison like a massive plantation. In fact, in 1905, the end of the prison's first year of operation, the state earned $185,000 from inmate labor, the equivalent of $4.5 million in 2009 dollars. The prison exploited, dehumanized, and repressed inmates, and was characterized for its racial injustice.[23]

During the Jim Crow era, local police departments often included Klan and White Citizens' Council members; they were known for framing blacks, and nobody with any power cared. Kennard developed cancer after being confined in prison, and *Jet* magazine ran an article on him, while he was dying in prison. The article influenced JFK and U.S. Attorney General Robert Kennedy to ask the Mississippi governor, Ross Barnett, to pardon Kennard or be ousted from office.

Kennard was released from prison without a pardon and was later admitted into the University of Chicago's Billing Hospital, where he fell into a deep coma and died. On May 17, 2006, the state of Mississippi corrected one of her past sins when a Forrest County circuit judge, Bob Helfrich, exonerated Kennard of the false felony charge that had followed his name for nearly half a century.[24] The case is a clear example of how racism and the unjust American justice system were used to silence people seeking freedom during the Second Reconstruction.

Following in the footsteps of others who tried to end segregation in higher education, Meredith was another thinker ahead of his time. He wanted to end the system of white supremacy. His school writings pointed out that he felt blacks were in a miserable existence, but he had put on his armor and was planning to get the most powerful man in the world, JFK, and his brother Robert Kennedy on his side to prevent him from becoming a casualty in what would develop into America's largest insurrection on American soil since the Civil War.

Meredith opposed nonviolence as a theory, which was an unnatural military strategy; plus, nonviolent protesters often faced violence, which was the very reason he refused to participate in protests. He felt that protesting was not an effective strategy in the black man's fight for equal rights. His opposition to nonviolent movement strategies put him at odd with his peers, but to him nonviolence was "non-sense," since southern blacks who openly participated in protests were being violently beaten and murdered at an alarming rate by whites.

Meredith felt that black leaders needed the support of the entire black community in order to break the system of white supremacy. He noted, "Non-violence influenced us to give up our constitutional right to bear arms, and turning the other cheek and begging did not produce many results for me and my kind."[25] Like Lloyd Gaines, Medgar Evers, Charles Dubra, Clennon King Jr., and Clyde Kennard, James Meredith decided to challenge school segregation as a means of breaking the system of white supremacy.

Meanwhile, Meredith mailed a follow-up letter to the University of Mississippi's registrar on January 31, 1961, which reads:

Dear Mr. Robert B. Ellis:

I am very pleased with your letter that accompanied the application forms you recently sent to me. I sincerely hope that your attitude toward me as a potential member of your student body reflects the attitude of the school, and that it will not change upon learning that I am not a white applicant.

I am an American-Mississippi-Negro citizen. With all of the presently occurring events regarding changes in our educational system taking place in our country in this new age, I feel certain that this application does not come as a surprise to you. I certainly hope that this matter will be handled in a manner that will be complimentary to the University and the state of Mississippi. Of course, I am the one that will, no doubt, suffer the greatest consequences of this event; therefore, I am very hopeful that the complications will be as few as possible.

I will not be able to furnish you with the names of six University Alumni because I am a Negro and all graduates of the school are white. Further, I do not know any graduate personally. However, as a substitute for this requirement, I am submitting certifications regarding my moral character from Negro citizens. All colleges previously attended have been contacted and my transcripts should be in your office or on the way. I am requesting that immediate action be taken on my application and that I be notified of its status, as registration begins on February 6, 1961, and I am hoping to enroll at this time.

Thank you very much.
James H. Meredith[26]

Four days later Meredith received a telegram from Robert Ellis stating that Ole Miss had found it necessary to discontinue consideration of his application for admission. He was also advised not to appear for registration. Meredith was inherently aware that showing up to register could cost him his limbs, liberty, or life. In the meantime, he received a letter from the NAACP Legal Defense Fund confirming its interest in assisting him to integrate Ole Miss. Miss Constance Baker Motley, one of the first female civil rights attorneys in the country, became the lead attorney in his case.

Meredith was not going to be able to register for classes at Ole Miss for the 1960–61 second-semester term because the deadline for registration, February 17, 1960, was approaching. Motley assured Meredith in a letter that the Legal Defense Fund would provide him with the legal assistance necessary to support his efforts to gain admission to Ole Miss.

In a letter dated February 21, 1961, Robert Ellis enclosed the $10 money order that Meredith had submitted for his room deposit. Meredith sent the $10 money order back to Ellis and stated that he intended for the school to consider his application for the summer semester. Meredith obtained a return receipt for each correspondence he sent to the university. He then wrote another letter to Robert Ellis the following March and asked if his transcripts had arrived from the universities where he had completed course work, but Ellis did not respond immediately.

Finally, on May 9, 1961, Ellis sent Meredith a letter acknowledging receipt of his transcripts. Ellis advised Meredith that his evaluation of his 90 credit course hours was not in any way a determination as to whether his application for admission would be approved or disapproved. On May 15, 1961, Meredith sent a $25 money order to the director of student housing as a down payment for occupancy of one of the student apartments so that his wife, Mary June, and his son, John Howard, could live on campus with him. On May 25, 1961, Robert wrote a letter to Meredith denying him admission to the University of Mississippi, because the university could not recognize the transfer of credits from the institutions that he had attended because they were not members of the Southern Association of Colleges.[27]

In addition, Ellis stated that the letters of recommendations that had been written by black citizens were insufficient. The $10 and the

$25 money orders were enclosed with the letter. The closing line had a note of finality: "Your application file has been closed." Meredith and his counsel had to decide on a strategy to proceed with his efforts to gain entrance into Ole Miss without becoming a casualty of white supremacists. He had learned one thing from Clennon King Jr. and Clyde Kennard—he needed to be protected if he were to appear at the registrar's office at an all-white college in the state of Mississippi.

CHAPTER 5

Breaking Jim Crow Barriers

In January of 1961 after the Christmas break, James Meredith and his wife returned to Jackson State College, and his lawyers resumed his legal battle to break Mississippi's segregation policies. In the meantime, white segregationists began a campaign of intimidation to deter Meredith.

Meredith's family, his legal team, and Medgar Evers were all concerned about his safety. Evers maintained that an armed guard should be posted at Meredith's apartment and suggested that he never go anywhere alone, while others suggested that he always travel with at least two cars and that the car that he did not occupy be armed. Meredith personally felt that the best protection for him would be the enemy himself.

A black principal of one of the schools in Kosciusko was called upon to deliver an intimidating message to Meredith's parents. The principal insinuated that either James Meredith withdraw his desegregation efforts or suffer severe consequences. Cap and Roxie Meredith assured the principal that their son had their full support. As parents, they felt their son had as much a right to attend Ole Miss as any of the white students. Mississippi whites were professional terrorists, and the incident was a warning.

The fear tactic definitely alarmed Cap and Roxie. During the wee hours of the morning, Willie Lou, Meredith's 16-year-old sister, arrived in

Jackson with Cap and Roxie in their pickup truck to warn him of the principal's message. Although his parents supported him and had advised him to do whatever he thought was right, they concluded that he should proceed with caution and were cautious themselves.

According to an anonymous source, "One evening J-Boy [James Meredith] was run off the road in Kosciusko on Highway 43 by two white men, but they were interrupted by an elder black, who was a friend of the Meredith family. He bravely drove his vehicle near Meredith's car and pointed a weapon at the men and demanded that they leave." This incident was another warning, but Meredith would not be deterred.

Meredith's family in Kosciusko began to be shunned by people in their community. Some people feared that their white employers would fire them for associating with the Merediths, so they began to limit casual conversations and visits with the family. In spite of being shunned, Roxie continued her regular routine. She was a loyal member of and devoted fund-raiser for Christian Liberty Baptist Church, the National Council of Negro Women, and Veterans of Foreign Wars. Roxie and Emma Mae Jamison led the building fund efforts for Central Mississippi College when it was destroyed by a fire. The facility is now used as a community center for Kosciusko residents.

Roxie and Willie Lou supported the social advancement of blacks and participated in a local march in Kosciusko. As Roxie and Willie Lou walked through the streets with a small group of citizens, most residents sat on their porches or looked through their windows and watched them walk by. Several years later, while a freshman at JSC, Willie Lou participated in a mass demonstration in Jackson and was detained at the Jackson Coliseum fairground, which was being used as a holding cell, because the jail could not hold the large group of detainees.

Although many local blacks supported Meredith's enrollment process, some were afraid to express their support of him. People had mixed feelings, and some of their opinions were negative. Meredith's effort to desegregate Ole Miss was definitely not welcomed by most of the white community. On the other hand, he gained hero status among the younger black generation who saw him as a champion for racial equality.

Efforts to intimidate Meredith continued. One of his neighbors in Maple Street Apartments was asked by a large, white man driving a Cadillac, "Yeah, you that nigger trying to go to Ole Miss?" He replied, "No." "Well you tell that nigger we are going to kill him," the white man said, then he got in his car and drove off.[1] Meredith recalled, "The message was designed to intimidate my neighbors as much as it was intended to put fear in me." After the incident, some of Meredith's neighbors organized the surveillance of his apartment and designed a car-parking pattern to hinder the entrance of outsiders.[2]

Meredith acknowledged in his memoir *Three Years in Mississippi* the danger he faced when he was trying to integrate Ole Miss. He said, "Contrary to what people might think, the one year that I spent at the University of Mississippi was not nearly as dangerous for me personally as the two years in Mississippi before I was able to gain admission to the school." He added, "The traditional practice in Mississippi has been to eliminate potential troublemakers before they get a chance to cause trouble." During the 1960s, blacks who questioned the status quo were lynched or simply disappeared.[3]

Overall, very few blacks supported Meredith's integration efforts. About 100 out of 1,300 Jackson State College students supported him. "Ninety percent of blacks opposed change, they wanted things to remain as they were," Meredith recalled "In the '60s, a college degree guaranteed jobs for blacks and families would sacrifice to educate one child so that child could provide support to the family," Meredith added. The advancement of one or two family members was progress to many, but many did not foresee that eventually there would not be enough jobs for all the blacks with teaching degrees.[4]

Meredith felt that it was important to have solidarity among blacks concerning efforts to obtain equality in this country, but gaining solidarity was hard work because few people believed change was necessary or possible. To garner more support, Meredith sent a statement to Mississippi blacks and to organizations in the state. A portion of the statement is follows:

I wish to explain why I plan to go to the University of Mississippi because I want the people of our society to know my reasons ...

First, there are my constitutional rights. It has been duly decided that no citizen of the United States can be denied the privilege of getting an education because of his race. The fact that no Negro has ever attended the school in question indicated to me that this right to an education has not been acknowledged ...

The Negro has his own educational facilities! My only answer to this statement is that there is a limit to the number of teachers that can be utilized in the state and a greater limit to the number of preachers needed, in addition to the fact that not every young Negro seeking to gain a position of leadership desires to be a teacher or a preacher ...

Problems. The greatest problem we face today, as I see it, is to stop the trend of our young Negroes toward an attitude of hopefulness. This is a demoralizing trend and will prove detrimental both to

Mississippi and the nation if it is not stopped. It will truly be hard for others to conceive of the fears and inferior feelings that prevail among our people ...

Fears of the so-called Negro leadership. "I'm going to lose my job." ...

White position. Most white people to whom I have talked, and I have talked to all with whom I have had the opportunity—from the man who installed my telephone to banking officials, agree that Mississippi carries segregation to unreasonable limits ...

Finally, I plan to enter the University of Mississippi for the good of my people, my country, my state, my family, and myself.[5]

George Harmon, who owned Harmon Drug Store in the Farish Street Historic District in downtown Jackson, empathized with Meredith and believed that the higher-learning curriculum for blacks should be expanded. In 1947, after serving two years in the military, Harmon left the state of Mississippi to attend pharmacy school at Xavier University in New Orleans, a Catholic school founded in 1925 to serve the higher-learning needs of African Americans and Native Americans. "My mother and everyone in my family wanted me to go to Alcorn or Jackson College, but I wanted to be a pharmacist, and I couldn't study pharmacy at Alcorn and Jackson College and none of the white colleges would accept me as a student back then," Harmon said.

According to George Harmon, when he was a boy he hated field work so much that he would cry in the field; his mother allowed him to take a job at Courtright Drug Store on Main Street in downtown Yazoo City when he was nine years old. People in the community looked up to E. G. Courtright. They would say, "That medicine you gave me sho' did help me!" Harmon worked at Courtright through high school and he aspired to be just like his white employer, even though everyone said it was impossible.

Harmon's former employer helped him find his first pharmacy job at Alamo Drugs on Farish Street in Jackson in the late 1940s. Harmon also worked at Alamo Drugs and MLS Drugs before he hung his own business shingle on Farish Street in 1953. Harmon's pharmacy was the second black-owned pharmacy on Farish Street. The first one closed in the 1940s. Harmon's Drug Store closed its pharmacy in 2011, but his wife ran a variety store there afterward.[6]

In general, college students had a pessimistic attitude about Meredith successfully integrating Ole Miss. One evening, a Jackson State College summer school student named Rudolph Jackson walked under the tree near the cafeteria where a group of guys had congregated. Meredith was discussing his plans to enroll at Ole Miss. Overall, students believed he would be harmed or silenced. Rudolph recalled hearing someone say emphatically, "That Negro ain't gone make it to no Ole Miss. He might end up in jail or at Whitfield [State Hospital,] like Kennard and the teacher."[7]

The attitude of Jackson and his peers was prevalent on campus and in the community. "I don't think he ought to be trying to go to them white folks school," a maid who was waiting to catch the city bus in North Jackson told Katherine Horhn Winters, who was working across the street from the bus stop as a private nurse. Winters replied, "If you keep thinking like that, we'll never get ahead."[8]

Meanwhile, Medgar Evers capitalized on his relationship with college students to build the Jackson Movement; he organized a NAACP chapter at Tougaloo College, a private school, but he had not been successful in organizing one at Jackson State College, a state-funded school. Evers organized a protest with nine Tougaloo College students at Jackson's downtown library. The students tried to integrate the library by sitting in areas closed to blacks and reading books. However, they were arrested and beaten by Jackson police officers.

The beatings angered Jackson State College students, and 50 student government association students organized a protest; by the time they reached Pearl Street, the crowd had grown to 200. Jackson police blocked the demonstrators from every direction. The crowd was not given the opportunity to disperse before the police shot tear gas at them, set dogs on them, and beat them.[9]

That summer Dorothy Benford, a student at Jackson State College, participated in all of the marches on Lynch Street, which was near JSC's campus. "If you can't go to jail, step out of line when you see the police," organizers had cautioned protest volunteers. Dorothy's husband was an instructor for the Mississippi School for the Deaf, her mother worked at a local restaurant, and her father was employed at a local dairy. If Benford was arrested, she could cost her family members their jobs and get expelled from school.

In spite of the risk to herself and family members, Dorothy lined up with the other students in front of the Masonic Temple on Lynch Street and started walking. By the time they reached Rose Street, someone yelled, "They putting people on the garbage cars." According to Benford, the police used the back of garbage trucks, which had open beds, to hold detainees when they arrested large groups.

Benford and a few students quickly stepped out of line to avoid arrest, and a lady standing on her porch noticed and yelled to them, "Come on," waving her arm indicating for them to come to her house. The students walked briskly through her front door, out the back door of her shotgun house to the next street, and headed back to campus. "A white police officer later recognized me as a protester and gave me a ticket," she added.[10]

JSC's president discouraged students from engaging in protests, but even he had boundaries. "President Reddex told me he never succumbed to the pressure from whites to ask my teachers to flunk me in order to disqualify me academically as a candidate for admission to Ole Miss," Meredith stated.[11]

News of Mississippi police brutality aired on national television. The violence against the students and citizens reached Premier Khrushchev of Russia, who sent a telegram to the mayor of Jackson protesting the treatment of blacks. A few months later, 27 white and black Freedom Riders, who were protesting segregated interstate travel, got off the bus in Jackson. The Riders were escorted from the bus to police vans and taken to jail. Meredith had driven his car to the bus depot to witness the event. By June 12, 1961, over 100 Freedom Riders had been arrested; some of them were jailed at Mississippi State Penitentiary in Parchman.

After witnessing the arrest of the Freedom Riders, Meredith felt even stronger that the movement could not be successful unless the majority of blacks participated in it. He felt there needed to be a solid following of blacks behind a movement or a leader and that a handful of blacks could not successfully challenge white supremacy.

In the meantime, Meredith's attorney, Constance Motley, did not have a license to practice law in Mississippi, so a local lawyer was needed in order for them to be able to file a lawsuit in the lower courts of Mississippi. They began to search for a local attorney willing to join the team. Jack Young, a black attorney in Jackson, was first asked to join but he declined. Finally, they approached R. Jess Brown, who was delighted to become a part of the Meredith legal team. R. Jess Brown had taken several high-profile cases to support the civil rights of blacks in Mississippi previously and was familiar with the judges and the legal system.

Jack Young, however, did support Meredith's effort to integrate Ole Miss. Even though he did not take the case, he drove James Meredith, Medgar Evers, Constance Motley, and R. Jess Brown to Meridian in his Pontiac to conduct their first secret meeting regarding the case, because Evers's car was too well known, Meredith's Cadillac was too noticeable, Motley said her legs were too long to ride in Meredith's Volkswagen, and Brown's Chevrolet did not have a backseat.[12]

In the end, some of the greatest thinkers of the time were a part of Meredith's legal and advisory team. Constance Motley had joined the

NAACP's Legal Defense and Educational Fund in 1945, while a senior at Columbia University School of Law. She was no stranger to the legal proceedings surrounding desegregation, for she had worked on school segregation cases since her law school years and had represented black plaintiffs seeking redress in housing, transportation, and many other issues.

A wealthy white philanthropist, Clarence Blakeslee, met Motley when she was a teen employed by the National Youth Administration. After hearing her speak on behalf of blacks at a community meeting, he was so impressed with her that he checked out her high school records. They were exemplary, and he offered to finance her entire college education. He kept his promise. Like Blakeslee, she became a philanthropist in a sense because she gave back to her race as a civil rights attorney.[13]

R. Jess Brown had a significant legal record too. In 1948, he and other attorneys filed a lawsuit seeking equal salaries for black teachers in Jackson. During the 1950s, Brown filed the first civil rights suit in Jefferson Davis County, Mississippi, seeking the enforcement of the right of black citizens to become registered voters. He had also been successful in obtaining the release of Clyde Kennard from Parchman Prison, and represented Clennon King when he was committed to Mississippi State Hospital.[14]

Additionally, Brown had filed a lawsuit for Mack Charles Parker in Pearl River County, Mississippi, who had been accused of raping a white woman. Brown was challenging the jury selection procedures including the lack of blacks in the petit jury venire, but Parker never made it to trial. He was abducted from jail on April 25, 1959, by a lynch mob led by J. P. Walker, a former deputy sheriff, shot, and thrown in the Pearl River before the trial began. Brown later served on the NAACP's Legal Defense Fund.[15]

Meredith and his legal team drove to the federal court in Meridian and filed a lawsuit in the office of Judge S. C. Mize, a U.S. district judge for the Southern District of Mississippi. The media had been tipped off and a news reporter for the *Meridian Star* took a picture of R. Jess Brown, Constance Motley, and James Meredith that appeared on the front page of the paper the following day.

The next day the paper ran an editorial on James H. Meredith titled "Never Say Die," with a call to fight against integration: "We must lock shields. We must fight for our race and for the South to the last bitter ditch. We must never lose heart. We can triumph—we will triumph—we must triumph."[16]

Meredith's first court hearing was in Biloxi, Mississippi, on June 12, 1961. He read the correspondence that had been sent and received regarding his integration efforts. Meredith, Motley, Brown, and Meredith's younger brother Arthur Meredith, who had just graduated from Gibbs High School in St. Petersburg, Florida, were the only blacks in the courtroom. Arthur's presence was very encouraging to Meredith.

After the proceedings, Judge Mize moved the case to Jackson, which was very convenient for Motley and the other attorneys, who were finding it hard to locate lodging accommodations and food in the small town of Biloxi. The move was also good for Meredith, who was enrolled in Jackson State College. Unlike the court in Meridian, the segregated courtroom in the capital city of Mississippi was jam-packed with blacks, who were required to sit on the right side, while the benches on the left were reserved for whites.

On February 3, 1962, Judge Mize stated his ruling in the trial, part of which follows:

> Plaintiff, James Howard Meredith, is a member of the Negro race and a citizen of Mississippi. He filed this suit against the members of the Board of Trustees of State Institutions, the Chancellor of the University of Mississippi, the Dean of the College of Liberal Arts, and the Registrar of the University. He alleged that he sought admission to the University of Mississippi as a resident, under-graduate, transfer student to that Institution and that he was denied admission solely because of his race. The complaint was answered by the Defendants, denying that he was refused admission solely because of his race.
>
> The only question now . . . is whether or not Plaintiff was denied admission because of his race . . . The evidence overwhelmingly showed that the Plaintiff was not denied admission because of his race. The Plaintiff, during this hearing on the merits, called as adverse witnesses, nearly every member of the Board of Trustees, who testified . . . that at no time had the question of the race of a party ever been discussed at a meeting of the Board of Trustees or at any other place and that so far as the members of the Board of Trustees was concerned all policies and regulations were adopted and followed without regard to race, creed, or color . . .
>
> The proof shows on this trial, and I find as a fact, that there is no custom or policy now, nor was there any at the time Plaintiff's application was rejected, which excluded qualified Negroes from entering the University. The proof shows, and I find as a fact, that the University is not a racially segregated institution.
>
> Inasmuch as Plaintiff has failed to meet the burden of showing by a preponderance of the evidence that he was denied admission to the University of Mississippi solely because of his race, the complaint must be dismissed.

The ruling against Meredith was a triumph for segregationists and a blow to the Meredith defense team, who appealed to the U.S. Fifth Circuit Court of Appeals. The legal team requested that the decision of Judge Mize be overruled and that a temporary injunction be issued so that Meredith could attend school in February of 1962, but the injunction was denied. Chief Judge Elbert Parr Tuttle gave a dissenting opinion. Tuttle said the record called for a granting of the injunction pending the appeal.

By the spring of 1962, Meredith had completed the requirements to graduate from Jackson State College. To stop the process of receiving his degree, he declined to pay the $4.50 graduation fee. Meanwhile, he had been accepted for admission to Howard University School of Law and had obtained a scholarship to study political science at Atlanta University Graduate School. In the meantime, he studied practically every subject offered at Jackson State, while awaiting a transfer to Ole Miss.

Seventeen months had passed since Meredith made his move to integrate Ole Miss, and the white power structure attempted to use the legal system to stall the process. On June 25, 1962, Meredith turned 29 years old, and as an unintentional birthday gift the U.S. Fifth Circuit Court of Appeals ruled that he should be admitted to the University of Mississippi. Judge John Minor Wisdom wrote the majority opinion, which is as follows:

> The Meredith matter is before us again. This time the appeal is from a final judgment after a trial on the merits. The judgment denies James H. Meredith, a Mississippi Negro in search of an education, an injunction to secure his admission to the University of Mississippi. We reverse with directions that the injunction issue.
>
> A full review of the record leads the Court inescapably to the conclusion that from the moment the defendants [school officials] discovered Meredith was a Negro they engaged in a carefully calculated campaign of delay, harassment, and masterly inactivity. It was a defense designed to discourage and to defeat by evasive tactics which would have been a credit to Quintus Fabius Maximus.
>
> After the trial on the merits, the district judge found "as a fact, that the University is not a racially segregated institution." He found that the state had no policy of segregation. He did find that segregation was the custom before *Brown v. Board of Education*...was decided in May 1954; he held, "there is no custom or policy now, nor was there any at the time of the plaintiff's application, which excluded Negroes from entering the University." The about-face in policy, news of which may startle some in Mississippi, could have been accomplished only by telepathic communication among the

University's administrators and the Board of Trustees of State Institutions of Higher Learning. As the trial judge pointed out in his opinion, "nearly every member of the Board of Trustees, testified unequivocally and definitely that at no time had the question of race of a party ever been discussed at a meeting of the Board of Trustees or at any other place and that so far as the Board of Trustees was concerned, all policies and regulations were adopted and followed without regard to race, creed, or color."

In our previous opinion of this case … "We took judicial notice that the state of Mississippi maintains a policy of segregation in its schools and colleges." … The facts raise a doubt as to the defendants' good faith in asserting Meredith was not in good faith in applying for admission to the University of Mississippi …

… Sometime in January of 1961 Meredith wrote the Registrar for application forms. He received a prompt reply thanking him for his interest and enclosed the forms. January 31 he wrote the Registrar, enclosing the executed forms. In this letter Meredith expressly informed the University that he was a Negro. This was not a gesture of defiance-the forms require a photograph and an indication of race-but a predicate for pointing out that although he could not furnish the names of alumni who reside in his county and have known him for at least two years, he was submitting certifications regarding his moral character from Negro citizens who had known him in the county of his birthplace. As is apparent from the letter, Meredith was "hopeful that the complications would be as few as possible." …

February 4, 1961, two days before registration began for the second semester, the Registrar telegraphed Meredith:

"For your information and guidance it had been found necessary to discontinue consideration of all applications for admission or registration for the second semester which was received after January 25, 1961. Your application was received subsequent to such date and thus we must advise you not to appear for registration.". …

We pause in narrating the facts to observe that the explanation is inadequate on its face. (1) It ignores the credits from Washburn, Kansas, and Maryland. (2) The "programs" from those institutions are of course "recognized" by Mississippi. As for JSC, its program was established and is supervised by the identical Board of Trustees supervising the program at the University of Mississippi. (3) The letters of recommendation refer to the requirement of alumni certification, a patently discriminatory devise …

We turn now to the reasons the University gave in its letter of May 25 for rejecting Meredith.

Alumni Certifications—Letters of Recommendation

One of the most obvious dodges for evading the admission of Negroes to "white" colleges is the requirement that an applicant furnish letters of alumni certifications. The Board established the requirement by resolution, November 18, 1954, just a few months after the Supreme Court decided *Brown v. Board of Education*. We mention it again at this point in the opinion because its adoption and incorporation in current Bulletins (Catalogues) of the University show affirmative action by the Board to evade desegregation ...

We draw the inference again that the assigned reason for rejecting Meredith was a trumped-up excuse without any basis except to discriminate.

Thus far, we have covered all of the specific reasons given in the May 25 letter. On the record, as of May 25, 1961, the University had no valid, non-discriminatory grounds for refusing to accept Meredith as a student ...

Reading the 1350 pages in the record as a whole, we find that James H. Meredith's application for transfer to the University of Mississippi was turned down solely because he was a Negro. We see no valid, non-discriminatory reason for the University not accepting Meredith. Instead, we see a well-defined pattern of delays and frustrations, part of a Fabian policy of worrying the enemy into defeat while time worked for the defendants.

The judgment of the district court is Reversed and the case Remanded with directions that the district court issue the injunction as prayed for in the complaint, the district court to retain jurisdiction.[17]

After the Fifth Circuit Court of Appeals ruled in favor of James Meredith, Judge Ben F. Cameron of the Fifth Circuit Court issued an order staying the enforcement of the mandate until university officials could apply to the U.S. Supreme Court for a writ of certiorari, which would bring the record of a lower court before a superior court. On July 28, the other members of the Fifth Circuit Court of Appeals set aside and vacated Judge Cameron's July 28 and 31 orders.

On September 13, 1962, the U.S. District Court issued an injunction against the University of Mississippi officials ordering them to admit Meredith to the university. On the very same day, Governor Ross Barnett, acting on behalf of the White Citizens' Council, issued a proclamation that vested the operations of the schools in himself and the duly elected and appointed officials of the state of Mississippi.

On September 18, 1962, the United States became a party to Meredith's case. The Fifth Circuit entered an order permitting the United States to appear as amicus curiae in the case. In essence, the United States was designated and authorized to appear and participate as a friend of the court in all proceedings relating to James Meredith and the state of Mississippi.

While all of the legal maneuvering was taking place, the local power structure decided that James Meredith needed to pay a visit to the county jail. One morning during the early hours, the local police knocked on his apartment door and presented a warrant for his arrest. The warrant claimed Meredith had committed voter registration fraud, for registering to vote in Hinds County; they were alleging that he lived in Attala County. However, Meredith paid $40 a month for his apartment in Jackson and had attended Jackson State College since the fall of 1960. He cooperated with the police and was allowed to change out of his sleeping clothes into dress clothes. Before he left the house, he made a quick phone call to Medgar Evers, whom he could depend on to send assistance.

Meredith was taken to jail; his trumped-up charges and brief confinement indicate what measures the state of Mississippi was willing to take to prohibit his enrollment in Ole Miss. A property bond had been refused, so he stayed in jail most of the day. Finally, by 5:00 p.m. attorney Jack Young was able to post bail and Meredith was released. Now, determining the best way to protect Meredith was on the table again.

_____ CHAPTER 6 _____

Crushing Southern Forces

Two years after the U.S. Supreme Court handed down the opinion in the *Brown v. Board of Education* case, which ordered the desegregation of schools "with all deliberate speed," the Mississippi legislature appropriated $50,000 to create the Mississippi State Sovereignty Commission, which was established to maintain segregation and white supremacy in Mississippi society. The states of Alabama and Louisiana followed suit and created similar agencies.

Ross Robert Barnett was appointed ex-officio chairman of the commission in 1960 when he was elected governor of the state. James Meredith's integration efforts posed a problem to the commission, which was seeking to combat the activities of the civil rights movement. Financial support of the agency was provided in part by Mississippi black taxpayers, even though the commission sought to oppress their race. From 1956 to 1973, the commission spied on civil rights workers, monitored black voter registration activities, and funneled money to pro-segregation causes.

The commission made financial contributions to the White Citizens' Council, whose goal was to preserve white power and the disenfranchisement of blacks. The council arranged for the names of black registrants to be published in newspapers, and they pressured white employers to fire their black employees who attempted to defy Jim Crow practices. Council members used violence, economic ploys, and terrorism to keep blacks away from the polls.

White Citizen's Council member James F. Byrne made a statement that illustrated the beliefs of the organization's membership:

> Frequently, the question is asked: "Where do we go from here?" Solomon with all his wisdom could not give a positive answer. We do know that the approximately 40 million white Southerners will do everything that lawfully can be done to prevent the mixing of the races in the school. Power intoxicates men. It is never voluntarily surrendered. It must be taken from them. The Supreme Court must be curbed.[1]

On June 11, 1963, President John F. Kennedy gave a televised address to American citizens and made it clear that he supported integration. He also pointed out that the high unemployment of black youth was a problem for all Americans. He contended that America was one country and that all who have come here should have the equal right to develop their talents. An excerpt of his address is below:

> Good evening my fellow citizens:
>
> This afternoon, following a series of threats and defiant statements, the presence of Alabama National Guardsmen was required on the University of Alabama to carry out the final and unequivocal order of the United States District Court on the Northern District of Alabama. The order called for the admission of two clearly qualified young Alabama residents who happened to have been born Negro . . . It ought to be possible for American consumers of any color to receive equal service in places of public accommodation, such as hotels and restaurants and theaters and retail stores, without being forced to resort to demonstrations in the streets, and it ought to be possible for American citizens of any color to register and to vote in a free election without interference or fear of reprisal . . .
>
> Too many Negro children entering segregated grade schools at the time of the Supreme Court's decision 9 years ago will enter segregated high schools this fall, having suffered a loss which can never be restored. The lack of an adequate education denies the Negro a chance to get a decent job.[2]

On September 19, 1962, the state legislature called a special session and enacted Mississippi Senate Bill No. 1501 aimed directly at the Meredith situation. The law ruled that no person shall be eligible for admission to any state institution of higher learning if he has a criminal charge of moral turpitude pending against him. Meanwhile, a warrant had been issued for Meredith's arrest.

He had previously been arrested and charged with false voter registration, which carried a one-year sentence. The white power structure planned to use the charges under the new law to legally stop Meredith from integrating Ole Miss. On September 20, 1962, the Mississippi Board of Trustees of State Institutions of Higher Learning adopted a resolution vesting Governor Barnett with the full power to act on all matters pertaining to Meredith's school admission.

Meredith and his legal team continued to debate the best way to handle his security, which had become their top priority. Attorney Motley felt that the NAACP's plan to get Meredith out of Mississippi was the best move to make, so she developed a plan that resolved the matter. She called Meredith and asked him to meet her in Memphis, Tennessee, at the home of A. W. Willis Jr. When Meredith arrived at Willis's house, Meredith asked, "Where is Constance?" A. W. confessed forcefully, "You've been tricked to get you the hell out of Mississippi!"[3] Meredith was not amused, but he went along with the plans and spent his first night in Memphis at a rooming house.

While in Memphis, Meredith contacted his first cousin Katherine and her husband, Robert Terrell, and stopped by the couple's house and visited them; his cousin Imogene Battle came by as well. Meredith and his relatives discussed race relations, the court case, and many topics during his visit. Katherine and Robert Terrell welcomed Meredith to stay with them for a while. Their hospitality kept him occupied, just as their home kept him safe for the next 12 days.

After a week or so, Meredith called A. W. Willis's office to check in with him. As their conversation continued, Willis asked Meredith to come to his office to meet someone. Meredith headed over to Willis's office, where he met Chief U.S. Marshal James J. P. McShane, who had served as chief of security for JFK's presidential campaign; he had been appointed chief U.S. marshal by JFK in 1962.

The only marshals Meredith knew were Wyatt Earp and Matt Dillon, but the U.S. Marshals Service is the nation's oldest federal law enforcement agency, responsible for conducting federal fugitive investigations, managing witness security programs, and other law enforcement activities. During their second meeting, Meredith was informed that the federal government was going to have McShane and several U.S. marshals escort him on campus when he attempted to register. Meredith had successfully acquired the support of the most powerful man in the world, JFK, who was commander-in-chief of the most powerful military in the world.

On September 20, 1962, Meredith was escorted from Millington Naval Air Station in Tennessee to Oxford, Mississippi, so that he could enroll in school. As they traveled on Highway 51, they stopped at the Batesville police department and several state trooper patrol cars joined the caravan. There were two state trooper cars in front, two cars were driven by U.S marshals, and another state trooper car was in the rear.

Once they arrived in Oxford and entered the campus area, they were greeted by a welcome sign that stated:

"Welcome to Oxford, the Reforestation Capital of the World." Whatever Mississippi does, it does zealously, whether it is playing football, crowning beauty queens, keeping Negroes in their places, or planting pine trees.[4]

The car carrying Meredith entered the campus through a side entrance. He was scheduled to register around 4:30 p.m. in the Continuation Center, which was 30 minutes after the regular registration period. State troopers were lined up shoulder to shoulder and there were 4,000 bystanders outside of the Continuation Center waiting to witness a showdown.

When Meredith entered the building, he was approached by a sheriff who served him with a set of summons. Meredith gave the papers to a Justice Department attorney. Governor Barnett shook the marshals' hands and was extremely courteous to everyone except Meredith. Barnett led them to the room prepared for registration. Barnett, Robert Ellis, the school registrar, and Meredith were seated at a long table. Ellis read a written statement that declared Barnett the school's registrar.

Barnett then read a statement to Meredith that declared as the school's registrar, Barnett was refusing to allow Meredith to register as a student at the University of Mississippi. Barnett gave Meredith a copy of the letter, and a representative of the Justice Department protested against Barnett's actions; but after a few moments, Meredith and the government officials left the building. Meredith's first enrollment attempt had been blocked by the governor of the state. The group quickly got into their cars; as they drove through the street, students and spectators threw rocks at their cars. Mississippi state troopers led the caravan to the Tennessee state line.

Meredith recalled in a *Saturday Evening Post* article feeling at times doubtful that he would be able to attend Ole Miss:

The court fight was long, and there were times when I wondered if it would be successful. I kept winning in court, but I didn't get any nearer to the university. Finally, after the Fifth Circuit Court of Appeal had said I should be registered, I felt the responsibility was in the Federal Government's hand; it was out of my hands to do anything.[5]

On September 21, 1962, the chancellor of the University of Mississippi, the dean of the College of Liberal Arts, and the registrar were charged with civil and criminal contempt by the appellate court. However, Judge Mize heard the case, ruled the officials not guilty, and dismissed the case. The next hearing was before the Fifth Circuit Court of Appeals in New Orleans, where university officials agreed to comply with the court's order to register Meredith. On September 24th, Governor Barnett issued another proclamation in defiance of the court's order. The Fifth Circuit Court issued a restraining order prohibiting Mississippi state officials from interfering with Meredith's registration.

Meredith and his legal team ended up in court in New Orleans for the contempt trial. Medgar Evers attended the trial as well and he had brought Mary June from the train station. The couple's reunion was very special because they had not seen each other in two weeks, and the court proceedings and travel had disrupted his family and school life. Mary June was hoping her husband's integration efforts would be successful and prayed for his continued safety. They felt a sense of hope because unlike the other segregation cases, Meredith was being escorted on campus by U.S. marshals.

During the morning hours of September 25, 1962, U.S. marshals John Doar and McShane picked up Meredith. As a precaution, they switched cars and drove to New Orleans's old airport. When they arrived, Meredith was refused service at the bar and had to go to the basement to use the "colored only" employee restroom. The group boarded a Cessna 220 and headed to Jackson so that Meredith could register for school in the Woolfolk building on West Street. During the flight, Meredith learned that John Doar was a Republican lawyer who had been appointed to serve in the Civil Rights Division by President Dwight D. Eisenhower.

When Meredith's party arrived in Jackson, they were met by a massive crowd assembled outside the building who taunted Meredith with racial epithets. Again, Meredith and the marshals were led into the building by Governor Barnett. Although Barnett had agreed to cooperate with the court order to register Meredith, he did not. He read another proclamation, which stated he was not going to allow James Meredith to complete his school registration in order to preserve the peace and tranquility of the state of Mississippi. Then, Meredith was handed a copy of the proclamation.

Meredith's comment on the governor's action later was:

I might add that I thought the governor put on a pretty good performance. The first time, when he turned us away at the university, he
reminded me of Charlton Heston, I believe it was, in a movie about
Andrew Jackson. Very dramatic.[6]

Governor Barnett's action led to another contempt trial in New
Orleans. His actions had been reported nationally and abroad on television, in newspapers, magazines, and on the radio. After the legal procedures were finalized, Meredith made another attempt to register for
classes. On September 27, 1962, the pilot, Meredith, and the two U.S. marshals flew from New Orleans to Oxford so that Meredith could register for
classes. Their party was greeted by newsmen, additional U.S. marshals,
highway patrol, and local citizens. The group was cursed, spat at, and
threatened as they were being escorted through the campus by the highway patrol.

As Meredith and his party approached the registration building,
Lieutenant Governor Paul Johnson and several men who were accompanying him formed a solid line across the sidewalk. Meredith and the marshals got out of the car, approached the line of men, and stopped. Johnson
and the men with him blocked the party from moving forward. Marshal
McShane tried to serve Johnson with a court order, but he refused the
papers, so McShane touched Johnson with the papers and dropped them
on the ground beside him. Johnson read a proclamation, which was similar to the document Governor Barnett had read previously.

McShane moved in on Johnson and demanded he step aside. The
cameramen present took a picture of McShane and Paul Johnson standing
face-to-face with their fists balled up. The registration of one man had
turned into a circus where clowns danced for the media and their constituents, but their theatrics gave a worldwide voice to southern hatred
and bigotry. A lot of pushing and shoving took place and Meredith
bumped one of the white men in line. When the man extended his fist to
hit Meredith, one of the marshals pulled him back and stepped between
Meredith and the man. Marshal McShane asked the lieutenant governor
to "let Mr. Meredith through," but Johnson declined. The party was frus-
trated that the registration process had been blocked again.

On September 28, 1962, the Fifth Circuit Court of Appeals ordered
Governor Barnett to pay a fine of $10,000 per day and for Lieutenant
Governor Paul Johnson to pay a fine of $5,000 per day unless they ceased
their interference with Meredith's registration. U.S. Attorney General

Robert Kennedy gave the marshals permission to use tear gas when they went back to campus in the event of a disturbance. Meredith thought it was ridiculous to send 50 unarmed men into a large crowd with tear gas where potential violence was imminent, but the president wanted to avoid sending troops to Mississippi.

On September 30, 1962, President John F. Kennedy issued a proclamation and executive order:

> Whereas the Gov. of the State of Mississippi and certain law enforcement officers and other officials of that State, and other persons, individually and in unlawful assemblies, combination and conspiracies, have been and are willfully opposing and obstructing the enforcement of orders entered by the United States District Court for the Southern District of Mississippi and the United States Court of Appeals for the Fifth Circuit; and
>
> Whereas such unlawful assemblies, combinations and conspiracies oppose and obstruct the executive of the laws of the United States, impede the course of justice under those laws and make it impracticable to enforce those laws in the State of Mississippi by the ordinary course of judicial proceeding; and
>
> Whereas I have expressly called the attention of the Gov. of Mississippi to the perilous situation that exists and to his duties in the premises, and have requested but have not received from him adequate assurances that the orders of the courts of the United States will be obeyed and the law and order will be maintained;
>
> Now, therefore, I, John F. Kennedy, President of the United States, under and by virtue of the authority vested in me by the Constitution and laws of the United States, including Chapter 15 of Title 10 of the United States Code 1, particularly sections 332, 333, and 334 thereof, do command all persons engaged in such obstructions of justice to cease and desist there from and to disperse and retire peacefully forthwith.
>
> In witness whereof, I have hereunto set my hand and caused the seal of the United States of America to be affixed.
>
> Done at the city of Washington this 30th day of September in the year of our Lord Nineteen Hundred and Sixty-Two, and of the independence of the United States of America the One Hundred and Eighty-Seven.
>
> John F. Kennedy[7]

President Kennedy's executive order authorized the secretary of defense to call into action for the purpose of carrying out the court order the Army National Guard and the Air National Guard of the state of

Mississippi to serve in the active military service of the United States for an indefinite period.

During an Ole Miss football game in Jackson at Mississippi Veterans Memorial Stadium, Governor Barnett spoke to a crowd of 40,000; many were waving Confederate battle flags as a symbol of white supremacy. "I love Mississippi...I love her people...her customs!" The crowd cheered him on; "Never, Never!" they screamed. Barnett said, "Never shall our emblem go from Colonel 'Reb' to Old Black Joe!" That night Barnett received a phone call from President Kennedy, who wanted to know if he was going to be able to maintain order. Governor Barnett said, "I don't know. That's what I'm worried about. I don't know whether I can or not."[8]

On Sunday, September 30, 1962, Governor Barnett had another telephone conversation with President Kennedy. The governor had to inform the president that there were hundreds of armed men around the campus who presented a danger to the campus. JFK informed Barnett that he had a responsibility to ensure that the least chance of violence would occur in Mississippi.

Earlier that morning, Robert and Dorothy Burton Henderson, a black couple who resided in Lexington, Mississippi, skipped church and were planning to drive to Oxford early to beat the traffic, before James Meredith arrived. When they drove onto Highway 51 north headed to Oxford, cars and trucks driven by rednecks were bumper to bumper. To make matters worse, their car broke down on Highway 7 between Coffeeville and Water Valley. Dorothy was so afraid that she sat in the car and cried until she became sick.

"Get out of the way, nigger," someone screamed at them as they sat in their disabled vehicle. Finally, a local resident gave them a lift to Oxford, to Elisah "Little Boy" Pegues's house, where Robert lived during the week, because he taught shop at Oxford Training School. Robert had borrowed Pegues's car to take Dorothy to Memphis, Tennessee, where she was a schoolteacher at Hanley Elementary School.

By the time they were about to cross Sorority Row, which intersects with Jackson Avenue, the traffic came to a complete stop. The mob was loud; they cursed the soldiers and yelled insulting remarks at bystanders. The guardsmen were pushing and being shoved. Later that evening hooded Klansmen started walking up Jackson Avenue trying to get on campus.

The streets were crowded with white, hostile men waving Rebel flags and screaming obscenities at any black in sight. Dorothy heard the helicopters flying over their heads taking the soldiers to the campus. It took them almost two hours to drive 26 miles from Jackson Avenue on Highway 6 to Highway 51, but they arrived in Memphis safely. Around 5 a.m. on October 1, 1962, as Robert was traveling back to Oxford, someone threw a brick through the rear window of the car he had borrowed.

"It was rumored that two black men had been murdered, and that one black man's body was discovered near the Ice House," Mrs. Henderson said. "People were hush, hush about the black murders," she added. However, there were never any official reports that any blacks died that night in Oxford, Mississippi.[9]

On September 30, 1962, on the other end of Highway 6, six miles west of Oxford, 12-year-old Leroy and his two siblings peeped through the window at all the traffic passing by. The children's parents, Ira and Ina Mae, sat in the sitting room listening to the radio, which gave several reports on the Meredith crisis. Their little house was close enough to the highway for them to hear the voices of people screaming out of their car windows. Leroy's family and another black family were sharecroppers on Young Waller's farm. Waller's nephew, William Lowe (Bill) Waller, would ironically later serve one term as governor of Mississippi from 1972 to 1976.

The loud noises and the crowded streets terrorized black residents in Oxford. The sleepy town gradually turned into one with a hostile atmosphere. Sundays in Oxford were usually quiet and heavy traffic rarely occurred. In fact, heavy traffic on Highway 6 generally was associated with college sporting events. "During the 1960s, Ole Miss had two football games in Oxford each year and both games were on a Saturday. We were glad that James Meredith was finally going to enroll at Ole Miss, but we were scared to death," Leroy stated.

As darkness covered the skies, the residents of Waller's farm could hear shots. Around 8:00 p.m., a shotgun blast burst through the wood-framed house. Then there was a second shot. Ira reacted quickly, grabbing his gun and directing his family to the back of the house. They were lying on the floor when a third shot sped over their heads and traveled through the back wall. They huddled on the floor for the rest of the night, because distant shots rang throughout the night.[10]

Earlier that evening, Meredith and Marshals McShane and Doar descended on campus to Baxter Hall and settled in an apartment, which included two bedrooms, a living room, and a bathroom. They could all hear the noise outside, but they did not find out until the sun hit their eyes the following morning what took place on campus while they were tucked away safety in their rooms. Trouble had been brewing in Oxford before people went to church for worship services. Thousands of whites had arrived in Oxford prepared to fight, die, or kill to keep James Meredith out of Ole Miss, for his success threatened the preservation of white supremacy.

Within an hour of Meredith's arrival, a white student became angry at the sight of a black male driving a military vehicle and attacked the driver, spraying him in the face with a fire extinguisher; the student's action incited a riot. Then, people started throwing cans, rocks, and bottles at state troopers, and overturning cars and lighting bonfires. The marshals threw tear gas and hid behind parked cars. A sniper fired a rifle from a campus building and people began to throw Molotov cocktails. Within hours, the riot escalated into an armed insurrection. Photographers were attacked and beaten, while some of them wandered through the streets, begging for their lives and holding onto their smashed cameras.[11]

French reporter Paul Guihard wrote in his last dispatch to the Agence France-Press, "The Civil War has never ended." Students had warned reporters to hide their cameras, but Guihard was anxious to take some photographs; he walked straight into the crowd and was shot with a .38 pistol. The bullet pierced his back and entered his heart. Ray Gunter, a local jukebox repairman who was participating in the riot, was struck with a .38 bullet in the forehead; he died before he reached the hospital.

After word reached President Kennedy that the marshals were in danger, he ordered the army to deploy some 20,000 National Guard troops immediately from Tennessee. Six hundred and fifty troops and 120 Jeeps and trucks were dispatched from Memphis, but the drive took six hours instead of two hours because segregation loyalists blocked the highway and deliberately slowed incoming traffic with large logs and railroad ties. The insurrection on the campus was the largest federal-state crisis since the Civil War.

In the early hours of the next day, federal troops were finally able to disperse the mob. The morning light revealed debris, smoke, overturned cars, shattered glass, and tire tracks. One hundred and sixty marshals were injured, 79 of whom had been injured by bullets, some seriously. Two white men had been killed on campus. Rumors circulated that two black men had been killed in the city during the night, but those claims were never officially substantiated. Afterward, 200 people were arrested, but less than a fourth of those were students of the university. The chaos of the insurrection had been initiated by Ku Klux Klan leaders, many of whom had traveled to Oxford from other states.

Around eight o'clock that morning, James H. Meredith, dressed in a gray suit with a red tie, walked to the registrar's office in the Lyceum Building, as calm as an actor entering a building where his 12th movie screening was being previewed, and registered for classes. Three hundred journalists from around the world had arrived on campus to cover the Meredith crisis. The headline in a Mexico City newspaper read "One Negro Rocks Uncle Sam"; in Copenhagen: "Bravo Meredith"; in Portugal: "Civil War Looms, Kennedy Uses Force."[12] A newspaper reporter asked Meredith if he thought integrating the University of Mississippi was worth the death and destruction that was caused during the riot. Meredith did not believe he had been asked a fair question, which annoyed him. He said in his 1966 memoir:

> Of course, I was sorry! I hadn't wanted this to happen. I believe it could have been prevented with responsible leadership in Mississippi. As for the federal government, the President, and the Attorney General had all the intelligence facilities at their disposal ...I think it would have been worst if they had waited any longer. Social change is a painful thing, but the method by which it is achieved depends upon the people at the top. Here there were totally opposed—the state against the federal government. There was bound to be trouble, and there was.[13]

After Meredith registered, he was asked by a reporter if he was happy to have registered. His comment to the reporter reflected his feelings: "This is no happy occasion."[14] On his way out of the Lyceum Building, he passed by a black janitor, who touched him with the broom in his hand and caught his eye. Meredith had the pleasure of formally meeting the gentleman later, who told Meredith that he touched him with the broom to let him know he supported him. Most of the black support staff at Oxford's elementary schools had elected to stay home. Therefore an airborne military division pitched in to prepare lunch for the children enrolled in the all-white schools.

Hundreds of weapons were seized by marshals and soldiers after the riot. Weapons were taken from the Sigma Nu House, which was under the leadership of Trent Lott, who would later become a U.S. congressman and a powerful long-standing senator. On Meredith's second day of class, an FBI informant reported that the United Klans of America held a meeting in Bessemer, Alabama, and decided to lay low for a while, and had planned to hang Meredith later from a gate on campus.

Meredith was escorted to his first class, Colonial American History, by Marshals McShane and Doar. Students booed and taunted Meredith, but he proceeded to class. A dozen students were in his class. One girl actually spoke to him but the rest of them remained silent. Nevertheless, Mississippi's total-segregation policies had been breached. The federal government provided protection for Meredith for two semesters at a cost of $55 million. No further violence occurred on the campus.

Meredith had hoped his wife and son could join him, but they could not because he had to share a room with an armed marshal who stayed with him the entire time he was enrolled in school to protect his life. His existence on campus was isolated and remote to say the least. The following month Meredith said,

> Personally the year will be a hardship for me. My wife will be in college in Jackson. Our son, John Howard, who will be three in January, is living with my parents in Kosciusko. I expect to see them often, but I don't think families should live apart.[15]

In general, blacks were as stunned as white citizens that Meredith had successfully gained entrance into Ole Miss. Rudolph Jackson's statement summed up the feelings of many JSC students: "When we looked up James Meredith was at Ole Miss."[16] The segregationists and the racist whites in the state had maintained a strong grip on preserving their way of life, which maintained a superior world for whites and an inferior world for blacks. Mary June said of his heroism: "Jay is a determined fellow. He likes to do things his own way." His mother-in-law, Mable Martin, said: "James is a very exact type of man. He likes things right and I guess he thought it was wrong for the University of Mississippi to be segregated and he had to do what he is doing."[17]

Being the only black student on the University of Mississippi's campus was at times unsettling for Meredith. He said in a 1963 article: "Just having a Negro in residence does not mean that the university has been integrated. Most of the time, I am perhaps the most segregated Negro in the world."[18] He was once asked years later if he had any friends on campus while attending Ole Miss. His response was: "I was not a student. I was a soldier in a war." Meredith also reported: "Students threw rocks and fire crackers at me. They insulted me, but I never allowed anyone to get close to me."[19]

In April of 1963, an article on Meredith appeared in *Look*, a women's magazine. In the article, he noted that no student should be subjected to the treatment that he had to endure during his semester at Ole Miss. "Though no price is too high to pay for liberation," he added.[20] Meredith received thousands of telegrams from supporters after he moved on campus at Ole Miss. However, some of the letters were hate mail; one letter included a piece of a rope, and another one included a poem: "Roses are red, violets are blue; I've killed one nigger and might as well make it two."[21]

Meredith later told a CNN reporter, "I considered myself engaged in a war from day one."[22] He wanted the Kennedy administration to enforce his rights as a citizen, and they did. He stated, "However as we slowly ascended the hill toward Baxter Hall, it appeared to me that the particular steps that I had chosen to take in an effort to carry out the mandate of my Divine Responsibility had been proper and timely."[23] He felt that above all, the integration of Ole Miss has been commissioned by God.

Off campus, most blacks in Oxford were afraid to talk to Meredith, while a few embraced him. The presence of the U.S. marshals, who drove him to the barbershop and to other locations in the city of Oxford during his school days at Ole Miss, was disconcerting for many blacks, whose normal response was to avoid the company of white men.

Susie Marshall, who was born Christmas Eve of 1913, was a resident of Oxford in 1962. She recalled that most blacks were glad James Meredith had integrated Ole Miss. "Blacks liked him, but they were afraid to openly talk to him or to invite him into their homes," Marshall stated. "I saw him many times, through the window of Thelma Price's place [a beauty parlor], or passing by in the federal cars headed to Cecil Nelson's Beauty Parlor on Depot Street and 6th Avenue. He would be over there with his people," she added.[24]

Meredith regretted that his aging parents were harassed and felt it was unfair to his father, who was 71 years old, to fear being violently attacked. During the Christmas holiday of 1962, Stanley Whitcomb, who was five years and six months old, lived next door to Cap and Roxie Meredith in Kosciusko. He recalled, "I was staring out the window when three cars, driven by Klukers [Ku Klux Klan], slowly pulled into our driveway one by one, drove pass the side of our house from the rear of our driveway off South Street, and parked in a line facing Allen Street."[25]

Within seconds of them driving off, they started shooting at the home of Meredith's parents, Cap and Roxie, in Kosciusko. The shots from the drive-by shooting barely missed Meredith's younger sister Willie Lou; no charges were ever filed against the shooters, which included Kosciusko police officers, though their identity was known.

A small percentage of the state's public school system was desegregated the following year. By 1965, Mississippi State University, the University of Southern Mississippi, and Millsaps College in Jackson were desegregated. James Meredith's enrollment at the University of Mississippi proclaimed that blacks did in fact have a right to attend any college of their choosing and to pursue nonteaching and other degrees.

James H. Meredith became the first black graduate of the University of Mississippi on August 18, 1962, obtaining a bachelor of arts degree in political science, history, and French. He placed a NEVER pin upside down on his shirt before he put on his cap and gown to remind his white classmates that they had lost the NEVER battle. During his registration attempts, white students had worn NEVER pins, which had been popularized by Governor Barnett as a symbol that blacks would never attend school with Mississippi whites.[26]

Fannie Alice Webb, a neighbor of his parents, recalled: "Me and Julia Carr rode with Mr. Cap and Miss Roxie to J-Boy's graduation. We were escorted from Kosciusko to Oxford by the U.S. Marshals." After the ceremony, the marshals escorted the family to Memphis for a dinner celebration at the home of Robert and Katherine Terrell. "Two cars [driven by U.S marshals] were in front and two cars were behind them. Then they told us, 'You on your own now.' Yes, Yes," she added.[27]

Meredith paved the way for other blacks to obtain an education at the University of Mississippi and to pursue various fields of study that were not offered at black institutions. Reuben V. Anderson was one of the first blacks to benefit from the road that was paved by Meredith. Anderson graduated from the University of Mississippi's law school in 1967. After graduation, he became an attorney for the NAACP Legal and Educational Fund and later become a municipal judge, a circuit court judge, a Hinds County court judge, and eventually the first black elected to sit on the Mississippi Supreme Court. He is currently a partner in the prestigious law firm of Phelps Dunbar LLP in Jackson, Mississippi.

Dorothy Burton Henderson, an eyewitness to the postriot activities on September 30, 1962, in Oxford, enrolled at Ole Miss four years after Meredith. She obtained a master's degree in elementary education in 1968 and became the first black instructor for the School of Education in 1978. "After Meredith, blacks started enrolling at Ole Miss. By the summer of 1966, there were a few blacks in several classrooms," Henderson stated.[28] The actions of one man changed Ole Miss forever.

James Meredith, and other students who withstood the agony of integrating all-white schools, must be commended for opening the doors that allowed so many to gain access to diverse educational and career opportunities. Meredith stood on the shoulders of Lloyd Gaines, Medgar Evers, Clennon W. King Jr., Clyde Kennard, the Arkansas seven, and others who opened doors. Although doors have opened, many new doors need to open.

Even in the twenty-first century, none of Mississippi's three historical black universities has a school of law or a school of pharmacy. Jackson State University (JSU) is the state's only urban university. It offers premedical and prenursing fields of study but does not have an undergraduate or a graduate nursing program. However, JSU's students can pursue medical and nursing degrees online through a relationship the university established with the University of Medicine and Health Sciences and the International University of Nursing, both of which are in St. Kitts in the West Indies. Otherwise, students can elect to pursue the above-mentioned fields of study locally through the University of Mississippi's Jackson branches. Alcorn State University is the only historically black university in the state with an undergraduate and graduate nursing program. Furthermore, Alcorn State University and Mississippi Valley State own antiquated football fields, which limit their capacity to generate revenues from their largest sporting events.

JSU had planned to build a football arena that would seat 40,000 people with property it acquired through eminent domain. On March 17, 2011, Governor Haley Barbour signed a bill into law giving JSU control of the University of Mississippi's stadium, Mississippi Veterans Memorial Stadium, which was the state's largest stadium, located in Jackson, Mississippi; it had been built in 1950 and expanded in 1980. Today, the stadium is primarily used for JSU football games and a few private events; hopefully in the future, the stadium will generate unprecedented revenues for JSU so that the university can continue to expand and flourish.

CHAPTER 7

Second Reconstruction Stories

Many stories about people who lived in the Jim Crow South were gathered through research and/or composed from personal accounts. The following narratives were collected from interviewees who shared their voter registration and other Second Reconstruction experiences from 1946 to 1966. Their collective stories introduce the reader to many previously unknown participants and shed new light on this historical era.

William White, a former carpentry teacher, grew up in Attala County and attended Attala County Training School with James Meredith's older siblings Lee Roy, Delma, and Thelma Meredith during the Great Depression. White taught building and construction and brick masonry, and was James Meredith's carpentry teacher for the 1947–48 school term.

In 1946, White and his wife, Christine, an elementary schoolteacher in Sally, went to the courthouse in the town square in Kosciusko and asked the circuit clerk to give them two voting registration forms. White had just returned to Kosciusko from active duty as a U.S. Navy seaman. White stated, "We had to each pay a $1 or $2 annual poll tax, and take a written and oral literacy test." The literacy test mandated the circuit clerk to ask a series of questions requiring the couple to interpret three sections of the Mississippi Constitution. The clerk was satisfied with the couple's responses and allowed them to register. "To my recollection, I don't recall that anyone was lynched in Attala County. When we watched movies at the Strand Theatre downtown, we sat upstairs in the balcony, while whites sat downstairs. We followed the rules and whites were peaceful."[1]

James Meredith's father, Cap, had registered to vote in the same courthouse in the early 1920s, but in those days many counties refused to allow any blacks to register to vote. Due to discrimination, only 6.7 percent of Mississippi blacks were registered voters, the lowest percentage of any state in the nation. Southern counties discriminated against black registrants by requiring them to take literacy tests and/or pay poll taxes.

Payment of the poll tax and literacy tests were not required in Shelby County, Tennessee, in the early 1950s. For instance, in 1953 18-year-old Robert Terrell drove to downtown Memphis, entered the courthouse on Front Street, and filled out a simple registration form. He was not required to pay a poll tax or take a literacy test.[2]

However, black registrants were required to pay poll taxes and take literacy tests as a voting prerequisite in Hinds County, Mississippi. Jimmie and Faye (they elected to omit their last name), a newly married black couple, drove downtown on Pascagoula Street in 1957, walked into the courthouse, and obtained two voter registration forms. "We were required to read and interpret three sections of the Mississippi Constitution and we both had to pay a $5 poll tax," Jimmie recalled.

The couple passed the literacy test on the first attempt, which was not the norm. Most blacks in the South were functionally illiterate and had a hard time interpreting legal or written documents. However, Jimmie and Faye were Mississippi Vocational and Technical College (now Mississippi Valley State University) graduates. Faye taught English at Rowan Elementary School in Jackson, and Jimmie was the chief financial officer/accountant at Utica Junior College, a black institution in Utica, Mississippi. He later became the president of Utica Junior College but lost his position when the school merged with Hinds Junior College during President Reagan's administration. Faye and Meredith's sister Hazel (Nell) became friends in college.[3]

In 1960, James Meredith, a 27-year-old junior at Jackson State College, registered to vote in Jackson, Mississippi, and was required to fill out a registration form. Black voter registration movements were picking up momentum, and Meredith and other students had participated in their school's student government association's voter registration drive.[4] At that time, there were no black elected officials in Hinds County and only six in the entire state. Those six lived in Bolivar County, a predominantly black county.

In 1961 two young men, Charles Sherrod and Charles Jones, went to Albany, Georgia, to organize voter registration drives. These men were among a new breed, willing to die to change the unjust and inhumane world they lived in. Charles Sherrod, field secretary of the Student Nonviolent Coordinating Committee (SNCC), was originally from Petersburg, Virginia, and Charles Jones was from Charlotte, North Carolina. Sherrod was born on January 2, 1937, and raised by his mother and grandmother. "I come from a humble background," he stated. As a boy, he belonged to the Boy's Club and was a member of a boys' choir that performed throughout Virginia. "I took all the money I earned home to my mother and grandmother to support the household expenses. My Scout masters, coaches, and uncles were my male role models. I had a strong love for God and believed men could overcome evil with good," Sherrod recalled.

When 24-year-old Sherrod arrived in Albany, Georgia, he believed in human rights and in the biblical concept "Love thy neighbor as thyself." He had a bachelor of arts degree in sociology and a master's degree in theology. He had mastered the study of people and different societies and was prepared to lead a flock. Sherrod became a resident of Albany; as time passed, he became a neighbor, a friend, a pastor, a brother, and an effective leader and organizer. Sherrod had the will to move mountains, and mountains of despair were on the earth where he and other black people trod. The masses of minorities were unemployed and many of them had lived in a cycle of poverty that had passed from one generation to the next.

Sherrod further recalled:

Our community included a few blacks owned shoe repair shops, cab companies, restaurants, and cleaning businesses, but they only employed a few of the town's black inhabitants. We boycotted several white owned businesses, because they wouldn't hire black cashiers, even though they were in our community making money off of us. We modeled our boycott after the Montgomery Bus Boycott [1955–56], which had been organized by SCLC. Our boycotts pressured white business owners to ask local politicians to end segregation because their businesses were declining. Smith Grocery was one of the businesses that did not survive the boycotts. It lost so much money that it had to close its doors.[5]

Sherrod and other members of SNCC participated in mass demonstrations in Albany, Georgia, between 1961 and 1962. Children as young as nine years old were walking around with picket signs. There were 22,000 blacks in Albany and about 5 percent of the total population was jailed for participating in protests. Sherrod always warned participants, "If you can't go to jail to stay, don't go." There was no bail bond money lying around, so if arrested, participants had to sit in jail until they were released on their own recognizance. "Back then, people used property bonds to get out of jail, but few of us owned property," Sherrod stated.

James Crawford, a black teenager from Albany, joined SNCC during this time period. Crawford started taking people to the courthouse to register to vote. One day he was approached by a deputy registrar and the following conversation took place:

Registrar: What do you want?

Crawford: I brought this lady down to register.

Registrar: (after giving the woman a card to fill out and sending her outside to the hall) Why did you bring this lady down here?

Crawford: Because she wants to be a first-class citizen like y'all.

Registrar: Who are you to bring people down to register?

Crawford: It's my job.

Registrar: Suppose you get two bullets in your head right now?

Crawford: I got to die anyhow.

Registrar: If I don't do it, I can get somebody else to do it. (No reply)

Registrar: Are you scared?

Crawford: No.

Registrar: Suppose somebody came in that door and shot you in the back of the head right now. What would you do?

Crawford: I couldn't do nothing. If they shot me in the back of the head there are people coming from all over the world.

Registrar: What people?

Crawford: The people I work for.[6]

Sherrod proclaimed, "I worked with hundreds, if not thousands, of young men like Crawford in Albany during the early 1960s." Albany's voter registration drives were responsible for registering around 500 blacks during the first year, and the following year, over 2,000 blacks became registered voters. They elected their first city commissioner in 1965, their second city commissioner in 1970, and Sherrod was elected as a city commissioner in 1976. He pointed out that today the city commission is majority black. Albany elected their first black mayor, Dr. Willie Adams, in 2004 and he was reelected in 2007. One of the gains of the majority-black school board was requiring all high school seniors of the city's four high schools to register to vote before graduating.

Sherrod coined the term the "Albany Movement." All of the activities in Albany were carried out under the "Albany Movement" heading.

Other cities modeled this pattern and named their movements: e.g., the Birmingham Movement and the Jackson Movement. SNCC formed alliances with the NAACP and many other organizations. Contrary to the media's perception that civil rights organizations were divided, they often worked collaboratively. "We were glad for any group to come and take a slap for us; we needed help; we also traveled to neighboring states and participated in the activities organized by other SNCC chapters and organizations," Sherrod said.

In 1964, Sherrod attended the Democratic Convention in Atlantic City; he recalled being asked by Fannie Lou Hamer, an SNCC worker from the Mississippi Delta, "How about getting me a glass of water?" Since she was an older lady who had a difficult time walking, due to injuries she and other civil rights workers had suffered the previous year, he kindly went to get her some water.

When he returned with a small glass of water, Fannie said, "Is this all you brought me?" He recalled, "I immediately went and found her a pitcher of water and she drunk the whole pitcher." He had never seen anybody drink that much water. So he started calling her "Tank Hamer." "The nickname was a private joke between me and Mrs. Hamer. When I greeted her I would say, 'What's up Tank Hamer?' "[7]

Civil rights organizations organized voter registration drives throughout the South. Martin Luther King Jr. and Malcolm X predicted that the ballot would be a means of obtaining political power in the future. Gradually, blacks were being elected to office. On the state level, Georgia blacks elected Leroy Johnson in 1962, who became the first black to serve in the Georgia General Assembly since the Reconstruction era of 1865–1877.[8]

On August 23, 1962, SNCC workers, Rev. James Bevel and James Forman, organized a mass meeting in Ruleville, Mississippi, at a local church to encourage blacks to register to vote. Of the 30,000 blacks in Sunflower County, not one of them was a registered voter. Race relations in the Mississippi Delta were extremely explosive and those who attempted to improve life for the Delta's black citizens were definitely putting their life at risk. Fannie Lou Hamer attended this mass meeting. At the end of the meeting, she and 17 other residents were inspired to become registered voters and signed a list promising to register at the Indianola courthouse the following Friday.

Although the group was risking their lives, Hamer and the other volunteers decided to challenge the electoral process. She reasoned that there was no difference between being physically killed and being alive yet dead. James Meredith had made a similar assessment of his race by stating that it was in a miserable existence. More and more, a small percentage of blacks, particularly youth, began to buck the system of white supremacy. When the Sunflower County group appeared at the courthouse in Indianola to register to vote, the clerk asked, "What do you nigras want?"[9] Hamer stepped into a leadership role and bravely replied that they were there to try to register to vote.

The citizens were initially given a form requiring them to write down their name, address, and place of employment, which was forwarded to the White Citizens' Council. The registrants were required to read and interpret several sections of the Mississippi Constitution. This test took most of the day. Afterward, the group left the courthouse and got on a bus headed back to Ruleville. En route, the bus was stopped by the police, who asked the occupants to step off of the bus. They were then instructed to reboard the bus and to return to Indianola. When they reached Indianola, they were detained and the bus driver was fined $100 for driving a bus of the wrong color. A local judge agreed to accept $30 for the fine and the group was allowed to leave.

When Mrs. Hamer reached home, she discovered that W. D. Marlow III, her employer, was furious that she had tried to register to vote. Marlow told her she would have to withdraw her voter registration or she would not be able to work for him anymore. Hamer said, "I didn't go down there to register for you, I went down there to register for myself."[10] She had baked cakes and sent them overseas when Marlow was in the war, had dutifully nursed his family when they were sick, had cleaned his house, had kept his books, and had handled his payroll; but she drew a line, for he was not about to influence her to withdraw the one act that would make her a first-class citizen. She believed voting would help change the deplorable circumstances of blacks.

Hamer knew firsthand what it was like to be black and poor. She recalled how her childhood had been in an article published by *Ebony* in 1966:

> Life was worse than hard. It was horrible! We never had enough to eat and I don't remember how old I was when I got my first pair of shoes, but I was a big girl. Mama tried to keep our feet warm by wrapping them in rags and tying them with string.[11]

The night after the group attempted to register to vote, Hamer left her home of 20 years and stayed with a black home owner named William Tucker and his family. Several weeks later, 16 bullets were fired into the Tucker home. Two young black girls were wounded during the incident.

After learning about the shooting, Hamer's husband immediately drove to the Tucker home and took his wife to another county to ensure her safety.

In the meantime, W. D. Marlow refused to pay the Hamers, fired them, and confiscated their car. Mrs. Hamer continued to go to the courthouse to take the "literacy test," and finally on her third attempt, January 10, 1963, she passed the test, becoming one of Sunflower County's first black registered voters. The other black registrants did not discourage easily and took the test as many as 26 times before passing and registering.

Local white racists used a series of harassment tactics to deter SNCC enlistees from their path. Hamer's husband, Perry, and her daughter were arrested, and they received a water bill for $9,000 even though there was no running water in their home. In fact, nearly half of the state's black population had no running water, and 66.4 percent had no indoor toilets. A local policeman known for his involvement in the Emmett Till murder personally threatened the Hamers. Their church was closed because the fire insurance was canceled. They were put on the "Black List," and no businesses would hire them; therefore they were forced to go on welfare, and food and financial support had to be collected for them.

Mrs. Hamer was the granddaughter of a former slave and the youngest of 20 children in the Townsend household. She had grown up in a family of impoverished sharecroppers who lived on a cotton plantation in Montgomery County, Mississippi. She married Perry "Pap" Hamer in 1942 and they became sharecroppers in Sunflower County. The stand that Mrs. Hamer took against Jim Crow customs came at a great personal cost to her.

Hamer escaped death several times. She and other civil rights organizers were brutally beaten after returning from a voter registration workshop in South Carolina on June 9, 1963. Mrs. Hamer's hospital recovery lasted almost a month, and her injuries made it difficult for her to walk. In the 1970s, Hamer was denied medical treatment in a Mound Bayou, Mississippi, segregated hospital facility and died a few years later on March 14, 1977. Like other brave souls, Hamer moved mountains of discrimination while she was on this earth.

A comrade of Medgar Evers, Dr. Ralph J. Bunche, the black undersecretary of the United Nations, addressed an audience at the 53rd Annual NAACP Convention in 1963. Following is a portion of his address:

I want to be as free as the whitest citizen. I want to exercise, and in full, the same rights as the white American. I want to be eligible for employment exclusively on the basis of my skills and employability, and for housing solely on my capacity to pay. I want to have the same privileges, the same treatment in public places as every other person. . . . I am as proud of my origin, ancestors, and race as anyone could be.

. . . In a competitive world [speaking to youth] you must rise to meet the competition. It also means building up confidence on the basis of demonstrated performance. In connection with preparation, the school drop-out figures for Negro youth are alarming. . . . don't let the fiction of race impair your vision or narrow your horizon of hope. Never think in terms of limitations—there need be none, at least none that you cannot overcome. . . . Train for what you want to do, break into it, face it with confidence. And above all, defend your dignity as men and women with all you have.[12]

Bunche was born in 1904 in Detroit, Michigan. His father, Fred Bunche, was a barber and his mother, Olive, was a musician. His parents both died when he was 13 years old; shortly afterward, his grandmother, Lucy Johnson, moved him and his two sisters to Los Angeles, California. Johnson was called "Nana," a Spanish term meaning "grandmother." She was a former slave who had the physical features of a white woman.

Bunche excelled in school; he was valedictorian of his graduating class at Jefferson High School in Los Angeles. He obtained a degree in international relations from the University of California in 1927 and graduated summa cum laude and valedictorian of his class. He obtained a master's degree in political science from Harvard University in 1927 and earned a PhD in 1934.

Although Bunche rose to the top of American society, he was no stranger to poverty. He knew what life was like for the ordinary black citizen. Bunche had sold newspapers in his youth to contribute financially to his family. He later served as a house boy for a movie star, laid carpet, and performed other odd jobs. His intellect led him to a career in public administration, a path that white society in general did not want blacks to aspire to pursue.

On Monday, June 11, 1963, two Alabama blacks, Vivian Malone and James A. Hood, attempted to integrate the University of Alabama. Hood was from Gadsden, Alabama, and Malone was from Mobile, Alabama. Alabama governor George Wallace stood in the door of the school to block the student's entry. He issued a prewritten speech similar to the speech that Governor Barnett had given a year earlier when he blocked James Meredith's registration at the University of Mississippi. Wallace eventually stepped aside and the students passed. Meredith passed the torch and paid Malone's and Hood's college tuition; his friend James Allen Jr. coordinated the transactions.

The next day Medgar Wiley Evers was assassinated. Evers had cried with the parents of lynching victims and had been one of only a few blacks to visit James Meredith while he was a student at Ole Miss, yet his life came to an end by a lone sniper. Evers was gunned down in his own driveway off Ridgeway Street in Jackson, Mississippi, when he got out of his car after a long workday. Charles Evers, Medgar's brother, recalled later that Medgar Evers's security detail required him to get out of the passenger's side of the car, where he would have been shielded by the car in the event of gunfire. On that night, Medgar got of his car on the driver's side. He died trying to make it inside his home to greet his wife, Myrlie, daughter, Reena, and his two sons, Darrell and Van.[13]

The morning of his assassination, Jimmie C. Robinson recalled that Evers came by the Masonic Temple on Lynch Street and briefly greeted people who were attending an NAACP meeting in Jackson. Robinson and Evers were members of the American Legion, which had been chartered in 1919 by Congress as a patriotic organization to support veterans. "Medgar came in the room with Joseph Broadwater and Albert Powell, wearing blue and gold American Legion caps," Robinson remembered.[14]

Floreada Harmon, co-owner of Harmon Drug Store on Farish Street, located in Jackson's black business district, recalled, "That evening before Medgar Evers was killed, he parked his car nearby and pointed to a police car which was being driven by white officers and I overheard him mentioning to George [Dr. George Harmon, her husband] that the police had been following him all day."[15]

The day after Evers was gunned down, Robinson visited Evers's home on Guynes Street, renamed Margaret Walker Alexander Street after a famous black author. Robinson recalled that reporters from the *New York Times* and other media outlets were there on that unforgettable day. Evers's assassin, Byron De la Beckwith, had used a long-distance scope on an Enfield army rifle to make sure his aim was accurate. Robinson was shocked when he saw the large hole a bullet left in the wall.

James Meredith was enrolled at Ole Miss when he heard the news that his friend Medgar Evers had been murdered. He was devastated. Meredith felt that Evers had sincerely represented the interest of his race. Meredith's name ended up on the Klan's hit list too; he was asked to leave Mississippi when he graduated that August, because the government could not protect him after graduation. After discovering he would have to leave Mississippi, he realized white supremacy would prevail. The day of his graduation, August 18, 1963, Meredith and his family left

Mississippi. They visited several countries in Europe, and he enrolled in University of Ibagan in Nigeria during the fall of 1964 and pursued a master's degree in economics.

Evers's legacy lives on, but unfortunately several generations of Americans are not aware of his contribution to our country. A street, a library, a post office, the Jackson Medgar Evers Library, Medgar Wiley Evers General Mail Facility, the Jackson-Evers International Airport in Jackson, Mississippi, and Medgar Evers College in New York City are a few of the institutions named for Medgar Evers.

Myrlie Evers and her children moved to California after her husband's death; she donated their former house to Tougaloo College in the 1990s. The house was converted into Medgar Evers Home Museum and is now a historical site. The home includes replica furnishing and the original refrigerator that was in the house when Evers was assassinated, donated by Charles Evers. A college employee, Minnie Watson, serves as the museum's tour guide.

The world's eyes began to focus on Mississippi, because death and terror had become commonplace, and people were watching to see the fate of Beckwith. Even though Beckwith's fingerprints were on the rifle scope, two all-white juries deadlocked in 1964 and Beckwith was set free. In those days, blacks could not sit on juries and white jurors were reluctant to convict white men and particularly known Klansmen. The unofficial laws of southern society gave racist whites the opportunity to adopt an "open shooting season" on blacks, and a wave of violence sweep through the South; this open season was similar to the violence of 1875 during Reconstruction, when black males, standing in line to vote, were shot in the streets by citizen-led firing squads.

SCLC opened a new office in Gadsden, Alabama, in the fall of 1962. Beulah Mae Sealey, a 40-year-old housewife, paid her SCLC membership dues, got involved in the Gadsden Movement, and became a voter education program volunteer. She drove her two-door 1959 white Chevrolet Impala to the SCLC office on 6th Street and Meighan Boulevard five days a week. "I got involved in the movement because I didn't think segregation was fair," she stated. Her husband, John Sealey, worked at the Republic Steel Plant, but he did not get involved with SCLC activities.

Beulah Mae Sealey was born in Etowah County, Alabama. Her mother was from Ballplay, a community in Cherokee County, and her father was from the small town of Clay. The family was subjected to Jim Crow laws and she despised the southern way of life. Although Sealey and other blacks paid the same amount of money for a sandwich at Woolworth's Diner, they could not sit down at the counter on a bar stool and eat their sandwiches. They had to get their sandwiches "to go" and walk and eat.

Many black citizens paid their SCLC membership dues, but they had to support the movement silently. Schoolteachers, maids, and other employees could lose their jobs if they openly participated in movement activities. She maintained a log of my mileage and received a gas stipend from SCLC for my services. Sealey taught adults basic literacy skills such as signing documents, basic reading skills, how to balance a checking account, and other life skills. When black citizens learned enough to complete a voting registration form, she drove them to the courthouse.

Her heart was filled with riches beyond money when she saw the joy written on the faces of those who had registered to vote for the first time. "I's registered" were beautiful words to hear. Blacks firmly believed the ballot would give them liberty, end segregation, and cure all societal ills.

Under the direction of SCLC leaders, Beulah Sealey organized 20 high school girls and Joe Flaukner organized 20 high school boys to participate in sit-in demonstrations to challenge Jim Crow laws in Gadsden. Sealey and the girls walked five blocks from the SCLC office to Main Street downtown and they crowded around Woolworth's lunch counter. The girls wore blouses and skirts below their knees and many wore oxford saddle shoes. "People didn't wear tennis shoes in those days," Sealey noted. Flaukner and the young men staged a sit-in demonstration at the Kress 5 & 10 Cent Store.

According to Beulah Sealey, after she and the girls reached the counter an employee cried out, "You will have to leave, we can't serve y'all." The protesters refused to leave the premises and sat and or lay on the floor in front of the lunch counter. The protesters had been trained to protect themselves from any violent reactions from white citizens by covering their heads with their arms and hands and bending their bodies in fetal positions.

The Gadsden demonstrators were not subjected to any violence and they were not insulted. In other cities, whites poured drinks on the heads of sit-in demonstrators and some protesters were even severely beaten. However, the store's staff reported the incident to the police precinct, which was located on 1st Street. Within minutes the patrol officers arrived driving a paddy wagon. Each protester was picked up and placed in the rear of the wagon. Flaukner and the boys were also arrested and confined in jail, where they remained for 10 days. During the next 10 days, an adult organized a group of boys and girls to gather at lunch counters to protest Gadsden's segregation laws. Each day a new group was arrested and the jail became overcrowded.

The prisoners were served bologna, bread, and grits covered with gravy for breakfast, and were given large bowls of black-eyed peas and corn bread for dinner. On November 29, Beulah Sealey turned 41 years old in the city jail. Her husband, John, went to the jailhouse to see if he would be allowed to visit his wife, but the jailer refused. "Well, today is my wife's birthday. Somebody got to sing Happy Birthday to Beulah Mae," Mr. Sealey demanded. The white guard walked to the cell, found Mrs. Sealey, and sang "Happy Birthday" to her.

Later that evening, Dr. Martin Luther King Jr. and Ralph Abernathy came to the jailhouse and the guards allowed them to make a brief visit. Both men walked through the hall, greeting the detainees and inquiring about their treatment. The food was the prisoners' biggest complaint. Sealey recalled that the most unpleasant part of her confinement was the watery coffee. "We had a good time while we were in jail singing freedom and spiritual songs," Sealey said.

Their topics of discussion included the integration of James Meredith into Ole Miss the previous month and JFK. Meredith's sister Hazel was Sealey's daughter-in-law and the mother of two of her grandchildren. By the time the 10th group was arrested, the jail was overflowing with people. "We were turned out at a trial."[16]

Over 6,000 people marched through the streets of Jackson on June 15, 1963, to protest the assassination of Medgar Evers. Rosie Clay, a 20-year-old freshman majoring in physical education at Tougaloo College, and several classmates parked their cars and joined the marchers who were walking up Capital Street, across Lamar Street. "As we approached Woolworth [near Farish Street], a large group of marchers tried to go into the front door to buy fountain drinks. When they [Woolworth staff] saw us coming, they locked the door," she said. The Jackson police maintained a presence by holding chained dogs as they stood on the outskirts of the crowd.[17]

According to Leon Goldsberry, at age 15 he was arrested while marching with protesters in Jackson who united and marched to protest the assassination of Medgar W. Evers. "We were jailed on the Fair Grounds. They fed us meal and water, and we had to sleep on the pavement," he noted. "Burt Case, a local news reporter, publically called us Negros when he gave television reports on our activities. The word 'Negros' was a fancy saying for niggers," he said.[18]

Dr. Jacob L. Reddix, the president of Jackson State College did not dismiss classes so that students could attend the funeral of Medgar Evers. "Mr. Reddix had expelled students whose names were sent to him for participating in protest previously. So we were very careful not to get caught or arrested," Dorothy Benford, a social studies major noted. Reddix prohibited students from getting involved in civil rights activities, but not all of the professors at the school shared his views.

Dorothy recalled her teacher Dr. C. C. Mosley saying, "I'm going to walk over to the blackboard and write your assignment for the next class, and when I turn around, I don't want to see nobody." The students were gone when Mosley turned around. As Benford was walking into the Masonic Temple to attend Evers's funeral, which was already in session, Martin Luther King and Ralph Abernathy were coming outside. She spoke to King and he replied, "How are you, daughter?" Dorothy was delighted yet surprised to see them. She replied, "I am fine, Dr. King."[19]

Three decades later, Evers's murderer was retried. On February 4, 1994, 73-year-old Beckwith was found guilty of Evers's murder by a racially mixed jury in Jackson, Mississippi. Because Beckwith was old when he was finally convicted, he served only seven years of his life sentence before he died on January 22, 2001. Many argue that justice was quite late.

Civil rights organizations and labor groups united in an attempt to unlock the doors of opportunity for blacks and other groups during the March on Washington for Jobs and Freedom on August 28, 1963. At the Lincoln Memorial in front of a crowd of 250,000, Martin Luther King Jr. delivered his "I Have a Dream" speech—"I have a dream that one day this nation will rise up and live out the true meaning of its creed: 'We hold these truths to be self-evident; that all men are created equal.'"—and SNCC advocate John Lewis said in his speech, "Some of our brothers are receiving starvation wages or no wages at all."[20]

As blacks attempted to break Jim Crow customs, whites became more violent. In 1963, Tallahatchie County, Mississippi, law officials shot three black protesters. Madison County police officers W. M. McNeer and Frank David shot Alfred Brown in the street and five youth participating in a voter registration drive in Canton, Mississippi.

A total of 1,000 protesters were arrested; shots were fired at workers, nine workers were beaten, and 25 black churches were burned. Unable to seek redress from the local judicial system, Robert ("Bob") Moses, a field secretary for SNCC, filed a complaint with the U.S. Justice Department. SNCC leader H. Rap Brown said, "Violence is as American as cherry pie."[21] He seemed to have a point. The defense to maintain segregation in Jackson, Mississippi, was more extreme than any other place in the United States, but violence was common in the Deep South.

Ninety-year-old Clint Alexander, a former member of the Alabama Christian Movement for Human Rights, witnessed southern violence during the last century too. "I found a smoking bomb behind Bethel

Baptist Church in Birmingham, Alabama in 1957. An expert moved the bomb away from the church, which saved the lives of members. The bomb blew a hole in the street big enough to sit a Volkswagen in," he recalled. A few years later, on September 15, 1963, four black girls (Denise McNair, 11, Carole Robertson, Addie Mae Collins, and Cynthia Wesley, all 14) were not as fortunate; they died when 16th Street Baptist Church in Birmingham was bombed.[22]

On November 22, 1963, as Americans watched their black-and-white television sets, news anchor Walter Cronkite with weepy eyes announced that President John F. Kennedy had been assassinated while sitting in an open black convertible beside his wife in Dallas, Texas. President Kennedy had one of the highest public support ratings of any American president. He and Jackie were the equivalent of a royal couple to the American public.

In June of 1963 Kennedy, who enjoyed widespread popularity among black Americans, had announced to the nation in a radio-television address that segregation was morally wrong and that Congress should act on the issue. Like his predecessors, Kennedy promoted token changes for the country's colored citizens, but his life ended during the middle of his first term in office. Nevertheless, he was loved by minorities because he spoke openly in favor of a new America and it was on the heels of his administration that congress passed new civil rights legislation.

A framed picture of JFK and Martin Luther King Jr. hung in the living room of millions of black Americans throughout the country for decades after their assassinations. The legacy of those who helped reshape America will be remembered for evermore. Katherine Nelson, who grew up during the Jim Crow South in Holmes County, Mississippi, had a gold-framed family portrait of King, his wife, and four children hanging on her living room wall for over half a century. "I purchased the portrait of King and his family in 1968 before he was murdered," Nelson recalled.

Even the threat of death could not keep some blacks away from the polls, and blacks continued to challenge Jim Crow customs. Rev. Bernard Lafayette, field secretary of SNCC and director of a voter registration drive in Selma, Alabama, was severely beaten by two white men and had to have stitches to close the multiple wounds he received. In Greenwood, Mississippi, about a dozen blacks, who had not broken any laws, were arrested while they sat on the courthouse lawn waiting for the voter registrar's office to reopen after lunch.

The soulful lyrics of Sam Cooke, "A change gonna come," echoed in the black man's heart, and the spiritual cry of marchers sounded out in the streets. The foot of oppression was on the black man's neck holding him to the ground, and he was struggling to rise up. In 1963, half of the black population in America was still living below the poverty level, compared to only one-fifth of whites. In the South, blacks were living on former plantations. In Harlem, blacks were living in rat-infested slums.

In June of 1964, youth workers went to Washington, DC, and testified concerning the daily terror they faced in Mississippi. They told President Lyndon B. Johnson, Attorney General Robert Kennedy, and representatives of the Department of Justice that numerous federal laws were broken by Mississippi whites. The president was silent and his administration did not respond to their complaints. Thirteen days later, three civil rights workers—James Chaney, a young black Mississippi native, and two whites, Andrew Goodman and Michael Schwerner— were arrested, released from jail, and shot to death in Philadelphia, Mississippi.

An informant's testimony eventually led to jail sentences for the sheriff, deputy sheriff, and others involved in the murders. Edgar Ray Killen, a Klan member and a preacher who had ordered the murders, was not convicted, because a white female juror refused to vote with the other 11 white jurors to convict a preacher. However, 40 years after the anniversary of the murders on June 21, 2005, Killen was retried and convicted of three counts of murder by a racially mixed jury and sentenced to serve three consecutive 20-year terms. Like Beckwith, Killen was a very old man when he was hauled off to jail.

During the 1960s, there was common consensus in the black community concerning the need for voter registration drives; although many blacks were terrorized when they attempted to register to vote, each community had different voter registration experiences. In May of 1964, an all-black high school in Georgia quietly administered voter registration drives without the threat of violence. That spring, 17-year-old Catherine McKay (now Catherine Coleman) stood in line to register to vote with her 500 classmates at Luther Judson Price High School, in Atlanta, Georgia.

Coleman recalled, "My registration card was mailed to me and I have been voting ever since." SCLC was involved in numerous protest activities in Atlanta and Coleman was invited to participate in their activities, but her mother would not allow them to join SCLC. It was dangerous to protest in those days, because participants were bitten by dogs, beaten, jailed, and in some cases tortured or murdered.

"When I was in school, we had to learn how to complete a federal income tax return, and were required to take typing. If the present school systems taught children how to fill out tax returns, and administered the good practices from the segregated school era, they would be better off," she concluded.[23]

On April 4, 1964, Malcolm X, the spokesman for the Nation of Islam, a black Muslin organization, who lived in Harlem, delivered "The Ballot or the Bullet" speech in Detroit, Michigan; he too believed voting would give blacks the political power needed to change America, but he opposed demonstrations. On July 5, 1964, Malcolm X spoke to a gathering of the Organization of Afro-American Unity. During the speech, he argued that demonstrations and protests were an outdated method for blacks to use in their quest for freedom:

> The days of demonstrations are over. They're outdated. All that does is put you in jail. You've got to pay money to get out of jail. And you still haven't solved the problem. Go and find out how much money has been paid by demonstrators for court, for legal fees, bail bonds, during the past five or six years. And then find out what has been gained from it and you'll see that we're in the red. We're broke . . . A demonstration is alright if it's going to get results.
> Oh yes . . . Don't say that you don't like what I did and you're going to walk in front of my house for an hour. No, you're wasting your time. I'll sit down and go to sleep until your hour is up . . .[24]

The ideology of Malcolm X was more popular in the North, for southern youth participated in protests and practiced the moderate "nonviolent" concept promoted by NAACP, SCLC, the Urban League, and Congress on Racial Equality (CORE). Though a southerner, James Meredith opposed demonstrations as well. He had witnessed the violence committed against the Freedom Riders in 1961 while a student at JSC, and he believed it would take more than demonstrations to change America. However, demonstrations gave voice to America's racial inequity, for the world witnessed police brutality and America's race problems.

CORE glamorized sit-ins to American youth. In November of 1963, an article entitled "All for the Cause: The Demonstrator," by P. A Bullins, appeared in the *Negro Digest*. The article started by saying, "Hey, man, what's happening? Have you made the scene yet? . . . What scene! . . . Like man ain't you hip to the battle? . . . Civil Rights, man. That's what's happening man. Like dig, haven't you read the press on the scene in Torrance, which was a town in California where demonstrations against housing had been staged."[25]

The article announced that if a protester went to jail on Saturday, he would be out on Sunday and that CORE would pay the bail bond. The author also assured the reader that he would not have to worry about missing school and that any charges would not prevent him from obtaining a civil service job.

On February 21, 1965, 16 shots were fired into Malcolm X's body by black Muslims while he was delivering a speech at the Audubon Ballroom in Harlem. His ideas gained national prominence after he was assassinated. The murders of Malcolm X, Martin Luther King Jr., as well as hundreds of civil rights workers took a toll on the movement, but blacks gradually made some political gains.

Because of racism, only 4 percent of black southerners voted in 1940. Fifty years later, two-thirds of all black elected officials in the United States were in the South.[26] After the 1964 Voting Rights Act, black voter registration in Mississippi jumped from 6.7 to 60 percent.[27] The Civil Rights Act of 1965 and the 1964 Voting Rights Act eventually helped curtail segregation and the disenfranchisement of blacks. The Voting Rights Act required federal examiners to monitor the elections in six southern states, part of a seventh state, as well as Alaska. The new law abolished literacy tests, and the following year the Supreme Court ruled the poll tax unconstitutional.

After the Voting Rights Act was enacted, federal registrars were dispatched into 25 Mississippi counties. In conjunction with voter registration drives, an estimated 268,440 blacks registered to vote by 1971.[28] The goal of black leaders was to obtain political power, but it took many years before they were able to elect enough blacks to increase their representation in government.

Of the 174 Mississippi state legislatures, there were still no black officials in 1964. In 1968, Robert George Clark Jr. became the first black elected to the state legislature since Reconstruction; he represented District 16, which was comprised of Holmes and Yazoo Counties. The Mississippi Freedom Democratic Party (MFDP), which was organized in April of 1964 by SNNC, the NAACP, and other organizations, had helped get out the vote and elect Clark. During the 1964 election year, out of 410 county Board of Supervisors positions, 4 blacks were elected. However, one black on a five-member board was not able to garner enough power to get the roads paved for his constituents.

Mississippi blacks continued to register to vote, and some county clerks were friendlier than others. On September 10, 1966, an Attala County registrant and a cousin of James Meredith was greeted by a friendly white clerk employed in the Kosciusko courthouse. Glennie Alston Kirkland, a 25-year-old woman who taught junior high school mathematics, went to the Kosciusko courthouse and registered to vote. Kirkland said, "Other people had paved the way before I registered to vote and I did not encounter any problems."[29]

The MFDP sought to hasten the political power of black Mississippians and to challenge the state's official Democratic Party, which had denied blacks the opportunity to participate in the electoral process. MFDP officials tried to win seats at the August 1964 Democratic National Convention.

The MFDP elected 64 delegates, including Laurence Guyot, Aaron Henry, Fannie Lou Hamer, Ed King, and Unita Blackwell. SNCC members Charles Sherrod, Leslie McLemore, and Frank Smith were studying in the Washington, DC, area that summer and organized the arrival of MFDP delegates. Guyot was chair and Hamer was the vice chair. Henry was the president of the Mississippi NAACP chapters, King was a white chaplain at Tougaloo College, and Guyot, Blackwell, and McLemore were SNCC organizers.

The presence of MFDP delegates at the 1964 Democratic National Convention was inconvenient for President Lyndon B. Johnson, who was seeking the Democratic Party's nomination for a second term. MFDP was arousing national attention concerning the widespread discriminatory practices against Mississippi blacks. White House staff unsuccessfully tried to quiet MFDP delegates by persuading them to wait.

Hamer testified in front of the convention's Credentials Committee. She talked passionately about the problems she encountered when she attempted to register to vote and the brutality imposed on movement participants when they were jailed in Winona, Mississippi:

> All of this is on account we want to register, to become first-class citizens, and if the Freedom Party is not seated now, I question America, is this America, the land of the free and the home of the brave where we have to sleep with our telephones off the hooks because our lives be threatened daily because we want to live as decent human beings—in America?[30]

President Johnson did not want Hamer to occupy one of the seats. He referred to her as "the illiterate woman." His administration called an emergency press conference in an effort to divert attention from Hamer's testimony, but her story aired nationally on the evening news. Johnson specified that Aaron Henry and Ed King could take two at-large voting seats, but the group refused to accept the compromise. Henry reasoned that Johnson was picking the black leader he wanted.

Hamer professed her disappointment with the offer by noting, "We didn't come all this way for no two seats, when all of us is tired."[31] Martin Luther King Jr. tried to persuade the delegates to accept the president's offer, and the MFDP delegation received national criticism for refusing to compromise with the president. Johnson preferred that the MFDP delegates simply go away, because southern delegates of the Democratic Party threatened to walk out if the Mississippi slate became integrated. Powerful Mississippi senators James Eastland and John Stennis, both known segregationists, opposed any integration efforts.

In the meantime, Johnson authorized J. Edgar Hoover to put the MFDP delegates under federal surveillance. MFDP was successful in gaining blacks more representation in the Democratic Party. Civil rights attorney Joe Rauh predicted that there would never be an all-white Democratic Party, and at the 1968 Democratic Convention a racially integrated delegation replaced the all-white regulars.

Rev. G. David Singleton, a white man from a farming community in Willows, California, sympathized with black southerners and relocated to the South to help change Jim Crow laws. He taught voter education to black Alabama residents from 1964 to 1975. In 1966, he became a poll watcher at the largest black precinct in Birmingham, Alabama. During that time, he met Rev. John W. Rice, Condoleezza Rice's father, a pastor of a church in Birmingham.

Singleton witnessed firsthand the continuing discrimination perpetrated by whites on Birmingham's black citizens. The white-led Board of Registrars would mail black voters instructions to report to new polling locations on Election Day in order to reduce black voter turnout. Many blacks did not have a chance to read their notice because they went directly to the polls after work and so were not able to find their new polling center in time to cast their vote.

Singleton confessed, "I will never forget the joy I felt when I saw blacks wall to wall on crutches and in wheelchairs standing in line until 2:00 a.m. in the morning waiting to exercise their right to vote in the March 1966 primary."[32] Rev. Singleton and thousands of youth helped change America and were instrumental in increasing black voter turnout during the Second Reconstruction. There were numerous casualties in this era, but gradually activists began to see the fruits of change.

CHAPTER 8

Fruits of Change

If America isn't for everybody, it isn't America.
—James Howard Meredith

In 1966, a branch of the MFDP was set up on Bill Street (known now as Yazoo Street) in Lexington, Mississippi, and Bea Ellis Jenkins became involved in the Lexington Movement, which facilitated voter registration drives and staged demonstrations. Fannie Lou Hamer encouraged Lexington residents to challenge the injustice in Holmes County, just as she and others had confronted discrimination in Sunflower County and throughout the South.

Jenkins was born in North Mississippi to property-less sharecroppers. When she and her siblings were 8 or 9 years old, they were required to pick cotton and perform field work. She was a few weeks shy of 11 when the stock market crashed in October of 1929; she remembered the Great Depression years vividly.

The children of sharecroppers were allowed to attend school during the fall and spring after they had gathered the year's crops. Jenkins, her relatives, and neighbors walked three miles (the equivalent of a one-way forty-five minute walk) to attend classes in a one-room school on the first floor of a two-story building. The facility was used for learning during the day, and members of Eastern Star and the Masons used the second floor after school hours.

Jenkins and her classmates sat on wooden benches in an open class-room. The school's human and class resources were limited. The younger children used the same primer book each year of the six grades Jenkins attended school. "Our principal was the janitor and teacher. The older boys had to go out into the woods to cut wood and start a fire on cold mornings. By the time the room warmed up, we had missed a good portion of our opportunity to learn," she stated.

White children were taken to school in their parents' buggies and were later bused to school. "We didn't have those advantages," Jenkins recalled. She remembered reading a passage in a book repeatedly— "Mary went to market to buy a stick of candy." Jenkins said the girl in the school book had a large pocket on the front of her dress. "Lord," Jenkins said with a slight laugh, "in those days, girls had pockets on the front of their dresses, but black girls tied their pockets up with ribbons, because we didn't have a penny to put in our pocket."

Jenkins moved to Lexington in the 1950s. Her husband, Louis, was a construction laborer and she was a maid for Will D. Wilson, the president of Holmes County Bank. She was responsible for cleaning, cooking, ironing, running errands, and caring for the Wilsons' child. Mr. Wilson gave her and her husband the bank loan to purchase the house and lot they lived in on Boulevard Street. She recalled Mr. Wilson telling her, "Anytime you want to march you can march, and if anybody say anything to you, you come tell me about it." Mr. Wilson's position was unusual because most white employers supported maintaining segregation and reported civil rights activities to the White Citizens' Council.

The doors to the MFDP office site in Lexington were open from Monday to Saturday. "In those days, didn't much move on Sunday. Sunday was the Lord's day," Jenkins noted. They elected Mary Hightower, a Durant resident, to serve as the president, and Georgia G. Clark, from West, as the secretary. Johnny Walls became their attorney, and Robert G. Clark Jr., a schoolteacher, was also a part of the Lexington Movement.

Members paid $5 annual dues, which helped support the operating costs of the MFDP. Jenkins's husband never got involved in the Lexington Movement. He had sugar diabetes and was not able to keep up physically, but he faithfully paid his $5 membership dues. Jenkins recalled that if she got off work at 1 p.m., she would go down to the MFDP office and perform whatever task was needed to be done that day.

Sometimes the group marched and sometimes Jenkins escorted black citizens to the courthouse so they could register to vote. "When we first went to register, the white folks denied our right to vote. They [the court clerks] yelled, 'Get out of here nigger, you ain't gonna register and vote up in here,'" she recalled. The marchers often sang inspirational songs. Jenkins still remembered a verse of one of the songs they often sang:

Ain't gonna let nobody turn me around.

We gonna keep on marching up the freedom highway.[1]

On more than one occasion, white police officers arrested Jenkins and the marchers, but they would not stop protesting. During one jail stay, Jenkins and the other protesters sang so loud that people could hear them around the corner. The jailers became annoyed by the noise and said, "Let them niggers out!" The protesters were released without posting bail that day, but there were times when bail had to be posted for protesters. The 1960s were dangerous times for blacks. "We were willing to die trying to gain the rights that we believed were due to us, but no one in our group was ever harmed," Jenkins said.

From her house, she can see children sneaking off from school and it makes her sick to see them hanging out doing nothing when they could be in school. "If children fail now, it is their own fault, because they have the opportunity to go to school and to get a good education," Jenkins complained. She added, "We paved the way for black children and yet some of them don't realize the advantages they have. I remember those days when there were no black police, sheriffs, elected officials, and limited educational opportunities."[2] Since this interview, Jenkins returned to north Mississippi and is now a resident of a nursing home there.

By 1966, the children and grandchildren of slaves in the Mississippi Delta, who were challenging the white power structure, were having a hard time. In reality, the Civil Rights Act of 1965 had not changed anything for the African American citizens in the Mississippi Delta. "They were giving us hell!" Unita Blackwell, a SNCC organizer, said frankly.

Blackwell was born March 18, 1933, in Lula, Mississippi. She lived on "Mr. Hamilton's" plantation. She said, "His name could have been Hampton 'cause my mama told me his name but she couldn't pronounce words good." Blackwell continued: "Virdia Mae did not go far in school; she had a third- or fourth-grade education. My father, Willie Brown, died many years ago, but mama died last month [August of 2005]. She was 90 years old; she would have turned 91 had she lived until August 25th."

The white landowners were evicting any black person whose name appeared on the county's registrar list. That year, Unita Blackwell met with people who had become homeless and she organized a protest.

People living on the plantations were living in three-room shacks. They wanted decent housing, fair pay, and to be treated like human beings. "About 70 of us moved in the airport; we had pots and pans; we were cooking and everything," she said.

When the group occupied the Greenville Airport, which was vacant, Blackwell and her husband, Jeremiah, were not living on the man's place (a plantation, where sharecroppers lived). They lived on a lot in Mayersville, Mississippi, on land that had been in her husband's family since Reconstruction. The Blackwells did not get evicted when they attempted to register, but they became the object of terrorists; they could never let their guard down after waking up to a burning cross in their yard. Because they received so many death threats over the phone, they had to sleep on the floor rather than in their bed.

Blackwell became active in the movement in 1964. She was encouraged to get involved while attending a meeting at a local church sponsored by SNCC. Like Fannie Lou Hamer, Blackwell was older than the average SNCC member. She was 31 when she became a field organizer and Hamer was 45. "I worked with the people, you see. We challenged the system, because we did not have any representation in the government," she added. Blackwell knew firsthand what it was like to work the man's fields from sunrise to sunset. She proclaimed, "Picking cotton can tear up your hands. I used to pick 250 pounds of cotton a day. Ain't many people can pick that much cotton."

After occupying the airport for a few days, the group was evicted by the Air National Guard; however, Blackwell and others continued to remain active in the movement. Blackwell became the first black female mayor in Mississippi in 1976; she served several consecutive terms and was responsible for installing a water system and raising funds for other structures. Her life story is recorded in her book, *Barefootin'*, which was published in June of 2006.[3] *Barefootin'* was cowritten by JoAnne Prichard Morris, a former acquisition editor of the University of Mississippi Press and the widow of Willie Morris, a personal friend of Blackwell's, who wrote the script for the film *My Dog Skip* (2000).

While SNCC workers were in the Mississippi Delta trying to dismantle the many barriers to black progress, SCLC staff and volunteers in Macon County, Alabama, were beginning to witness the fruits of change. The predominantly black county is home to Tuskegee Institute. The Tuskegee Civic Association had administered voter registration drives since the 1940s to local residents, who were primarily educated and middle class.

On May 3, 1966, 75 black candidates ran for public office in the Black Belt counties. Gradually, Alabama blacks began to see the fruits of their labor. Lucius Amerson, a 32-year-old Korean War veteran, became the first black sheriff since Reconstruction in Macon County. The voters also elected a black tax collector and a black county commissioner. Fred Gray, a civil rights attorney, lost the 1966 election because his white opponent used the ballots of dead men to rig the election, but Gray was elected to the Alabama state legislature in 1970. In 1972, Johnny Ford, of Tuskegee, became the first black mayor in Alabama.

The 1967 election year in Mississippi was significant because 22 blacks were elected, marking the first time since Reconstruction that blacks had achieved significant political representation. A headline in the Greenville, Mississippi, paper the *Delta Democrat-Times* said, "Negro Vote Is Now Potent in the State."[4] MFDP member Robert G. Clark made history too by becoming the first black elected to the Mississippi state legislature since Reconstruction. He defeated a three-term legislator, J. P. Love, who was a Delta planter and the chair of the House Education Committee.[5]

In spite of the positive changes taking place, the majority of blacks feared the white establishment, and Mississippi blacks saw less political progress than neighboring states. James Meredith returned to his home state in May of 1966 and organized the "Walk Against Fear" to help alleviate the black man's fear of the white power structure. He told a *Times* reporter, "I want to test whether or not a Negro in Mississippi really has to fear to walk down the road and to stand up and to be men, and also to urge people to register and vote as a kind of way of asserting whether Negroes are really men in Mississippi."[6] At that time, Meredith and his family lived at 25 Claremont Avenue in New York City on the fourth floor of the Peter Minuitt Building, which was across the street from Barnard College and within walking distance of Riverside Church, where Dr. King delivered his famous "A Time to Break Silence" antiwar speech.

Meredith was a student at Columbia University School of Law; his wife, Mary June, was teaching at a junior high school in Manhattan; and their six-year-old son, John, was in the first grade. Meredith associated with people from all walks of life including reputed black gangster Bumpy Johnson and James Baldwin, a writer and activist. "We lived in the same neighborhood. He [Meredith] was very open and friendly," Afeni Shakur recalled later.[7]

On June 5, 1966, Robert Terrell, a Memphis resident, drove Meredith to the Mississippi-Tennessee state line to meet companions who started walking with him down Highway 51 south. "When I dropped James off, there were around 25 people waiting for him," Terrell recalled.[8] The Walk Against Fear was scheduled to continue for 225 miles down Highway 51 south until the group and those who joined them reached

Jackson, Mississippi. FBI agents and state troopers followed the walkers, and news reporters drove slowly ahead of the group.

Meredith distinguished walking to be quite different from marching. "Walking is the act of exercising one's right as a citizen to use the highways and byways of the United States, but marching is protesting, and I ain't never participated in a protest," Meredith said emphatically. In essence, people who chose to walk were exercising their right as private citizens to walk.[9] Nevertheless, whether walking or marching, both actions were attempting to defy an existing system, which is essentially protesting.

When Meredith announced his walk, he welcomed any able-bodied man to join. "I insisted that women and children should not have to take the risk of walking up Highway 51," he said. For this reason, Mary June and John did not join him. "My goal is for me and my kind to dominate the world. When me and my kind become rulers, we will rule the world the right way," he said, waving his arms in the air. "Most human beings want satisfaction in their lifetime. Destroying white supremacy will give me satisfaction, but I realize that I may not see the system destroyed during my life." So, all he believed he could do was lay the groundwork that will eventually destroy this system.[10]

Meredith, Rev. Robert O. Weeks, and other men who had joined the Walk Against Fear spent the night at a home across the Mississippi state line; they continued walking the morning of June 6, 1966, and FBI agents, state troopers, and local police officers trailed the small group on day two of the walk. After walking a total of roughly 30 miles, the walkers reached the small town of Hernando, Mississippi. "Every black leader in the county [Desoto County] was ahead waiting to join us," Meredith recalled.

According to the article "Big Changes Are Coming," as Meredith and friends walked up Highway 51 they saw a few small stores, some old decaying mansions, and many old decaying board houses where blacks lived in Hernando, the first town in Mississippi coming from Tennessee. Meredith walked up to the main square of the town and started talking to black residents. "I told them that a new day was coming, that we were going to get all the rights and privileges we were entitled to," he said. He urged some to register to vote. Some said, "We gonna register." Meredith also told residents the old order was passing, that they should stand up as men with nothing to fear.[11]

The group walking with Meredith included Mohammad Rauf of the *Washington Daily News*; Sherwood Ross, a white Washington radio broadcaster who had volunteered to serve as Meredith's press coordinator; Rev. Robert O. Weeks, a white Episcopal minister from Monroe, New York;

and Joe Crittendon, a Memphis Negro businessman. Shortly after walking through Hernando, Claude Sterrett, a friend of Meredith's from New York, joined them after they had passed through the town and said breathlessly, "Jay, I met a man down the road who said someone's waiting for you with a gun. He's gonna shoot you."[12]

Suddenly, Meredith heard a voice behind him. "James," the voice said. "I only want James Meredith. All the rest of you stand aside." James turned around and saw a man standing in the roadside foliage. Meredith said:

> This was the face the southern Negro has been staring at through 350 years of history: the hard eyes, the fleshy face, the hard line of mouth. You've seen the same face in dozens of pictures. It is the face of the deputy sheriff, the face of the man freed by the all-white jury after murdering a Negro, the face of those vicious young men carrying Confederate flags who hit civil-right workers with ax handles.[13]

"Just James Meredith," he said, moving toward the shoulder of the road. "I wished suddenly that I had brought a gun, things were happening so fast," Meredith recalled. Then he threw himself on the ground and was hit in the back by shots from Aubry James Norvell. Within moments, Meredith was lying on his side stretched out on the pavement of Highway 51 in agony. He had been wounded by shotgun pellets. Norwell was in the area bird hunting and shot James Meredith when he recognized him.

Photographers and reporters, who were riding slowly in vehicles ahead of the group, jumped out of their cars and took several photos of Meredith lying against the pavement. Rev. Weeks surveyed Meredith's wounds and pleaded with onlookers, who were asking questions and taking notes, to get Meredith to a hospital. Lying on the ground, Meredith heard the commotion around him. "It was, I suppose, as close as I had come to being killed," he later said. Meredith knew what millions of people would not know for at least an hour—that he was alive because initially it was reported that James Meredith had been killed instead of just wounded.[14]

Meredith was driven to William F. Bowld Hospital in Memphis. As soon as he was alert enough to make a phone call, he called his wife in New York. She was in a state of shock after hearing the reports on the news. He tried to call his 62-year-old mother, Roxie, but she had broken down after hearing the news and was under sedation. "It would be two days before she could be told that I was alive," he recalled.[15]

Meredith did not rest well that first night in the hospital. When he woke up the next morning, he noticed a bouquet of flowers on the shelf,

which was from Dick Gregory, one of his friends. Gregory was a
renowned comedian and a civil rights activist. He, his wife, and family
had flown in to visit Meredith. Gregory had left home thinking Meredith
was dead. He planned to resume the walk at the location of where
Meredith was shot and went to survey the area.

Some of the original walkers were waiting for Meredith to recover so
that they could continue the walk with him. However, news of the shooting reached other leaders, and Martin Luther King Jr., the spokesman for
SCLC; Stokely Carmichael, the SNCC chairman; Roy Wilkins, the executive director of NAACP; Floyd McKissick, the national director of CORE;
and Whitney Young, director of the Urban League, united and decided
to continue the walk in Meredith's name.

"The Big 5 [King, Carmichael, Wilkins, McKissick, and Young] visited
me while I was in the hospital. They let me know they wanted to continue
the walk," Meredith recalled. The civil rights leaders asked Meredith who
he wanted to be in charge in his absence and he replied, "Martin Luther
King Jr." When asked if Carmichael could use the words "black power"
in his speeches, Meredith said, "Absolutely." Wilkins and Young could
not come to a consensus with the other leaders about the logistics of the
march and they flew back to New York.[16]

With Meredith's blessing, King and the other leaders invited people
from all over the country to join them; they changed the name "Walk
Against Fear" to the "Meredith March Against Fear." The walk was
resumed at the location where Meredith had been ambushed in
Hernando. Like a bandwagon, as the marchers reached new communities, more people joined. Meredith urged the leaders not to do anything that would be detrimental to the million blacks who would still
be in Mississippi after they left, and shared his concern about the
safety of women and children and a large group in general. Charles
Evers visited Meredith in the hospital too. He had concerns about the
impact that the march would have on Mississippi blacks after it was
over.

Norvell, a native of Forest City, Arkansas, was an unemployed white
resident in Memphis. He was quickly apprehended and arrested, wearing
a white shirt and a pair of sunglasses at the time of arrest. Norvell was
sentenced to serve a five-year prison sentence for his crime, becoming
one of the first southern whites to be convicted for committing a violent
crime against a black citizen.

After being a victim of a violent crime, Meredith made a public
endorsement of the Deacons of Defense and Justice which had formed in
Jonesboro, Louisiana in 1964 as an armed self-defense organization to

protect civil rights workers from Klan and police violence. Meredith noted that he would have been better prepared had he been armed when he heard Norvell shout to him. Meredith said:

> Dr. King is quite an impressive man, but there is much feeling that his philosophy of nonviolence is no longer tenable. There are many Negroes, myself included, who believe that we no longer can guarantee the white man is Mississippi that we will not strike back . . . My own feeling is that nonviolence is incompatible with American ideals. America is a tough country, and a man has to look for his own, to be his own man . . . I believe in the next few years, you will see fewer and fewer Negroes supporting nonviolence . . . It is not an American idea to abandon willingly any personal control over your own life; and this philosophy of nonviolence requires this.[17]

Dr. King and the other leaders resumed the march in Hernando at the location of Meredith's ambush in his honor. On several occasions, white spectators sat outside as the marchers passed by and yelled insulting remarks at the participants; some of the marchers were attacked on side roads. Many local whites wore Confederate clothing and held the Confederate flag up as a gesture to marchers that white supremacy reigned in Mississippi. During the march, some 5,000 blacks registered to vote for the first time. One marcher held up a sign that read, "Remember Jimmy Jackson Register and Vote." Jimmy Lee Jackson had died as a result of injuries he sustained from a beating by police officers when he attempted to register to vote the previous year on February 26, 1965, in Marion, Alabama.

Each evening the marchers set up campgrounds in rented circus tents and slept outdoors. The tents were paid for with funds that had been donated to the march by politicians, entertainers, and movement sympathizers. Stokely Carmichael's and Martin Luther King's philosophies clashed. Carmichael, who was 25 years old, promoted black power, which mainstream America considered radical. King was a more conservative 37-year-old, who did not feel it was appropriate for Carmichael to use the controversial term "black power." King was also being pressured by donors to persuade Carmichael to tone down his black power rhetoric. But Carmichael had joined King and the others with the sole purpose of promoting black power.

Carmichael believed black economic independence, black unity, self-defense, and political power were the ingredients necessary to advance the black race. During a mass meeting in Greenwood, Mississippi, Stokely exhorted marchers by demanding, "What do we want?" and then leading the response, "black power." With their fists balled up, he and the participants would raise their right arms straight toward the sky, as a symbol of black power. The press aired the "black power" slogan during the Greenwood activities, and the message spread throughout the country. Five months later, Huey Newton and Bobby Seale formed the Black Panther Party in Oakland, California, and the black power movement was born.[18]

SNCC field secretary Charles Sherrod said "black power" was the affirmative of everything that society said was bad about being black. The youth of his day began to affirm that black was beautiful and nappy hair looked good, and promoted self-pride. Later, James Brown put it this way: "Say it loud, I'm black and I'm proud."[19] "Black power was never about hate, even though the media claimed it was," Sherrod added.[20] James Meredith called what he saw emerging in his community in August of 1966, the Negro movement:

> The root of this is a deep pride in one's own race, in one's own traditions, one's own manhood. A pride, if you will, in being Negro. Bravery comes directly from pride, and there will be a lot of Negroes prepared to die before the crisis is over.[21]

At the time, many newspaper reporters wrote very biased articles and printed inflammatory statements against blacks. The media referred to the "black power" ideology as a racist movement. Charles Evers, older brother of Medgar Evers, recalled that the white press in Jackson, Mississippi, once printed, "Although he [Sidney Poitier] won it [an Oscar], well, you know, we don't approve of it."[22] Charles Evers said, "Like all of us, he [Stokely Carmichael] was a victim of the press; they never accurately printed what Stokely and others really said."[23]

Fannie Lou Hamer organized a group of 100 to participate in the march, and she insisted that marchers stop to register to vote. She said, "Dramatizing is all right, but we're tired of all these folks marching through leaving the people behind worse off than they were before."[24] Hamer proudly walked up front with Martin Luther King and led the group in singing freedom and civil rights songs.

By the time the group reached Yazoo City, Percy W. Bufkin, a brakeman for a railroad company, and his coworkers saw the marchers headed toward them while they were sitting in railroad cars on the track. "The marchers were four or five abreast. It was a lot of people!" he recalled. "Since we had the railroad crossing blocked, we cut it in two so they could get across the tracks," he added. At that time, Bufkin lived in an all-white neighborhood in South Jackson, Mississippi.[25]

Around June 22, 1966, the marchers reached Belzoni in the Mississippi Delta. "The Meredith March is coming to town," a black male yelled with excitement. "Say what?" another man inquired. "Yeah, the marchers are coming with Reverend King to Belzoni," the male replied. Tyrone Davis, a 16-year-old black teenager, overheard this conversation and became excited. "That evening the marchers camped out on the grounds of Green Grove Baptist Church, which was pastored by Reverend Thurman, who died in 2005 at age 105," Tyrone Davis stated.

Davis could not wait to go and meet the marchers. That evening, he walked to the church grounds and spoke to everyone he saw. There were white and black people in the crowd; black men were wearing low-cut afro hairstyles and some of them had on dashikis. A lot of men had on overalls and wore wide hats on their heads.

The people in Davis's community heard that James Meredith had gotten shot earlier that month and then a rumor started that he died. When Davis heard a friend of his friend's father say the Meredith March was coming to town he thought, "I am going down there to meet that man." Davis added, "Initially, I assumed I would have the opportunity to meet James Meredith." Even though Davis was only 12 years old when James Meredith was trying to integrate Ole Miss, he had followed the story, which was the biggest event in the news for a long time.

After speaking to the marchers and listening to their stories, Davis went home and lay in his bed, but he simply could not rest. "In my mind, I could hear one of the women saying, 'We are leaving here early in the morning walking to Louise,'" Davis stated. Knowing that his mother would never give him permission to walk with the marchers, he quietly left home before dawn and joined the marchers without his mother's consent.

As they walked up Highway 49 west, they sang freedom songs. The protesters walked 18 miles from Belzoni to Louise that day and camped out on a farm owned by a local black that evening. The next day they walked to Yazoo City and camped out that evening at Oak Grove Baptist Church. That evening, Davis went and sat on the church steps and thought, "I'm going to find Reverend King." He recalled, "Two men were guarding the tent when I approached. They asked me what I wanted. I told them I wanted to talk with Reverend King and one of the men told Reverend King, 'Someone out here wants to see you.'"

Reverend King told the men to let Davis in his tent and he went in. King asked his name and how old he was. Then he asked him where his parents were. "When Reverend King discovered that I had left home without my parents, he took me under his wing. They found a place for me to sleep," he said. The following morning they discussed making sure he was taken back home safely.

The next morning the marchers started walking up Highway 16 toward Yazoo City. That evening, as the car King and Carmichael were driving in came close to the school in Canton where the marchers were planning to camp out, a man yelled out, "Reverend King, they are fighting ahead." Carmichael asked the crowd not to run and Reverend King tried to keep the crowd calm, but people panicked. Within moments, the police shot tear gas into the crowd. Davis was injured during the incident and he did not go any farther with the marchers. He ended up going to his aunt's house in Canton. He never saw Reverend King again alive. He attended King's funeral in Atlanta, after he was assassinated in 1968.[26]

Leon Goldsberry, known now as "Dr. Dirt" because of his expert knowledge of gardening practices, was 18 and his sister, Christine White, was 16, living in Edward, Mississippi, in June of 1966 with their parents in a home that was built by their great grandfather Samuel Oliver in 1895. They grew up across the tracks from the Southern Christian Institute, known now as the Bonner-Campbell Institute. It served as a primary school for blacks until 1926 and became a teachers college in 1931. The college closed in 1953 when it merged with Tougaloo College.[27]

During the 1960s, the facility was used by Bob Moses to provide training in nonviolence and to host mass meetings. In June of 1966, Leon and his sister rode with Millie White, a civil rights organizer, to Canton and walked with the marchers to Tougaloo. Leon recalled the speakers mentioning Medgar Evers and feeling so much joy. "The speeches made you want to cry," he recalled. Leon proclaimed, "We didn't want the same life that our parents had. We didn't want to take what they had taken." He recalled that his mother was once raped on the other side of the tracks from his house, but no justice was served on her behalf.

Mississippi whites used to love to go coon hunting. "We were the coons," he said. He mentioned that one of his uncles had been lynched, though the event was too painful for him to discuss. "The preferred hanging tree was the sycamore tree because the branches were so strong that they did not break," he stated. He mentioned despising being called "spearchuckers," a racial epithet.

"James Meredith had guts to walk through Ole Miss in 1962 and to help take away the fear that African men had to walk the streets and byways in 1966," he concluded.[28]

Although the tear gas incident in Canton had deterred some people from going farther, more people joined the march as they walked from Canton to Tougaloo. James Meredith had recovered from his hospital stay

The two girls in front and their family lived in Tougaloo, Mississippi, off State Street near Tougaloo College during James Meredith's March Against Fear, June 26, 1966. (Photo by the late John F. Phillips, a photographer who captured hundreds of social justice photographs during the 1960s and 1970s. Licensed from www .baldwinstreetgallery.com.)

and spoke to the crowd on the campus of Tougaloo College, which was north of Jackson. The godfather of soul, James Brown, one of the most popular entertainers of the time, was one of the people in the crowd. He performed on stage and his presence was inspiring to his fans.

Jackson native Tommy Robinson, who lived within blocks of Medgar Evers's homesite, said, "Everybody in our neighborhood attended the Meredith March." He added: "We all hung out with James Meredith in West Jackson. He was the smartest one. That's why he was chosen to break that barrier." After being entertained and hearing the speeches, the crowd left Tougaloo College and walked up State Street toward downtown Jackson.

Katherine Horhn Nelson, a private-duty nurse in Jackson, sent her teenage sons to her brother Archie Horhn's house in Holmes County, on June 25, 1966, so that they could march the following day. Archie and his cousin Rosetta drove a pickup truck up Highway 51 and rode alongside the marchers. Her nephew Jimmie Lee and Nelson's sons J.D. and Walter Winter rode on the back of the pickup truck for a while and walked with the marchers for a while. "He [James Meredith] did a God-sent thing," Nelson recalled. "You ought to be brave and strong like James Meredith," she told her sons.

Katherine's sons did not have to look far for role models. The Horhn men were law-abiding citizens who helped their family climb out of poverty. "We were sharecroppers on a farm between Goodman and Pickens [Holmes County, Mississippi]," she noted. Katherine was the third of 10 children in her household. "Four (Fannie Mae, Johnny Will, Charlie, and Tommie) of the smartest children in our family went to college. All of us picked cotton; our money went in one pot, and Daddy took care of the household expenses and paid college tuition once a month," she said.

Half of Charlie's tuition was paid by an anonymous donor. Her mother, Emma Lee Williams Horhn, believed the donor was Hoover Maxwell, who had taken over the farm after his father, Clyde Maxwell, died. Mr. Hoover was nice to them; he added three rooms to their three-room house, after their four cousins moved in, because he saw that it was a strain on their family to live in such a small house after adding four more children to their household. "Mama passed in 2003 at age 100; she lived to see her son, Charlie Horhn, become the district director for Congressman Bennie Thompson, and her grandson, John Horhn, become a state senator, District 26 Hinds and Madison County, Mississippi," Nelson added.[29]

The Meredith March Against Fear was the last and largest mass mobilization of citizens during the Second Reconstruction. The march ended on June 26, 1966, in Jackson at the state capitol. One eyewitness, Jo Freemon, photographed various segments of the march including the event at the state capitol as James Meredith, Reverend King, and others sat on the podium. *Time* magazine writer Jack Thornell estimated the crowd at 18,000 people.[30] However, historian Lerone Bennett, Jr reported that 30,000 attended the rally.[31] The atmosphere of the audience was one of elation and people cheered with excitement.

Even though the Meredith March Against Fear did not encourage the masses of black citizens to cast aside their fears of the white power structure, people felt a sense of progress. Over five thousand blacks registered to vote during the 26 days of the Meredith March Against Fear, but black Mississippians still did not have enough voters to elect enough candidates to office to truly represent their political interests. James Meredith wanted to reach as many black Mississippians as possible through the walk, but as the saying goes, "Nothing happens overnight." As he said, "I want me and my kind to be on top." Collectively, he and his kind were a long way from the top; in fact, over half of them were living below poverty in extreme poverty.

James Meredith's March Against Fear crowd approaching the Mississippi state capitol, June 26, 1966. (Photo by the late John F. Phillips. Licensed from www.baldwinstreetgallery.com.)

Later that summer on August 21, 1966, Martin Luther King Jr., Roy Wilkins, Whitney Young, James Meredith, Floyd McKissick, and Stokely Carmichael appeared on *Meet the Press*, an NBC television and radio production. The host used divisive language by classifying James Meredith and Stokely Carmichael as black power advocates and calling Martin Luther King Jr., Roy Wilkins, and Whitney Young "old guard" civil rights leaders.

When asked his feelings about being described as a loner and as a man with no organization and no clear-cut philosophy, Meredith said, "The group with which I most closely associate myself is the Negro. This is a misnomer, this 'loner' business." Meredith also made the following statement:

We have 25 million Negroes. My position has been and probably will remain for some time that in order for the Negro to accomplish what he deserves and needs, we are going to have to find something that everyone can attach to, say like the Democratic Party. You have Senator Kennedy, you have Senator Eastland, you have Senator Wayne Morse—all members of the same party, but men with different views. I think that the Negro is going to have to do the same thing. We are going to have to have something that Dr. King, or Dr. Jackson or Mr. Wilkins, or Stokely Carmichael and all the other people in this country . . . can attach to and work toward.

On his opinion concerning the difference between nonviolence, self-defense, and being physically attacked, he said:

What really happened with nonviolence, they took the Negro as he was in 1960, or whenever it was, and they attached this name "nonviolence" to him and thereby gave legitimacy to a particular movement. This changed nothing. It just gave a name to what already existed and gave the implication that if this were not the case, there would be violence. The Negro has never entertained the idea of taking up arms against the whites and they cannot . . . I know the people that shot in my home years ago. They know the people that killed all of the Negroes that have been killed. The community knows them . . . White supremacy will not allow itself to remove these people from its society. If they don't find a way, the Negro has no choice, but to remove these men, and they have to be removed. You can't have killers running around in the society killing people.[32]

At the time that Meredith was interviewed on *Meet the Press*, blacks did not have any significant political representation by the Democrats or the Republicans. Senator Kennedy supported integration, while Eastland supported segregation, and Morse was a maverick against the Vietnam War. Those senators all had different views, but they were a part of a political force. Meredith reasoned that blacks would have to unify and a find common ground in order to change their social, political, and economic underclass status in society. He felt that white society would have to make whites accountable for committing violent crimes against blacks or blacks would rebel, as in the old adage "If you put too much pressure on a pipe, it will burst." He had noted the previous week:

Negroes are dying bravely alongside whites in Vietnam, and when that generation comes marching back to small and large towns in America, they will not easily put up with the inequalities they have suffered in the past.[33]

In the mid-1960s, black youth were tired of segregation, police brutality, poverty, widespread white-on-black murder, community degradation, and the ills of racism. Some of them declared that they would no longer go to the back of the bus or turn the other cheek, and eventually police brutality and violence bred violence.

The 1965 Watts Riots was the most violent urban outbreak since World War II. Thirty-four people were killed, 1,034 people were wounded, and 4,000 were arrested. Ten thousand blacks revolted for six days during August 13–16, 1965. By the third day of the riots, blacks had looted gun stores and were heavily armed. They shot at helicopters, damaged buildings, and burned local businesses, sparing businesses marked with terms such as "Negro owned" and "Blood brother."[34]

It took thousands of police and soldiers including an entire infantry division supported by tanks to confine the riots. The property losses totaled over $35 million with 200 buildings destroyed and 600 damaged.[35] A California gubernatorial commission investigated the riots and discovered that high unemployment, poor schools, and inferior living conditions led to the riots, yet no efforts were made to address those root problems afterward. As a result of the riots and other issues, California created SWAT teams, which incorporated military tactics with police work to crush future riots or social upheavals, but employment remained stagnated.

The Watts riots were provoked when Highway Patrol officer Lee Minikus pulled over Marquette Frye and started hitting him and his brother Ronald. A crowd gathered, and as they witnessed the police brutality, they became agitated. Ronald and Marquette's mother, Rena, arrived and tried to speak up for her sons, and the police arrested all three of them. An angry bystander threw a bottle that hit a patrol car and "the rest is history."

Twenty-seven-year-old Big Bob was living in Los Angeles and witnessed the second and third days of the riots. He said, "During the early '60s, the Los Angeles police department hired white racist, high school graduates, from Texas to join the police department." California was different from southern cities. In Watts, the Muslims and the people in the community were not going to stand by quietly while racist cops mistreated them. "Malcolm X prophesied that the city's practice of hiring racist cops would be the downfall of the black community in Los Angeles," Big Bob added.

The Watts riots continued in part because of incidents like when white cops shot a black man in the head, without cause, who was taking his pregnant wife to the hospital. White police were committing murder under the guise of their badges, but murder is murder. People were still angry that the police fired multiple shots into a Muslim mosque, claiming the Muslims had pointed weapons at them. It was known that the police threw the water pistol in the mosque. According to Big Bob, the youth of the '60s were activists, and it was them that helped change America.

Activists did not walk around singing. "The militant brothers were the ones who started the riots. They were the foot soldiers who were willing to die for the advancement of black people," he added.

"Many so called civil rights leaders were 'political trough-eating niggers' who take money from white supporters for self-advancement instead of working for their black brothers," he noted. Many "trough eaters" got wealthy. He argued, "A pig don't care where the slop comes from or who puts the slop in the trough, a pig eats everything thrown in the trough including the garbage from the enemy of his people." Selfish politicians delayed the black man's progress by supporting the white power structure for economic gain for themselves.[36]

The roots of discrimination including joblessness, poverty, and de facto segregation caused riots to break out in northern and southern cities. The National Commission on Urban Disorders reported 8 major uprisings, 33 outbreaks of violence, and 123 disorders across the country in 1967.[37] The commissioner reported that the average rioter was a young, high school dropout.[38] However, Big Bob said, "Watts's rioters were people who lived in the community from all walks of life, but looters were primarily young people."

The media echoed two chants from rioters, "Get whitey" and "Burn, baby, burn,"[39] but failed to emphasize the conditions that led to the riot. The blacks in Watts were not poverty stricken. They lived in a neighborhood of well-kept streets and single-family homes. Half of the homes were owner occupied.

By the summer of 1967, segregation and poverty created a destructive environment in ghettos and urban areas. Riots erupted in Newark, New Jersey, and Detroit, Michigan, setting off a chain reaction in neighboring communities.[40] The Kerner Report of 1967 concluded, "Our nation is moving toward two societies, one black, one white—separate and unequal."[41]

By the mid-1960s, the Second Reconstruction, better known as the civil rights movement, was on its last leg. Activities were being fueled by new recruits, while older participants were becoming disheartened. The assassinations of Malcolm X, Medgar Evers, and countless others silenced movement leaders, but a new consciousness had awakened in black youth, who were inspired to fight for a new world.

Julius Lester, a young black writer, wrote about the new expressions of young militant SNCC workers:

Now it is over. America has had chance after chance to show that it really meant "that all men are endowed with certain inalienable rights." ... The days of singing freedom songs and the days of combating bullets and billy clubs with love ... They used to sing, "I Love Everybody" as they ducked bricks and bottles. Now they sing:

Too much love,
Too much love,
Nothing kills a nigger like
Too much love[42]

In 1967, Albert Gibbs Jr., a premed major enrolled at Tougaloo College in Tougaloo, Mississippi, joined every social organization available to students including CORE, SNCC, SCLC, and the NAACP. Gibbs recalled: "The movement was fueled by 20 percent of our race. Some people, told us to go home. Others asked me and my friends, 'Why do you want things to change?' Other people wanted things to change, but were not willing to pay the price for change."[43]

When Gibbs was growing up in Vicksburg, Mississippi, blacks accepted their second-class status in society. They went to the back of the bus and used the colored-only facilities. "I was born into the Jim Crow culture; we never challenged the system; it was our way of life," he stated. He had spent his first two college years at Alcorn A & E College in Lorman, Mississippi, where civil rights activism was basically mute.

Gibbs had been inspired to get involved in the civil rights movement at Tougaloo College. "Once I got involved, nothing could turn me around," he said. Tougaloo was a different world from Alcorn. College professors at Tougaloo taught African history, gerrymandering, civil disobedience, and other subjects that were not taught at state-run colleges. "Tougaloo College hosted numerous speakers like Angela Davis, Stokely Carmichael, Dick Gregory, and other activists who were not welcomed at state institutions," Gibbs recalled.

He once attended a camp at the Southern Christian Institute in Edwards, Mississippi, hosted by Bob Moses, which taught voter registration tactics such as staying in a straight line to maintain order. Facilitators taught participants to make sure voter registrants had their poll tax receipts and their proper identification documentation with them when they arrived at the courthouse. "Even though the Voting Rights Act outlawed poll taxes, it was late in effect because many counties continued to use poll taxes and literacy test to delay the voting registration of black citizens," he added.

By 1968, the Mississippi Sovereignty Commission perceived that Gibbs was a threat to its goal of preserving white supremacy so they began to spy on him. Their investigation tracked Gibbs and his wife's indebtedness, former addresses, current and former employers, and their involvement with civil rights organizations and activities. Gibbs declared, "Evidently an informer was among our group for the commission to be able to keep up with our daily activities." He recalled that he would not have verbally discussed movement activities had he known his conversations were being reported to the Sovereignty Commission.[44] A July 30, 1968, commission report stated:

> A colored male by the name of Al Gibbs, about twenty-four (24) years of age, who is employed by the Community Action Program with offices at 320 North West Street, are reportedly heading up the OBAY Group while Spencer [Howard Spencer] is gone. He is married and his wife's name is Dorothy, and she is now with Friends of Children. Gibbs is not known to be a radical type of person. He has stated that he is going to merely try to hold the OBAY Group together and will take them on picnics at the Reservoir and other social type activities.
>
> Inquiries were made to determine the background of Gibbs. Albert Gibbs, Jr. was a student at Tougaloo College and one (1) time resided with his wife at 1405 Apple Street. They are believed to reside somewhere on Gault Street, in the Lynch Street Sub-Division # 2 . . .
>
> In May of 1967, in Jackson, White Auto Sales entered suit for $16.00 which has not been paid. Their credit is being reported unsatisfactory by banks and businesses during 1967 and 1968.
>
> The groups consisting of the NAACP, MFDP, and AFL-CIO, has again changed their plans for precinct meetings with regard to the challenge of the Mississippi Delegation to the Democratic National Convention. They had planned to meet this morning, July 30, at the Masonic Temple on Lynch Street in Jackson. The Masons were using the building and they put off their meeting until later in the day. They plan to handle their precinct meeting at the Masonic Temple by having people from the various areas sit together and have their meetings right there. Hodding Carter, III, from Greenville is involved in this challenge.
>
> Investigations will be continued.[45]

The Mississippi Sovereignty Commission investigated Gibbs for at least five years. It once noted that Gibbs was trying to organize a demonstration. Reports noted that Gibbs associated with Bennie Thompson, who is presently a representative for Mississippi's second congressional district. The report stated:

Gibbs plans to call a press conference this date next door to the Central Methodist Church on Farish Street. He plans to publicly criticize the fact that Hemmingway [Joe Hemmingway, director of Community Action Program] has ordered a cut off of the funding for NYP [Neighborhood Youth Program].

Gibbs has stated that the white employees of CAP are no good and should be removed.

Benny Thompson, colored male, of the Tri-County Community Center on Rose Street is supporting Gibbs. Thompson is believed to have handed out communistic type literature in the past. Thompson plans to run for mayor of Bolton.

There is a possibility that Gibbs will try to lead a group to the CAP offices after his press conference to cause a demonstration and physically remove the white employees from the building. At this writing during the morning, the press conference has not yet been called.[46]

The commission maintained thorough reports on civil rights activities, which was disadvantageous to movement participants because law enforcement and even the Klan could be tipped and alerted to the make and model of vehicles that activists drove. The commission's report for a Solidarity Day program, an outdoor event on Lynch Street near JSC, illustrated how inclusive the details were. The Solidarity Day report stated:

According to information . . . Congressman Ronald Dellums of California, who is scheduled to speak . . .

R. B. Cottonreader, Mississippi Field Representative, Southern Christian Leadership Conference (SCLC), Hosea Williams and Joe Hammond, member SCLC, are to attend and Cottonreader has already arrived.

Information received that estimated 108 persons will attend from Washington, D.C. via two buses, one of these busses will bring students from Howard University, Washington, later bus has arrived in Jackson.

A green Ford van . . . has been obtained from Albert Gibbs, manager, Age of Aquarius, Jackson, which is to be used during Solidarity Day Activities.

Angela Davis, black militant who has reportedly been in Cuba writing a book, appeared at Wounded Knee . . . it is not known at this time whether or not she will attend Solidarity Day.[47]

The sophisticated snooping of the government of movement workers and the murders of black leaders severely hindered the progress of the black power movement. The assassination of Dr. Martin Luther King Jr. in 1968, made some blacks feel hopeless, and set off a wave of riots. Even Mississippi youth were emboldened to attempt to copy-cat urban rioters. Leon Goldsberry was a college student at Rust College when King was murdered. Rust College is a historical liberal arts college in Holly Springs, Mississippi, 35 miles southeast of Memphis. The college was founded in 1866 by the Freedman's Aid Society of the Methodist Episcopal Church. James Meredith's oldest sisters, Delma and Thelma, had obtained teaching certificates from Rust College in the early 1940s.

Goldsberry was in the student union when a news report flashed across the television screen announcing the assassination of King. "Students were crying. We were angry and had a deep sense of rage," he recalled. Some of the male students decided to act, and they purchased some gasoline in which they soaked towels, set the towels on fire, and throw them on U.S. Highway 78. Although no injuries occurred to travelers on the highway as a result of the students' actions, just as Meredith predicted after he was ambushed in 1966, the nonviolent approach of turning the other cheek was ending.[48]

Gradually, the 1965 Voting Rights Act proved to be the most effective piece of civil rights legislation ever passed by Congress. Over the next 20 years, black voters were able to elect more candidates to office due to the sharp increases in black voter registration. For example, in March 1965 only 19.3 percent of blacks were registered voters in Alabama, while in November 1988 68.4 percent were; the changes were similar in a number of southern states.[49]

The Second Reconstruction renewed interest among the black race to improve their standard of living in America. Thousands of protest activities took place, thousands of demonstrations were staged, and numerous laws were challenged and enacted to give the black race the first-class citizenship rights that had been guaranteed to them by the U.S. Constitution.

According to Peniel E. Joseph, northern black militants were inspired by the direct action of civil rights protesters in the South and disenchanted by southern racial violence. To distinguish the black power movement from the civil rights movement, Joseph proposed that black power movement encompassed every facet of African American political life in the United States and beyond.

Northern activists were concerned with national injustice against blacks. In 1961, New York advocates including Maya Angelou, LeRoi Jones (Amiri Baraka), and Mae Mallory demonstrated on the floors of the United Nations in New York City against the assassination of Patrice Lumumba, first prime minister of the Democratic Republic of Congo.

They felt Lumumba had been assassinated for defying American foreign policies.

Black college students protested for curricular changes, which resulted in the development of black studies programs. African American politicians used the black power base to build political machines and elected black mayors in Cleveland, Detroit, Atlanta, Newark, and Gary, Indiana. It was upon this base that the Congressional Black Caucus was built.[50]

In his article "The Black Power Movement: A State of the Field," Peniel Joseph described the effect the black power movement had on politics, noting:

> Black power militancy proved decisive in inaugurating the first generation of black elected officials and producing the eclectic array of multiethnic and multithemed social movements that the historian Jeffrey Ogbar memorably characterized as "rainbow radicalism."[51]

The Black Panther Party for Self-Defense, which was formed in Oakland, California, by Huey Newton and Bobby Seale, was the most visible black power group. The Black Panthers borrowed their name from the Lowndes County Freedom Organization, which was nicknamed the Black Panther Party. This southern group had been formed by black sharecroppers in Lowndes County, Alabama. Black Panthers in Oakland served free breakfast to schoolchildren in cities such as Oakland, New Haven, Connecticut, and Winston-Salem, North Carolina. Female members Kathleen Cleaver and Elaine Brown achieved iconic status. Because of them and others, women's issues became a central theme of the organization.[52]

From Lowndes County, Alabama, to Philadelphia, black power advocates organized antipoverty programs. The term "black power" was popularized by Stokely Carmichael in Greenwood, Mississippi, during the Meredith March in 1966, but the phrase had previously been used by Richard Wright in 1954 in his nonfiction treatise about the liberation of the West African Gold Coast. The term "Negro Power" had also been used by Paul Robeson during the 1950s and by Congressman Adam Clayton Powell Jr. in 1966. White Americans viewed the term "black power" as a "declaration of war. . . . *Time* magazine characterized the term as 'a racist philosophy' that advocated reverse discrimination."[53]

Peniel Joseph considered the August 1965 riots in Watts and the heckling of Martin Luther King by inner-city residents who rejected his pleas for nonviolence as the end of the civil rights era. King's advocacy of open housing and slum clearance in Chicago signified a wave toward black militancy and the civil rights struggles' shift to the north. Chicago militants' rejection of King nonviolent ideology, the election of Stokely Carmichael as chairman of SNCC, and Carmichael's popularization of black power in Greenwood, Mississippi, prompted the genesis of the black power era.[54]

Joseph observed that "the embrace, at times, of violent rhetoric, misogyny, and bravado by black power advocates have made them and their struggles easy targets for demonization and dismissal."[55] The movement's destructiveness poisoned a generation of activists and helped steer the drive for civil rights off course and ultimately destroyed the potential of civil rights movement to establish new democratic frontiers.[56] James Meredith had noted in his *Meet the Press* interview in August of 1966 that a military call for American blacks to engage in a physical revolution was unattainable.

After the Second Reconstruction and the black power movement ended, Americans witnessed massive drug epidemics, overcrowded prisons, urban industry decline, and the deterioration of the family structure. As the twentieth century came to a close, new challenges became evident and the cloud of economic inequality, which had lingered since the Emancipation Proclamation was issued, persisted. Few have climbed the economic ladder in society, while the masses of people of color have remained undereducated and in poverty.

CHAPTER 9

The Living Legend, 1966–2012

As I understand chess, you have to set the game up so you can win.
—James Howard Meredith

James Meredith is a strategic thinker and a careful planner. Before responding to a question, he often pauses to gather his thoughts. When he heard Senator John F. Kennedy's civil rights platform he felt that if Kennedy was elected, America would be headed in a new direction. Meredith did not just haphazardly decide to break down Mississippi's integration policies; he had considered doing so when Central High School was integrated in Little Rock, Arkansas, in 1957.

When Kennedy was inaugurated on January 20, 1960, as the 35th U.S. president, Meredith acted on his thoughts and wrote an admission letter to Ole Miss. Though he made every effort to avoid being the victim of violence, he was ambushed by a white male on June 6, 1966, on the second day of the Meredith Walk Against Fear. He had launched this 225-mile walk from Memphis, Tennessee, to Jackson, Mississippi, to encourage black voter registration and to underscore the black males' fear of the white power structure.

Fifty years after Meredith broke Mississippi's segregation laws, religion had begun to consume his philosophical thoughts. Even in his younger years, Meredith was driven by his divine responsibility to foster social change, and he had a keen capacity to interpret the present atmosphere. A parable of Jesus illustrates that signs dictate when changes in society are under way.

Jesus said to the multitude in Luke 12:54–56:

> When you see a cloud rising in the west, you say at once, "A shower is coming" and so it happens. And when you see the south wind blowing, you say, "There will be scorching heat," and it happens. You hypocrites! You know how to interpret the appearance of earth and sky; but why do you not know to interpret the present?

Meredith saw the cloud rising and moved immediately after graduating from Ole Miss; but he did return, and he never stopped trying to use his voice for the betterment of his race. After graduation, James Meredith and his family moved to Nigeria. He enrolled in University of Ibadan and obtained a master's degree in government and economics in 1965. Meredith developed a lifelong friendship with one Nigerian student, Dr. Jimor Osakwe, at Ibadan University and lasting relations with others. In 1966, Meredith published a memoir with Indiana University Press. He dedicated the book to his father, Moses "Cap" Meredith (1891–1965), who had died at age 73 the previous year. A *Newsweek* magazine review stated:

> Seldom is a piece of violent history so dispassionately disserted by one of its participants as it has been by James Meredith in this three-years-later study of his breakthrough at the University of Mississippi. Part report and part legal brief, part manifesto, part tract, it is a valuable and fascinating account.[1]

James Meredith is a self-made businessman who held a few jobs after completing law school. He worked as a stock market broker (1968–70), taught African American studies at the University of Cincinnati (1984–85), worked in Congress as an advisor to Congressman Jesse Helms (1989–91), and taught at a private school called Thomas Christian Academy (1993–94) in Yazoo City, Mississippi. He was standing on the podium at the academy in a cap and gown when his youngest child and only daughter, Jessica, received her high school diploma. He started off as a tree farmer in the 1960s and later became a landlord and real estate investor. He was very successful in business. During the 1970s and 1980s, he operated two nightclubs (Chimneyville and Broad Street Lounge) in Jackson, Mississippi.

Meredith has been dubbed eccentric, arrogant, and crazy by critics, while those who champion his legacy have called him a thinker ahead of his time, a philosopher, a genius, and a brave one. Chief NAACP attorney Jack Greenberg, who helped guide Meredith's legal case, said,

> Meredith has been so calm, so reasonable, so-good-humored that I guess ordinary people would have to think he was a little crazy . . . after all we generally assume that a guy should be somewhat neurotic in a situation like this. He is always sober, witty, and quiet.[2]

Meredith said, "Many things written about me have been wrong."[3] Writer Robert Fay said Meredith unsuccessfully tried to unseat Adam Clayton Powell Jr.[4] Though he had considered it, Meredith never ran against Powell. Journalists have claimed Meredith ceased being a civil rights activist in the late 1960s, but this is also quite far from the truth. In 1968, Meredith walked 1,000 miles from Chicago to New York to underscore the de facto segregation and discrimination that existed in the North. Technically speaking, the deaths of Medgar Evers in 1963, Malcolm X in 1965, and countless others paralyzed the civil rights struggle and the nonviolent theory. Some historians marked the Watts Riots in August of 1965 and the Meredith March Against Fear in June of 1966 as consummation of the black power movement.

Meredith had returned to America from Nigeria and enrolled in Columbia School of Law in New York City in 1966. Several years later, Mary June gave birth to twins, Joseph Howard and James Henry. Their oldest son, John Howard, was in the second grade when his two younger brothers came home from the hospital. All three boys were taught at home and as they grew up they were encouraged to strive for academic excellence. An "A" was the standard. James Henry said:

> Growing up, education was an important part of my everyday life. I was able to do well academically because my parents invested in me—by spending time and helping me to learn the basics. By knowing the fundamentals at an early age, I developed a desire to learn and with that desire, I was able to grow in intellect and prosper in education.[5]

In the early 1970s, Meredith once again returned to his home state. Who remembers when James Meredith sat in the courtroom in Jackson, Mississippi, during the mid-1970s and observed court proceedings or when he cried bloody murder because he perceived that the Jackson Police Department was railroading a 16-year-old male into the prison system. The teen was being represented by a young black attorney named John Walker who fought hard to no avail to defend his client against the charges. The teen's mother called the trial an open-and-shut case and recalled that Judge Russell Moore would not allow Walker to cross-examine the white witness nor allow black witnesses to testify. Meredith used his voice through his magazine *Outlook* to expose injustices and run political news, but the magazine was popular mainly because it listed the weekly arrest records and marriage license applications of Jacksonians. The arrest records were often an embarrassment to private citizens and their families and a source of gossip for others.[6]

Louis Armstrong, a 23-year-old army veteran who was a senior at Jackson State University for the 1974–75 term, recalled: "James had a big impact on me. When I was in college James formed the Independent Political Party. We met every Sunday and ran a slate of candidates for a local election that year. We ran for every slot. I ran for state legislature." Meredith noted: "Louis Armstrong was a young man when he ran for office. He was the first of the candidates in our organization to become elected to office." Armstrong became one of the first blacks elected to city government in 1985. According to Armstrong, the Independent Political Party was founded so that they could forge their own political path because the Democratic Party was not representing the interest of black people at that time. "Local black leaders who had ties to the Democratic Party were opposed to the idea," Armstrong noted. However, Armstrong and other college students felt there was a need for blacks to forge their own political presence. Armstrong is presently the deputy director for the City of Jackson.[7]

While Meredith engaged in various entrepreneurial and political activities, Mary June was a teacher at Jim Hill High School in Jackson; she was teaching full-time at Jim High upon her untimely death in 1979. Both James and Joseph were students at Saint Andrews Episcopal School, and John was a student at Morehouse College in Atlanta. Their oldest son, John, was a product of the public school system and a graduate of Provine High School in Jackson. Their sons were model students. The twins attended some of the most prestigious schools in America: North Country School, Lake Placid, New York; and Phillips Academy, Andover, Massachusetts. They went to school with some members of the famous Kennedy family. Joseph recalled years later in a speech at the dedication of the statue of his father at Ole Miss that his dad made such a sacrifice to drive them across the country to get a good education.

In 1981, James Meredith met Judy Alsobrooks. She would become his second wife. His mother, Roxie, had been his father's second wife, 12 years his junior. His paternal grandmother Francis had been his paternal grandfather Ned's second wife. Francis was 16 years younger than Ned. Like his forefathers, Meredith blended the families from two separate units and made them whole. Alsobrooks recalled the details of how she and James Meredith became acquainted:

> We met in Gary, Indiana, on a cold December day. It was actually the day after Christmas 31 years ago. I was visiting my friends Carrie and Tommy Williams who had been friends with James for many years. They didn't know he was driving through Gary on his a way to a family funeral in South Bend, Indiana. He was living in Jackson at the time and I was a music teacher in the Maywood, Illinois, school district. Tommy immediately introduced me as a "single woman." James's wife June had passed away a couple of years before. We exchanged numbers and regularly communicated by phone. In less than two months later in February, I came to Jackson to visit for my birthday. He proposed to me at the airport and placed an engagement ring on my finger.[8]

After their engagement, Judy stayed with Meredith's younger brother Arthur and his wife, Mary, for a short time. "Never in my wildest dreams did I think I would ever visit Mississippi let alone live there. But on March 14th, just two and a half months after we met, we married at the Williams home in Gary where we met," she stated.[9] After completing the school year, she and her son Kip (by a previous marriage) moved to Jackson in June.

She recalled, "James's oldest son, John, was serving in the army and the twins, James and Joseph, were in prep school in upstate New York when we married." Their daughter, Jessica, was born a year after their marriage in Jackson, Mississippi. Mrs. Meredith enrolled in graduate school at Jackson State University shortly after moving to Jackson, where she obtained a master's in communication and started a television news career. Being a wife, a full-time student, and a mother kept her pretty busy, but achievement is built from one's labor. She was ambitious, he supported her, and she was delighted with the new chapter in her life. She said, "So, to meet and then marry such an historical icon was very interesting, to say the least." Though considerably younger, Judy remembered the historic events leading up to Meredith's integration feat. She recalled:

> Jay is 16 years older than me but I remember vividly the long legal process of his integration into Ole Miss. My church in Gary offered

prayers for his safety and success during that period. My parents stayed glued to the television every day to see if "he made it through the night."[10]

In 1983, James Meredith was offered a visiting professor position in the African American Studies Department at the University of Cincinnati. During a visit to Cincinnati, Judy submitted résumé tapes from her work as a television reporter/anchor at the stations in Jackson. "When we returned home, I got a call from a news director there who was interested in interviewing me," she noted. When they moved to Cincinnati, Judy started working at WLWT-TV. They lived in a home a block away from the university.

While a toddler, Jessica traveled across the country with her father to practically every one of his speaking engagements. He is truly a nurturing parent. His mother, Roxie, thought Jessica would be better off at home with her mother. But he managed; on out-of-town trips, Meredith and Jessica would stay at the homes of friends and relatives and the woman of the house would comb Jessica's hair and groom her. Though generations apart, Jessica still enjoys hanging out with her father and is continuing to learn business lessons from him.

On July 27, 1983, Meredith's mother, Roxie Meredith Weatherly, passed. She was 83 years old. She had been one of his greatest supporters. She had lived a life of service, having made notable contributions to her community and her state. At the time of her death, she was a member of the National Council of Negro Women, the Veterans of Foreign Wars Auxiliary, Christian Liberty Baptist Church, and Church Circle No. 1. She was serving as president of a fund-raising project to raise funds for the construction of a youth camp in the Kosciusko area. Over the years, Weatherly had served on numerous fund-raising committees. She had helped raise funds to rebuild Central Mississippi College after it burned in the 1970s and made other contributions to her place of worship and her community. *The Clarion-Ledger* said of her:

> Mrs. Roxie Weatherly, 83, mother of civil rights activist James Meredith died Sunday at Hinds General Hospital in Jackson . . . Myricks Funeral Home is handling the arrangements . . . Mrs. Weatherly was the widow of Moses "Cap" Meredith and Coleman Weatherly.[11]

After the passing of his mother, Meredith served as an assistant professor for University of Cincinnati from 1984 to 1985. "He continued with speaking engagements and operated various businesses. I continued working for WLWT for five years," Mrs. Meredith said. When the Merediths were in the process of moving to San Diego, California, Meredith received a call from Senator Helms's office in Washington with an offer for a position in Helms's office, which he accepted. "So, for the next two years we commuted from Washington to San Diego," Judy noted.

When they moved to San Diego, Jessica entered kindergarten. "I felt pressured as a child to live up to my father's academic standards," she recalled. On weekend visits, Jessica was required to write and learn dictionary words. "Dad taught me practically every word in the dictionary and my times tables," she added. Jessica tried to live up to the academic precedent of her older brothers. Though she was an honor student, she found it hard to bring home a perfect report card. "I felt inferior to my older brothers because they were straight 'A' students," she admitted. However, the folk saying "God gives everyone talent" is relevant because everyone can become the master of something. Though Jessica could not achieve academic excellence, under her parent's guidance she is acquiring business acumen. She is also continuing to learn and grow as the presiding officer of Heirs United Investment Club, a family entity which was formed in 1997 to provide financial literacy to members while investing their assets in the stock market.

The twins in particular were brilliant and academically gifted children. Judy once told a story about the twins accompanying her to the grocery store and the boys telling her "Wait" as they calculated the cost of the grocery item she had selected to give their assessment on which item on the shelf would give the family the "best bang for their buck" without taking into account food quality or brand, they rendered a verdict on every product. When the twins were in the fourth grade, they had a very mature vocabulary because they dedicated a lot of their time to mastering the English language. As teens, while their peers were working to earn money or perfecting their basketball game, they were working hard at being smart.

In 1991, the Merediths returned to Jackson, where they have resided ever since. Meredith established a publishing company, Meredith Publishing, and completed 11 books. He had previously obtained the rights from Indiana University Press to publish his memoir, and he started printing *Three Years in Mississippi*. He outsourced the binding of hardback copies to a press at the state penitentiary in Parchman.[12] To date, Meredith has published over 20 books.

Judy obtained a job at a local television station, and in 1994 she became the general manager and principal developer of W23BC, Jackson State University's first television program. By then she had been in the industry as a reporter and anchor for more than a decade. The program provided internships for students and aired local talk shows and a variety of television programming.[13] W23BC continues to have a positive impact in the community. Katina Rankin, who is presently a morning anchor for WLBT, a local television station in Jackson, was one of the station's [W23BC] early interns.

Meredith formed the Meredith Institute in 1995 to serve as a learning vehicle for citizens. Though he was fiercely criticized for his views against blacks learning Ebonics, he held true to his convictions. He advocated that learning the English language can help black males turn into intellectual giants. He is highly intelligent and raised several intellectuals. He never caught hold of the Internet, e-mail, or e-commerce, and continues to advocate that the library is one of the best learning resources in the community. He types correspondence on a Smith Corona typewriter, overlooking typing errors these days, and sends messages to friends in Africa via e-mail through family members.

In 1996, Meredith reinvented his 1966 walk from Memphis to encourage blacks to go to the library.[14] On June the first, Meredith attempted to walk up U.S. Highway 51 to reach Jackson on June 25, his 63rd birthday. "Slowed by prostate cancer surgery in April, he had to be driven the last 50 miles."[15] At that time, he was physically frail from weight loss. The following year, he donated his personal materials to the J. D. Williams Library at Ole Miss rather than to Jackson State University or Tougaloo College. The Meredith collection included manuscripts from his famous book *Three Years in Mississippi* as well as copies of the book in several foreign languages, awards, photos, letters from community and business leaders, newspaper and magazine clippings, and his political campaign material.[16]

Meredith made several unsuccessful attempts to enter politics after completing law school. In 1972, he ran as a Republican against powerful Mississippi senator James O. Eastland. He ran as a Democratic as well as a Republican candidate for Congress. At age 59, Meredith campaigned to fill the vacant seat left by Agriculture Secretary Mike Espy in 1993. He walked a 100-mile trek through the Delta and highlighted black-on-black crime, calling it "genocide." His campaign platform listed tax breaks for the poor, welfare reform, a nationwide prohibition on gambling and lotteries, and the reinstatement of religious training and prayer in public schools.[17]

Meredith's campaigns were primarily self-funded and never seemed to take off. He was not able to garner any significant votes either, which was a testament to his low popularity as a political candidate and the result of his limited campaign budget. Whether people agreed or not, Meredith used his campaigns to share his views with voters. Meredith said of Harvey Johnson, Jackson's first black mayor:

> My assessment is one of hopefulness. If Harvey Johnson can keep the people from leaving Jackson, then we have hope. Jackson has the potential to be one of the greatest cities in America, but, it also has the potential to be another Gary, Indiana, which has just recently quietly elected a white mayor.
>
> The key for Jackson is to keep the tax base. Jackson will not be getting money from the federal government that we have been getting. That is why I am stressing so much on individuality. Mom and Pop businesses, land ownership and independence.[18]

Forty years after Meredith integrated Ole Miss, his son, Joseph,received the "Outstanding Doctoral Student Achievement Award" from the school's Finance Department. As an alumnus of Ole Miss, Dr. Joseph H. Meredith delivered a speech on October 1, 2006, during the dedication of the U.S. civil rights monument at Ole Miss, which featured a 17-foot limestone portal topped with the words "courage, perseverance, opportunity, and knowledge." The monument was built with $160,000 in grants and private donations and included a statue of James Meredith. Actor and Mississippi native Morgan Freeman said during the festivities, "Mississippi is a much better state today because of James Meredith, and this is a much better university."[19] U.S. Representative John Lewis, a Georgia Democrat, delivered the keynote address that Sunday evening, He said:

> This is a day to rejoice! With the unveiling of this monument, we free ourselves from the chains of a difficult past. Today we can celebrate a new day, a new beginning, the birth of a new South and a new America that is more free, more fair, and more just than ever before.[20]

The rear of the civil rights monument included a life-size bronze likeness of James Meredith. The statue portrayed him walking, an action that he had used repeatedly to deliver messages to citizens and on behalf of social change. An online biography of James Meredith said of the dedication event:

> The very school that closed the door to him and his kind up until October 1, 1962 erected a Civil Rights Monument and a 6'2 life size statue in his honor, which was unveiled October 1, 2006, 44 years after

he attended his first day of class. As the statue unveiling program unfolded, James Meredith sat on the podium next to his pretty wife, Judy, in a tailored white suit with a black and white bowtie as cool as he had been when he walked across the campus, for the first time, in 1962 escorted by U.S. Marshals. In 2006, his thick, manicured, black and white beard gave him a distinguished look, and he is just that—one of a kind. James Meredith is his own man in his own right.[21]

Two years later Dr. Joseph H. Meredith died of complications from lupus, a disease he struggled with for 39 years. At the time of his passing, he was an assistant professor in the College of Business Administration in the Division of International Banking and Finance Studies at Texas A&M International University in Laredo, Texas. He left a legacy of achievement behind. When Joseph turned in his dissertation to his professor at Ole Miss, his committee suggested he revise only *one* word, a testament to his excellent writing skills. James Meredith distributed a pamphlet to visitors who viewed Joseph's body before the funeral. In it he said:

> My son Joseph was totally self-motivated. I never once had to tell him to do his best. For him it was automatic . . . From the age of six Joseph attended the best educational institutions in the nation and made only one "B" from first grade at St. Andrews Episcopal School in Jackson, through his graduation from Harvard—Magna Cum Laude in Economics.
>
> That one "B" came in his second year at Harvard. It was so important to him that as soon as he finished the final exam he made the only collect call to me during his whole life. I suppose that he wanted to put me on notice that the next report card would not be perfect. Schools were still sending the report cards to parents at that time.[22]

Mrs. Meredith obtained a doctorate degree from Mississippi State University in public policy and administration in 2007. She published her dissertation entitled *The Glass Ceiling: Women in Administrative Capacities in Public Universities in the Deep South* after completing her studies. Dr. Judy A. Meredith, known as Ms. A to former student anchors, later faced a career and emotional backlash, and filed a multimillion-dollar age and sex discrimination lawsuit against her employer, Jackson State University, in May of 2009. Her comment was, "It has been resolved to the satisfaction of the parties." She is presently a professor in Jackson State University's Department of Mass Communications.

The Merediths have their own American story, but Mr. Meredith, age 75, said he was propelled by God to carry out earthly missions, and he

Meredith Coleman McGee and Blanch Kern who was born on August 31, 1919 at the 100th Celebration for Center Church of God in Center, Mississippi (June 26, 2011). Blanch is James Meredith's oldest living first cousin through the Patterson lineage. Their grandfather William Patterson donated the land for the church, and their grandmother Roxie Hickman Patterson and a group of women recruited the church's first members. (Meredith C. McGee Collection)

opened dialogue for his friends in Africa to American diplomats in 2009. That same year he retorted, "I ain't dead yet."[23] From May to June of 2009 during his 200 Mile Walk for the Poor, he repeated that phrase periodically, indicating that he had more missions to carry out in the years ahead. When he walked people joined him, and walking gave him the opportunity to discuss various issues with residents and community leaders.

Meredith was wearing a white straw hat, white shirt, white slacks, and black diabetic shoes when he launched the walk on Sunday, May 24, 2009, on Old Highway 61 south, in Tunica, Mississippi, to focus the Christian Church on its responsibility for care of the poor in its community. A blogger for the *Clarion Ledger* called Meredith's focus on church resolutions toward poverty a typical conservative response, but Meredith pointed to scripture, Psalms 72:4: "He [the king] shall judge the poor of the people; he shall save the children of the needy, and shall break in pieces the

Photo at the state capitol in Jackson during SCLC's 2009 Campaign for the Poor with the film crew of the upcoming documentary *Mississippi Messiah*. To the left of James Meredith is Dylan Nelson, who was nine months pregnant during the shooting of the film in which they documented Meredith's activities during the summer of 2009. Clay Haskell is on the right. Nelson and Haskell directed and produced the film. (Meredith C. McGee Collection)

oppressor." An article on the Tunica trek described Meredith's physical fitness:

> Most walk participants slowed down from exhaustion after walking five or six miles, but Meredith and his brother, Arthur Meredith, kept a steady pace ahead without stopping to take a break. They were physically fit for walking, having exercised regularly for years; when they were children they lived in a rural community in Kosciusko, MS and walked one hour to school and one hour from school. Though, Meredith broke down Mississippi's color barrier to higher learning in 1962, the poor in today's world do not always have access to a quality education, a reminder that the fight for a better world must continue.[24]

Today, the kings are judges and elected officials and the oppressors are loan companies, rent-to-own companies, banks, pawnshops, and business bullies, who exploit consumers and workers including those in foreign countries and earn record profits through high-interest instruments. Meredith pointed out that usury practices are contrary to Christian principles (Leviticus 15:36). He passed out literature discussing the responsibility of the rich to the poor to clergy and reporters during his 2009 Walk for the Poor. Though Christianity is the driving religious force in America, the profits keep rolling in, and from 2008 to 2009, bank overdraft fee profits had doubled.

Meredith said later to McArthur Straughter, mayor of Yazoo City, Mississippi, during his 2009 Walk for the Poor, "Somehow we got to tell our people *Brown* was a sham."[25] But back then, blacks in general had no way of foreseeing that America would defy the law set forth in *Brown* and preserve segregation. Meredith preached home school preparedness as a means of reducing the complicated public school problems in hopes that his message would be received.

"Forty years ago we wanted the opportunity to vote; today we are the rulers," Meredith told an audience in Lexington, Mississippi, during the second week of the walk at a community meeting (referring to the fact that most of Lexington's elected officials are black). Meredith never stopped trying to improve life for him and his kind—a Negro of Choctaw descent. According to Dr. Judy A. Meredith, in May of 2012 Latinos came to the Deep South to draw attention to racism and immigration laws in the United States, and reenacted the 1966 James Meredith Walk Against Fear from Memphis to Jackson, when Meredith was shot by a sniper after crossing into Mississippi from Tennessee. The walkers represented Latinos from across America, Mexico, and South America. They began walking from the Lorraine Motel in Memphis were Dr. King was killed and they later held a rally at the state capitol on May 7, 2012, in Jackson. Protesters called the event the Walk Against Fear 2012. One sign said, "No Human Being is Illegal."[26]

Like other great men, Meredith's name has been tarnished by gossip and falsehoods. "People who hold center stage have just about as many people who hate them as they have who admire them," Meredith noted.[27] He was dubbed "a tom" for endorsing Klansman David Duke in a Louisiana gubernatorial race. But according to his wife Judy, he said [of Duke], "I can't say that a man can't change." Meredith agreed with Duke from a policy standpoint that welfare should be reformed, because he believes welfare policies implemented by liberals in the 1960s helped disintegrate the black family by forcing the male out of the home.

In fact, David Duke claimed in a sit-down meeting with Meredith that he had changed. However, Meredith's uncle Bennie advised him

Fred Watson (front left) traveled from Atlanta Georgia, to walk with James Meredith (front right) during Meredith's Walk for Education & Truth on Highway 51 in Memphis, Tennessee, May 25, 2012, near the Mississippi/Tennessee state line. (Photo by Meredith C. McGee)

not to attend any meetings with Duke, because he was such a controversial figure. Meredith did not heed his uncle's warning, and his enemies buried his character after he became an ally of Duke. However, no one can accurately say that Meredith supported an antiracial agenda against blacks, because Meredith had spent his life working to end white supremacy.

Meredith was said to have opposed the Martin Luther King Jr. holiday, but he personally said: "The Martin Luther King holiday was one of the greatest things that happened for black people. I never opposed the holiday; I opposed the holiday commission promoting the nonviolence concept to black people. I have always opposed nonviolence, which encouraged blacks to give up their right to protect themselves and their property." Meredith said he and Martin Luther King Jr. debated the concept of nonviolence every time they saw each other. "Martin admitted to me that he opposed nonviolence as a theory, but used it as a means to accomplish goals," he added.[28]

Senator Jesse Helms, Meredith's employer from 1989 to 1991, openly opposed the Martin Luther King Jr. holiday when it was first proposed. But Helms's views belong to him, not Meredith. An aide to Helms said, "There is a great consonance of political thinking between the Senator and Meredith on matters like religious values, abortion, and development in Africa."[29]

Meredith made a living off various business ventures and became self-sustainable. Notably, tree farming produced for him his greatest profits. He used the proceeds from tree sales to purchase his last home. As he aged, he became extremely conservative, having nothing to do with the toys under the Christmas tree and birthday celebrations but everything to do with his grandchildren and great nieces and nephews singing their ABCs fast, then slow and counting to 100 and by twos. He made learning competitive and fun by engaging his family members in group songs.

Meredith took pride in his responsibility to provide homework assistance to his grandchildren by Jessica, who moved under his roof for a few years after her failed marriage. He dutifully transported her children to and from day care and school, and loved his existence as granddaddy and his role as a father figure. He owns a two-story building called the James Meredith Business Complex in the Historic Farish Street District in downtown Jackson, where his daughter, Jessica, operated a convenience store for a brief period. The building is now the home site of Jackson Taxi, which he owns and Jessica manages. The company's taxi drivers service the greater Jackson metropolitan area and the Jackson Evers International Airport.

Meredith is one of a handful of blacks who own property in the historic district. The Big Apple, Collins Funeral Home, Dennis Brothers, the *Jackson Advocate*, Harmon's Drugs, Peaches Restaurant, and People's Funeral Home are a few of the businesses remaining that were in the district before integration, when the district was bustling with economic activity. Plans to revitalize the historic black district have fallen apart under three mayors—Kane Ditto, Harvey Johnson, and Frank Melton.

In the past quarter of a century, a few businesses have located in the district, while most of the buildings have been gutted and lie dormant. New promises to revitalize the district into a tourist area similar to Beale Street in Memphis and Bourbon Street in New Orleans are renewed practically every election season. Like Beale Street and Bourbon Street, Farish Street was the city's first black settlement after slavery. Owners of existing businesses in the district including Meredith have at times found it hard to hold on financially in an area filled with vacant buildings and inactivity. Meredith briefly put his building and lot up for sale a few years ago, and Peaches Restaurant received donations after losing business because of slow street repairs. Revitalization could definitely provide the city's predominantly black population with needed jobs. One thing is for sure—a low-wage retail or service job is better than no job at all.

In August of 2012, Meredith coauthored a memoir with historian William Doyle entitled *A Mission From God: A Memoir and Challenge for America*, which was published by Simon & Schuster. Patrons stood in long lines waiting to buy his new memoir at his book signings when it hit the market. However, book sales will not likely outpace the sales of his first book, *Three Years in Mississippi*, which was translated into multiple languages; plus it is still selling in the marketplace today.

In 1966, James Howard Meredith was a household name in America and was known around the world for integrating Ole Miss. Today, Americans under age 40 are becoming acquainted with him and rightly so, because he risked his life 50 years ago to dismantle the Jim Crow system, which exposed blacks to a repulsive life. Secondly, he is a living legend in whose name massive voter registration drives in his home state were established during the Meredith March Against Fear. In the future, he will be introduced to more Americans through various films. His character is featured in an eight-hour television miniseries, *The Kennedys*, and in the Mississippi-based documentary *Mississippi Remixed*. New information about Ole Miss's 1962 football team aired on ESPN in *30 for 30: Ghost of Mississippi*. Lastly, the documentary film featuring Meredith, *Mississippi Messiah* is forthcoming.

His new memoir challenges Americans to improve public education. However, he refused to participate in the University of Mississippi's "50 Years of Integration: Opening the Closed Society" celebration, which was held September 26 through October 10, 2012, on campus, asserting that the poor quality of education today gave him nothing to celebrate. He opted out of the integration festivities, but he proudly sat in the skybox with Chancellor Daniel W. Jones at Ole Miss's football games that season. His statue on campus is admired by all students, but particularly black students who are reminded that Ole Miss has come a long way when they pass by the Confederate Memorial not far from the Civil Rights Memorial.

Today, Meredith proposes that children should receive the proper spiritual and academic training from birth to age five at home in order to excel academically and prosper in society. He believes the lack of school preparedness is the root cause of student failure, and advocates that parents and grandparents send their children to school equipped with a basic academic foundation. In addition, James Meredith believes the message for our present time is based on the biblical principle, "Train up a child in the way that he should go and he will never depart from it." He believes we should train our children and throw away the idea that they learn what is necessary at school. In the article "Message for Our Time," James Meredith noted that moral and commonsense training is as important as the ABCs and the 123s. He claimed:

> We can develop a healthy community that lives right with God and enjoy its results only if we do the hard work of getting alone with each other, treating each other with dignity and honor. No more lies. No more pretenses. Tell your neighbor the truth. When you lie to each other. You lie to yourself. All the glory be to God alone.[30]

James Meredith noted, "We don't have a spiritual commonness." He wants the message by which people symbolize his legacy to include the message from God that we must train and teach our children.[31] Meredith's wife, Dr. Judy A. Meredith, gave her view of his legacy:

> I believe James's legacy would be that of a philosopher, a thinker, and as one who defies acceptance of the "status quo." Life should always improve for humans, and societal problems should always be confronted rather than covering them under the proverbial carpet of denial. But I think he should also be known as a great example of a husband, father, and grandfather. His family knows him as dependable, honest, and straightforward. His grandchildren adore him and he cherishes his role as "granddaddy."[32]

And Jasmine Meredith, a high school sophomore and the only daughter of the late Dr. Joseph H. Meredith, shared her view of her grandfather's legacy:

> I definitely feel that even today my grandfather is doing what he can to engrave his mark in history. He is one of the most motivated men I know. He tells the truth, he did not let himself get watered down by mainstream hero worship. My grandfather wants to make a difference, he wants to make a change, and it all begins with the younger generation. We are the future. I think my grandpa is making a great impact on our lives and doing the right things to get the job done.[33]

Meredith's legacy will first and foremost include his integration of Ole Miss on October 1, 1962, at the age of 29, and his becoming the first black to graduate from an all-white college on August 18, 1963, in the state of Mississippi. He was definitely a model child. He had a keen admiration for his father, though he loved his mother dearly. Meredith valued their

From left to right: Bill Chandler, executive director of Jackson-based Mississippi Immigrants Rights Alliance, James Meredith, and Mississippi state representative Jim Evans, chatting during SCLC's Poor People's Campaign, June 26, 2009, at the Mississippi state capitol. (Photo by Meredith C. McGee)

farm as a resource so much that of all his father's 10 children, Cap Meredith gave James Meredith the opportunity to purchase the farm.

Meredith would be characterized as a black male who is 5 feet 7 inches tall, of medium build, and highly intelligent. If one wants to view him as slightly narcissistic, perhaps they will consider that God walked with Meredith 50 years ago when he broke down Mississippi's segregation policies, and God is still walking with him. Leon Goldsberry, alderman of Ward 3, Edwards, Mississippi, who walked in the Meredith March in 1966 said: "We as a people don't always honor our black heroes. We don't honor James Meredith, but he had guts."[34]

Perhaps in the coming decades, Canon James (Meredith's newest family member by James Henry) and his generation will appreciate the deeds of his grandfather, James Meredith, and others who changed America at a great personal sacrifice to themselves. And hopefully, Canon James and his peers will tackle the issues of their times and forge their actions into the pages of history as well.

CHAPTER 10

America's Economic Landscape in the Twenty-First Century

This chapter provides an overview of America's economic landscape, for the economic gap between the haves and have-nots in American society is a pertinent issue today. Political power was restored to blacks during the 1960s, but they have made few economic gains since the clock passed the twenty-first century, and many people of color have become property-less. Educational opportunities have not changed the living conditions for many since the integration accomplishments of James Meredith and others in the twentieth century.

Discrimination is still the root cause of economic lopsidedness. The NAACP filed a racial discrimination class action lawsuit against a dozen banks, including Wells Fargo, on July 11, 2009. The Illinois attorney general conducted an investigation of Wells Fargo for violating fair-lending and civil rights laws by steering blacks and Latinos into subprime high-interest loans. A *New York Times* study found that blacks and Latinos were getting subprime loans at alarming rates, while whites in the same income bracket obtained regular low-interest loans.

According to China's *Report on U.S. Human Rights Record in 2000*, 1 percent of U.S. citizens own 40 percent of the property in the country, while 80 percent of the population own only 16 percent. Since the 1990s, 40 percent of the wealth went into the pockets of the rich and only 1 percent went into the pockets of the poor. In 1992, the income of corporate executives in the largest U.S. companies was 100 times that of ordinary workers; by 2000 it was 475 times higher.[1]

President Lyndon B. Johnson declared a war against poverty, yet we have been losing that war since Johnson declared it.[2] A generation ago, the distribution of income in America was comparable to that of other industrialized countries, but today the United States is not in line with countries in Europe. Then, America's poverty was connected to the unresolved legacy of slavery. However, the U.S. gap between the elite and the middle class was no larger than it was in Europe. Today, America's wealth gap is wider than other industrialized nations. The share of income held by the top 1 percent is twice the rate of that in Britain and three times of that in France. However, Latin America wealth gap is comparable to the United States.[3]

Today, the government's mandatory minimum wage of $7.25 is not even a living wage. James Meredith noted, "No one can live off the minimum wage."[4] Does our government endorse exploitation? Some argue that the government looks the other way when corporations provide low, inadequate wages to employees.

Collectively, blacks have not been able to rise above the tides of poverty and despair, but some have always managed to beat the odds. The Reconstruction-era leader Isaiah Montgomery, a former slave and Mississippi state legislator, founded Mound Bayou, Mississippi, in 1887 and developed a business district over a century ago that included a bank, a law firm, and agricultural enterprises. In the 1920s, black businesses in Tulsa, Oklahoma, prospered and became known as the Black Wall Street. By the 1970s, many stable black business districts disintegrated, employment declined, and wages decreased.

Many argue that welfare recipients who live in air-conditioned homes and own cell phones are not poor. However, when a segment of the population lacks a political voice, poverty is translated into poor education and inadequate government representation. Meredith said, "People are poor because their condition is a consequence of social factors, particularly injustice; poor people are needy, without power, and abused by those with power."[5]

America's poor public education system is one factor that contributes to the growing economic disparities in this country. More than 30 million low-income Americans cannot afford to send their children to college, which prohibits families from supporting the educational advancement of their children.[6] The working poor need adequate education, savings, and advancement to well-paying jobs to pull themselves out of poverty.

These ingredients have not been available to the masses for decades, leaving scores of people of color in persistent poverty.

The conditions of twenty-first-century poverty are devastating. On the morning of August 29, 2005, Hurricane Katrina revealed that many poor people resided in inadequate living environments. Some of the predominantly black residents of New Orleans's Ninth Ward were not able to evacuate their city before Hurricane Katrina ravaged their communities and took the lives of its residents; most of the residents did not own cars and were black low-wage earners, welfare recipients, and have-nots.

New Orleans, Louisiana, known as the Big Easy, takes in millions of tourist dollars daily but is home to some of the poorest people in this country. The tourist industry provides thousands of low-wage jobs. Most low-wage jobs perpetuate poverty. On the eve of the hurricane, New Orleans's poverty rate was almost triple the national average. Jobs on Bourbon Street, in the French Quarter, and in the casinos are mostly low-pay service and retail jobs. With abundant educational institutions available in the area, more than three-fourths of the city residents do not have a college degree. More than 40 percent of the public school children are illiterate, half drop out before graduation, and Angola State Prison eventually becomes the home of many of them.

New York City's poor have headaches too—homelessness, joblessness, and poverty—and today, the city's garment industry, which was once its largest employer, has become almost extinct. America once produced 100 percent of this country's clothing. Staggering unemployment due to the 2008 recession poses economic challenges for a new segment of the population—white-collar workers—who were once highly paid. The poor economy has created new forces that have rendered millions of haves into have-nots.

New York's working- and middle-class jobs in the manufacturing, distribution, and administrative services have disappeared. Nationally, high-wage jobs have been replaced with low-wage employment in the retail, food service, and home health care industries.

Most haves invent and or have direct ownership of products and services such as coffee, oil, steel, vacuum cleaners, beer, and real estate. For example, William ("Bill") Gates founded Microsoft, Sidney Frank created Grey Goose vodka, and Jeffrey Bezos founded Amazon.com.

Some black entrepreneurs have been able to rise to the very top of American society. Hickory, Mississippi, native and Black Entertainment Television (BET) founder, Robert ("Bob") Johnson became the first black billionaire when he sold BET to Viacom, parent company of CBS, MTV, VH-1, and UPN, in 2000 for $3 billion. Born in Kosciusko, Mississippi, television personality Oprah Winfrey is the second of two black billion-aires worldwide and one of the most influential women in the world. She climbed to the top of American society as a high end income earner and as a result of her prosperous business ventures.

Unlike the rich and famous, poor people are primarily consumers, who lie at the bottom of the economic cycle. The wealth disparities for people of color and immigrants are huge, and closing them will require complex solutions. James Meredith believes there must be a need for the labor of poor people, who must tap into educational resources available in this country in order for them to be able to earn better wages and climb out of poverty. He says today's issue is not black versus white but rather rich versus poor. In the next chapter, Meredith and other Americans share their perspectives on how the wealth gap can be closed.

CHAPTER 11

Closing the Economic Disparities in the Twenty-First Century

You should let no excuse stand in your way.

—James Howard Meredith

At the dawn of the twenty-first century, Mississippi had more black elected officials than any state in the United States but few judges of color. Nationally, the wealth gap had widened instead of closed since James Meredith became the first black student to graduate from the University of Mississippi on August 18, 1963.

James Meredith's legal battle from 1961 to 1962 had successfully broken Mississippi's integration policies; he had been a warrior for humanity; he had launched the Meredith Walk Against Fear where he had been gunned down on the second day; he also walked from Chicago to New York in 1966 to oppose northern de facto desegregation; he had written 26 books, presented lectures, documented racial problems, and used his voice throughout his lifetime to further American race relations.

Half a century after Meredith integrated Ole Miss, the state of black America is still in crisis mode. In 1969, General Motors was the country's largest employer, and AT&T enjoyed a government-guaranteed monopoly on phone service. GM's chief executive, James M. Roche, earned $795,000, the equivalent of $4.2 million today, but GM workers were paid well too.

They received excellent benefits and were generally middle class. Today, Walmart is the largest corporation in America. Its top executive earns $23 million—more than five times Roche's inflation-adjusted salary. Walmart's nonsupervisory employees are paid $18,000 a year, which is less than half what GM workers earned in 1969. Plus, only a few of Walmart's workers have health benefits.[1]

A group of racially mixed individuals from different socioeconomic backgrounds, including politicians, community leaders, educators, community activists, business owners, entertainers, haves, and have-nots, have shared their views and perceptions concerning what is needed to shrink the economic disparities in America. The interview participants live in Davis, California; Atlanta, Georgia; Clinton, Mississippi; Flowood, Mississippi; Jackson, Mississippi; Pelahatchie, Mississippi; Buffalo, New York; and New York, New York. Two participants were evacuees from New Orleans, Louisiana. Interviews ranged from five minutes to two hours, and the responses varied from one paragraph to multiple pages. Each interview respondent was asked to answer the following single open-ended question: What can be done today to close the wide economic gap between the haves and have-nots in America?

Certainly, there are multiple and complex issues relating to the wealth gap in America. James Meredith said, "Black and white is the old issue; the new issue is rich and poor." He feels it is his responsibility to put the wealth gap on the table today.

"We were able to close the wealth gap with muscle years ago," James Meredith contended. He added:

> The black male was brought to America in the first place, because he was strong. Today, there is very little need for brute strength in America's service economy. In today's economy, a person that can lift 300 pounds can be just as effective as someone that can lift only 50 pounds. Twenty years ago, an employee at the post office was required to lift and sort mail. Today, postal workers need to be computer literate just to fill out a job application.
>
> The minimum wage was the worst thing that ever happened to poor people in America, because it eliminated the moral sanction to pay a living wage. Nobody can live off of minimum wages. Before Congress enacted the minimum wage standards, employers were under a moral pressure to pay their employees a living wage. Now, employers follow the law and they do not provide employees with a living wage. Years ago, the community and the church put pressure on employers to pay living wages or provide other amenities to employees.

A homeless person in America is rich compared to a homeless person in Brazil. Poor people in Brazil do not have access to food stamps, health care, or a good education. The fact that blacks in Brazil have limited educational opportunities prevents them from being able to close the economic gap. America has the best education system in the world and we need to take advantage of it.[2]

Meredith told a group of citizens in a city hall meeting in Tchula, Mississippi, during his 200 Mile Walk for the Poor:

> Because of Obama, we have no more excuses. Obama's mother taught him his ABCs and how to count before he turned five years old, that's why he is who he is. The best teacher in the world can't teach a child who doesn't know the fundamentals when he or she enters school. Everyone in this room has a child, niece, nephew, or grandchild under age five. Most children, who are not prepared for school, don't make it through the school system. It's the responsibility of us old people to teach the children in our family. Parents, grandparents and guardians should begin teaching their children basic reading, writing, and math skills when they are toddlers.[3]

Meredith believes that school preparedness is the responsibility of parents and grandparents. He noted:

> Children should be prepared for kindergarten at home and parents should not rely solely on the school system to teach their children. Parents should review their children's lessons, assist them with homework, and help children prepare for tests. All families should have a hardback children's dictionary, which includes pictures and sample sentences. To say any more about that subject would be a waste of words.[4]

That last sentence was said emphatically, and with that he ended the discussion.

Mississippi state representative Alyce G. Clarke, in 1985 became the first black female to be elected to the Mississippi House of Representatives; she is James Meredith's cousin, and she declared that one key factor to closing the economic disparities in America is to impress upon the have-nots the importance of getting a good education, which hopefully will get them a good job. She noted:

> College freshmen can make more informed career choices if they research which fields pay well and which career paths offer the most

job opportunities. Have-nots should get involved politically by voting and making regular contact with their local, state, and federal representatives.

The haves can help close the gap by making concerted efforts to enlighten, inform, and inspire youth, and impressing upon them the importance of economic development. I think youth should understand that "he or she who has the gold rules." My mother used to tell me: "You don't know what you can do unless you try." Youth should try to increase their opportunity to get good jobs. Some two-year trades pay more than jobs requiring college degrees, which is why youth should research career opportunities.

The haves should do everything within their reach to reduce the prison population. Today, 70 percent of those confined in Mississippi's state penitentiary are black, yet blacks only make up 37 percent of the state's population. Several decades ago, there were 143,000 black men in prison and 463,600 in college, but the incarceration rate increases each year. Making good career choices, holding elected officials accountable, and reducing the prison population can help close the wealth gap.[5]

Beulah Greer, director of the Community Students Learning Center, Lexington, Mississippi, agrees with James Meredith and Representative Alyce Clarke that education is significant, but she considers possessing skills and business development to be significant as well. Greer said, "It is important for family members and educators to promote valuable learning experiences and to build on the strengths of children rather than focusing on student weaknesses." She added:

> The school system should implement Individual Educational Plans for students and revise traditional educational models. Practical learning experiences such as plays and extracurriculum activities are important to the educational process. Public schools should allow students to participate in plays all the way through high school, because plays offer valuable learning experiences for students interested in drama.
>
> Every individual has a special talent. The late Peter Jennings, former anchor and senior editor of ABC News, climbed the television broadcast business ladder without a college degree because he built on his talents and mastered them during the course of his career. Youth can broaden their talents just as Jennings did in order to allow their talents to lead them to greater job opportunities.
>
> It is important for people to learn how to save and invest their money, because people must be able to effectively manage their

money in order to manage their finances. Parents should teach their children how money works while they are young. All families need a financial game plan, which includes a plan for investing and retirement.

Educators should make an effort to learn ways to make receiving an education fun to children, and should poll children in order to discover what children's perceptions are concerning what will make learning fun. If learning is enjoyable, children will excel academically and be motivated to become academic achievers. Meredith said in a speech at an NAACP program in Holmes County that people fail their children because they assume it is not their responsibility to teach their children, and secondly, they assume they cannot teach them. We must take responsibility for preparing our children to enter school armed with the basic fundamentals, and we must train children how to survive in a capitalist world by teaching them financial literacy.[6]

When asked what can be done to close the wealth gap, the publisher of *The Jackson Advocate*, Charles Tisdale, said frankly, "Black America should kill the Uncle Toms and preachers." He clarified his statement:

The preachers collect thousands of dollars on Sunday, and on Monday they take the money to Trustmark, Amsouth [now Regions], BancorpSouth, and other banks. Money from the church is deposited in the bank, and once there, the money is seldom loaned to black bank patrons. The preachers are stewards of most of the money that is funneled in the black community, yet many of them won't take the money and do anything significant for the communities they serve. The misallocation of funds and community neglect are the most devastating deterrents to the progress of the black community. An example of fund misallocation occurred during Kane Ditto's mayoral term, when a black minister was hired by the city of Jackson, Mississippi, to oversee $38 million of HUD funds. The funds had been allocated by HUD as loan funds to build minority businesses and new homes. However, all of the monies were distributed to the white community and not one red cent was used to support black businesses or to construct new homes for blacks.

Too often, poor people are neglected by the church. A *love offering* is collected every year to buy preachers a new Cadillac, but tithes and offerings were intended to be used to help the widows and the poor and not to fatten the preacher's pocket. The Bible says, "Blessed are the dissatisfied and blessed are the hungry for they shall be filled." If a $25,000 love offering was used to assist the poor instead of going in the preacher's pocket, conditions for poor people would change, but the preacher is getting stuffed and the hungry are not getting fed.

Fiscal abuse exists in the black community, because black people are often ill informed. The public school system teaches children not to read, not to write, and discourages children from being inquisitive. The community can become more informed by neighbors talking to each other and sharing important issues among themselves. If one neighbor shares with a neighbor, who shares with a neighbor, eventually the entire community will be informed.[7]

Black people can begin to hold preachers and politicians accountable when they are aware of the misdeeds that their leaders perpetrate on them. "When blacks kill Uncle Toms, greedy preachers, and make leaders accountable the black community will improve," Tisdale concluded. Mr. Tisdale died from respiratory failure at age 80 on July 7, 2007, in a Jackson hospital. He was a lifelong activist for the black community. On November 3, 2009, the Jackson City Council voted to rename the public library on Northside Drive in Jackson, Mississippi, the Charles W. Tisdale Public Library.

Jimmie Louis Stokes, president of Utica Junior College (1969–85), now called Hinds Community College–Utica campus, said:

The biggest economic challenge for blacks is the fact that blacks often own very little. We are the biggest consumers, percentage rise, who often buy things that do not appreciate in value. Black people are laborers, who paint cars, but do not make paint, who repair houses, but do not build subdivisions, who fix cars, but do not own the patent to design any. Not enough black folks in general support black-owned businesses.

Two grocery stores set up businesses near my community in North Jackson. The black owned grocery venture called New Deal Supermarket opened on Northside Drive and they went out of business. Blacks would not patronize the black-owned business and eventually the business was not able to compete. But, Piggly Wiggly, which is white owned, received so much business from the black community that it had to expand.

In addition, black people need to learn and understand the significance of the financial pages in the daily newspapers and learn financial strategies in order to access their rightful place in this capitalistic economic system. Black Americans are the richest blacks on this planet, but we are the largest consumers among ethnic groups, and we have the smallest net worths. Instead of blacks purchasing consumer goods, those who have not should establish a financial underpinning by saving and invest in the businesses of America. By investing we become stockholders and we create wealth in that process.

I disagree with those individuals who believe that if and when blacks in America acquire enough formal education that would be the deliverance factor into the political process, the power process, and the economic process. In addition to having negotiated the formal educational structure process, which many of us have successfully done, we must also acquire the strength to analyze the psychological aspects of our existence in order to benefit from both aspects. Too many black people don't like and won't support each other, and some of us don't even like ourselves.

We must remember that there are lots of highly, formerly, educated blacks in America and this formal successful navigating has not gotten the masses of us out of poverty.[8]

By 1994, only 624,000 blacks had master's and doctorate degrees, but by 2004 1.1 million blacks had acquired advanced degrees. "Therefore in order to make full contributions to democracy and capitalism, we must push ourselves forward to become the producers of goods and services instead being predominantly consumers," Stokes added.[9] Paul Krugman too asserted that pointing to education as the problem with inequality is a myth. He claimed:

> The richest twenty percent are those standing between 800 to 1,000. But even those standing between 800 and 950—Americans who earn between $80,000 and $120,000 a year—have done only slightly better than everyone to their left. Almost all of the gains over the past thirty years have gone to the fifty people at the very end of the line. Being highly educated won't make you into a winner in today's U.S. economy. At best, it makes you somewhat less of a loser.[10]

Like Meredith and others, Dr. Leslie Burl McLemore, a political science professor at Jackson State University (JSU), pointed to education as a means of closing the U.S. economic gap. He said, "Providing a quality education to all of American citizens will serve as a panacea for all of society's ills, because education is a cure-all and an equalizer for all of the inequalities in society."

"I am from Wall in Desoto County, Mississippi. We were sharecroppers. A tenth-grade scholar taught my daddy how to write his name," McLemore recalled to an audience at Koinonia Coffee House on Adams Street off Jackson State University's parkway on July 30, 2010. In his younger days, he was a field secretary for SNCC (1960–64). In that leadership role, he fought to obtain civil rights for black people. Now every summer, he presides over the Fannie Lou Hamer Institute on Citizenship and Democracy, which seeks to foster and expand the meaning of citizenship and democracy by exposing school-age children to the exploration of the civil rights movement.

McLemore entered politics by filling a council seat that had been vacated by Louis Armstrong after facing legal troubles. Armstrong was one of the first three blacks to be elected to the Jackson City Council in 1985, when the city changed from at-large districts to a seven-ward system. McLemore served as a city councilman for Ward 2 from 1999 to 2009. As president of the City Council, McLemore was sworn in on May 7, 2009, as acting mayor upon the death of Frank Melton, who died from a full cardiac arrest two days after losing his election bid. McLemore served as acting mayor until July 5, 2009. Harvey Johnson, the city's first black mayor, was sworn back into office on July 6, 2009. He had been defeated by Melton four years earlier.

The following year, McLemore was named the acting president of Jackson State University on May 19, 2010, after President Ronald Mason resigned, ending a 10-year tenure, amid controversy over his recommendation to create Jacobs University, which proposed to merge Mississippi's three black historical colleges into one institution of higher learning. His popularity declined after his merger idea was exposed; he went from being adored to being publicly booed by students. However, he quickly received a job to head Southern University Systems in Baton Rouge, Louisiana.

McLemore noted:

Education is an important framework for an individual. A person's life alliances are built upon one's educational background. W. E. B. Du Bois considered education a means that can bring about a change in one's circumstances. In many cases, an individual's achievement can be pointed back to one's teacher who often inspires their student's future endeavors.

It is important for educators to find better ways to deliver education to our children, to discover lessons learned, and to point out the best teaching practices to serve as models to improve our school systems. A quality education trains children to think, how to analyze, and how to think through problems; parents are wise to try to reach their children by reading and singing to them when they are in the womb. Good teaching practices train students how to break down problems into small component parts in order to solve them. A dilemma exists today, because few teachers take the initiative to search for lessons outside of the textbooks. The history of people of color is taught in an episodic manner, but they should be taught about themselves through textbooks, just as European history is merged into our lessons. Narrowing the teaching of history through months, provide students with only fragmented history lessons.[11]

During a Cultural Diversity Committee roundtable discussion at the University Club in downtown Jackson, Mississippi, in November of 2005, McLemore proclaimed that black people were the only group in America to obtain political power without obtaining economic power. The black community was left in a poor economic state when the civil rights movement ended. McLemore concluded, "Providing all citizens with a quality education will expand the economic pie and increase economic opportunities of all Americans, because a quality education is one of the most important variables that can increase one's economic standing."[12]

Sean Devlin, executive director of American Civil Rights Education Services (ACRES), Brooklyn, New York, offered the following reflections on closing the wealth gap between the haves and have-nots:

From the standpoint of ACRES, to close the wide economic gap between haves and have-nots in America, the answer is clearly to improve educational opportunities for all who seek such services.

The *Brown v. Board of Education* ruling in 1954 clearly holds that one of the most important functions of the state is to provide an equitable education for all its citizens. I believe that everyone deserves an equal opportunity for a quality education. Once the educational playing field is leveled for all in a truly democratic fashion, then I have no objection to citizens conducting themselves in accordance with the laws of the marketplace, the dynamics of a meritocracy, or what some might call economic Darwinism "survival of the fittest."

Clearly, the great civil rights challenge in education, for which your family member James Meredith fought so courageously in 1962 and beyond, is still before us. Resegregation and inequitable resources in our public school systems are on the rise and most adversely affect people of color and the economically disenfranchised. The social revolution that is needed to overcome these challenges can be aided by the law and by nonviolent direct action; however, I emphatically believe that lasting change in the field of education can only be achieved when the hearts and minds and souls of all human beings are transformed by divine love.

Perhaps in this lifetime, you, James Meredith, myself, and ACRES may only touch and transform a hand full or maybe dozens of souls.

But those whom we touch will reach out and lift up others and what began as a ripple of hope can turn into a tidal wave of positive progressive social change.[13]

Sean Devlin passed away in 2009, but not before exposing thousands of New York students to the stories of veterans of the civil rights movement. The program had a great impact on students, who noted that their journey to the South encouraged them to improve their grades.

Marcia Weaver, a former councilwoman for the City of Jackson, Mississippi, said: "Everybody who has an opportunity to work, should work. Young folks need the opportunity to obtain as much education as they can get before they enter the workforce, and wages need to be fair for the work that people do."[14]

Frank Taylor, a member of Winston County Self-Help Cooperative in Louisville, Mississippi, contended that the wealth gap can be closed when poor people become smart consumers or by creating profitable co-operative forms of business. He stated:

> Community leaders should identify the general needs of consumers in order to educate them, because being a smart consumer saves money and improves one's economic standing. For example, smart car owners get regular car tune-ups, maintain their tires at the proper inflation to save gas, and get regular oil changes to preserve the life of their motor; smart borrowers obtain prime interest loans of 7 percent or less and uses credit sparingly.
>
> Cooperative forms of businesses is one of the easiest ways to help the little-business man increase his purchasing power by pooling money with others, which saves money, while sharing expenses reduces overhead costs, and exposes co-op members to higher business profits. There needs to be a direct campaign to educate consumers on how to pool their resources to create business enterprises, which can turn consumers into entrepreneurs, and help them gain a larger piece of the economic pie. By joining a co-op, consumers switch their position in the money cycle by becoming entrepreneurs, who sell goods or services to other consumers.[15]

Lakeshia Walters, a support staff member of the Rural Development Leadership Network, in New York City, assumed that the most important factor that will close the wide economic gap in America is getting good people on the Supreme Court, who will interpret the Constitution fairly. She noted:

Judges who are against affirmative action will continue to create laws that will help widen the economic gap. I feel that we [minorities] are going backward rather than forward, and I pray that my generation [young adults] will wake up and smell the coffee. Corporate America can contribute to closing the gap by paying fair wages like Ford [Ford Motor Co.] did years ago. Ford gave a lot of minorities the opportunity to reach the middle-class status in society. I support affirmative action because this policy helped have-nots become a part of the have group.[16]

Betty Mason, a retired public schoolteacher who lives in Jackson, Mississippi, contended that someone in the community should assume the responsibility of teaching disadvantaged children how to tap into the resources that can help them get into college as a path to help level their economic standing. She noted:

A lot of students don't seek education beyond high school, because they don't have guidance, and many do not know how to apply for college loans and scholarships. Public school counselors often have huge case loads and can only assist a few students with college preparation. Plus, youth don't do the math—high school diploma, $7 per hour—two-year trade, $20 per hour.

One of the greatest mistakes minorities make is investing in luxury cars and materialism that increases their indebtedness. Young couples who are planning to marry should save down payment money toward home ownership and make financial plans. When possible, families should invest in home computers and educational software. Children need to be taught to be ambitious, independent, competitive, self-supporting, and should be encouraged to strive to make their lives better.

Parents should teach children the importance of purchasing life, property, and disability insurance, because insurance protects a family's income and property. Young parents must understand that having no savings can lead to financial hardship and bankruptcy, if the head of the household gets fired, laid-off, or injured on the job. Therefore families should understand the importance of practicing effective money management strategies; public school systems need to improve career-counseling programs, and when necessary adults can lend a hand to a neighbor's child who needs college guidance.[17]

A real estate investor, who lives in North Jackson, Mississippi, named Cressie Nelson Hopkins asserted that black business owners should learn how to operation competitive businesses. She proclaimed:

We don't have decent black-owned businesses in our community. Years ago, Lake Hico Shopping Center was a vibrant shopping area. Jack in the Box, a dollar store, a beauty salon, and Winn Dixie operated businesses in the Lake Hico Shopping Plaza.

During the early 1990s, New Hope Baptist Church opened a grocery store in the old Winn Dixie facility. In fact, the church purchased the entire commercial shopping center. The church's grocery store business was called Bromer. They sold cigarettes, but refused to sell beer and eventually the business folded. Management claimed they went out of business because they experienced high thief problems. The way I look at it, they could have hired a security company to reduce their thief problems, but I personally believe they lost valuable business because they refused to sell beer, which reduced their competitive edge.

Today, Lake Hico Shopping Plaza is completely vacant and New Hope Baptist Church has become a negligent landowner. The entire commercial plaza is one of the worst eyesores in North Jackson. No property owner should be allowed to neglect their property, plus property neglect deteriorates the community.

Small businesses will survive if they have good service and competitive prices. Property owners must upkeep their lots, buildings, and yards in order for us to have healthy communities. When local businesses hire people in the community, money will flow back into the community, crime will decline, employment will rise, and the community will improve.[18]

A Mississippi hip hop artist named Brad Franklin (Kamikaze) asserted that an education and good work ethics are important factors that can help increase one's income. He said:

The number one factor that will lift have-nots to the next level is education, because the best jobs go to the best educated. There was a time in this country when a high school diploma would be sufficient for someone to build a successful career in the industrial manufacturing industry. However, today people need to obtain an education beyond high school to get good jobs. A job applicant with a master's or specialist's degree will get a job faster than someone with a bachelor's degree, and someone with a college degree will get a job faster than someone who holds a high school diploma. Regardless of whether a person is black or white or from the North or the South, an education can open more opportunities for people.

The community suffers from the decline in family values, and there is a generation gap between elders in our community and young people, but the community will benefit from having a connection between the two generations. Older people have a lot of wisdom to share with young people who are willing to listen. The older generation believed in putting in a hard day of work and they tried to do the best they could do. A lot of young people do not understand the value of hard work. Some youth obtain degrees and job opportunities, but they lack good work ethics, which is why some of them cannot hold a job.

An education, skills, and good work ethics are ingredients that can take have-nots and put them in the have level. Advancing is a process that takes planning and effort. Success doesn't come easy; it requires hard work. Once a person arrives to the have level, he or she should reach back and pull someone else up. If we continue to pass the torch, things will get better.[19]

Hollis Watkins, President/Founder, Southern Echo, Inc., a nonprofit organization in Jackson, Mississippi, believes the root causes of this country's economic disparities are linked to racism and the poor quality of public education available to have-nots. In 1961, Watkins, a Tougaloo College student, met activist Robert "Bob" Moses in McComb, Mississippi, and became a foot soldier for SNCC. That year, he participated in the first lunch counter sit-in in McComb, Mississippi.

Watkins was prompted to become a proponent for social justice many years ago after winning first place in New Farmers of America Contest during the 1955–56 school year for singing a popular radio song. When they reached the state contest level, the organizers unjustifiably deducted points from them because they did not appreciate the lyrics the group sang and did not want them to have more points than their white challengers. The point deductions cost them first place on the national level. Watkins unsuccessfully tried to lead a protest against the organizers, but that incident sparked the flames of his activist life. A verse of the song is below.

You load *sixteen tons*, and what do you get?
Another day older and deeper in debt.
Saint Peter, don't you call me 'cause I can't go,
l owe my soul to the company store.[20]

This song depicted the predicament of poor people. Little has changed; the debt used to be to one store, now the debt is spread out. In the past, racism was linked to the killing and murdering of blacks which caused them to deeply fear demanding changes relating to education and access to jobs. Acquiring a good education would have allowed have-nots to develop economic opportunities 40 years ago, and an quality education can open doors today.

Racism has been the mechanism that provides have-nots with a poor public education, and it has also helped widen the economic disparities. Have-nots must first overcome our fear of challenging the status quo. One way to overcome fear is for us to unite, because there is strength in numbers. Uniting means we must pool our monetary and human resources together. Have-nots must pool brain power to create large effective enterprises, become educated, and determine how the haves have maintained their economic strong hold over us.

First and foremost, have-nots must understand that haves will never establish a free public educational system that will equip have-nots with the knowledge to create businesses that will compete with their companies. If haves provide have-nots with the same level of education that they receive, they would equip us with the tools to become equal to them. The haves will not provide the training to have-nots that they need to lift themselves from poverty. If have-nots gain the proper knowledge, we can change our own circumstances; we have plenty of opportunities to learn; everything we need to learn is available in books, courses, in the library, and on the Internet.

If have-nots become equal to haves, they will not be able to exploit us. The haves' ability to exploit have-nots helped widen the economic gap in this country. Corporations exploit people all the time. For example, a particular corporation pays an executive $250,000 to run a company and may employ 14 employees who earn $8 per hour for production. In this example, the executive earns more than the entire workforce. The exploitation system elevates a few people and leaves the majority behind. America was built on the free labor of Indian and African slaves and the cheap labor of the Irish, Jews, Japanese, and Chinese.

If the owner of the company makes a profit of $1 million in a given year after he has paid his expenses, then the business owner's economic gap is even wider than the executive's gap between the workers. Of the 15 people employed in the company, only 1 person earns a large salary. The 14 employers responsible for production earned only $15,360 per year, which is not even a living wage. Once people realize that an $8-per-hour job is the equivalent of sharecropping, he or she will want to use his or her skills to create a situation where he or she can earn a profit himself.

Have-nots can take into consideration some alternative business enterprises to create a more balanced earning scale. A cooperative form of business will elevate more people and eliminate greed. Co-op development is one alternative to help close the economic gap, because the profit distribution is more equal.

People have been conditioned to assume that there are no alternatives to earning minimum wage pay rates, and this state of mind is the equivalent of a mental slavery. The plantation system was the worst form of exploitation, but there are similar plantation systems today in city, county, and governmental agencies. The coal mine was a plantation and anybody today who does not earn a living wage is on a plantation because they have just enough money to keep from starving.

Large company stockholders, corporate board members, politicians, and top executives benefit from the exploitation system. Vice President Dick Chaney overlapped into the corporate and political world. The Bush administration gave Halliburton and its subsidiaries contracts to rebuild the Mississippi Gulf Coast during Hurricanes Katrina and Rita. Chaney used to be the CEO of Halliburton and directly benefited from Halliburton's profits as a stockholder. On the Gulf Coast, Halliburton was the plantation, and immigrant workers were exploited.

The Mississippi Delta has been a closed society since slavery ended, and people in the region are still exploited. There are a lot of plantations in the Delta, where cotton is king. Today, the descendants of former slaves work on cotton, soybean, and catfish farms for low wages. Some of them work in factories earning low wages and most of them do not have health care or retirement benefits. Like their forefathers, most of them are not landowners.

Low-income workers are fed a false perception that life is better now than it was for their fathers who worked on the land as sharecroppers, but in reality little has changed. Periodically, some of them get a 20 cent raise, which is only $384 per year. How far can that go? Have-nots can elect candidates of their choosing these days, but many elected officials need to receive training in order to provide effective representation to their constituents.

Elected officials often see themselves as separate from community, which divides them from their constituents, and sometimes they themselves become oppressors. Elected officials should call town meetings and enter into collective discussions with citizens to stay close to the people and to discover solutions to help lift the have-nots from the pits of hell. After integration, a lot of the businesses in the black community closed. White flight from cities/towns contributed to economic and job loss, but our local economy would strengthen if we support local businesses; then, there would be no need to drive out in the suburbs to shop or to find employment.[21]

Arthur Meredith, James Meredith's youngest brother, shared his views on this topic as well. He said:

Have-nots must master specific skills in order to be able to compete. He recalled his father, Moses "Cap" Meredith, telling him: "If you are a master of your trade, then no one is better than you." The master of any trade will not have to worry about having something to do because he will always have work to do and a means to earn a living, because the master is the best and the best is always in demand. I believe that the principle that a boy should know what he plans to do in life by the age of 13 should be followed today, because planning and dreaming are important components in the development process.

The state of idleness was one of the worst things that ever happened in the community. Idleness begins at home, when parents allow their children to get out of bed and step over their clothes in the middle of the floor. Idle children often become unproductive adults. People must be productive in order to become the masters in their fields. Good parenting is essential, because parents can teach their children to be resourceful or wasteful. Children who respect their parents will most likely submit to teachers and other authority figures. Good home training is essential to the development of children, who must learn to be competitive, plan for the future, and become masters in their fields in order to increase their economic positions in society.[22]

Kendrick Portis, an evacuee from New Orleans, Louisiana, as a result of Hurricane Katrina who performed concrete finishing work in Pelahatchie, Mississippi, assumed that closing the economic disparities are fueled at home by parental guidance. He claimed:

The lifestyle of parents can influence children not to be the best that they can be. If parents drink, smoke, and curse at home in front of their children, the children are influenced negatively and do not try to do their best. Fathers should be leaders and mothers should be wives.

The father figure in a house holds a lot of weight. Where I am from, if the man didn't work, but things got paid, he was either robbing people or businesses or selling drugs and this life is a poor example for a son or daughter. Children have to be strong and must realize that they don't have to do what everybody else does. Children should try to do what is right, by following good role models, which can keep them out of the criminal justice system and put them on a road out of poverty. I want to tell children: make a dollar and save a dollar, because if you spent every dollar you have you won't have anything to fall back on.

Poverty where I am from was low and deep like floodgates. People were barely paying their rent; some people used to walk from door to door begging for food and money. There is a great despair among poor people who don't have hope. It is not easy to escape poverty when a person doesn't have hope and stops dreaming; without hope and dreams, a man has nothing, and it is hard to make something out of nothing. My God helped me make it through (he said this smiling).

Dreaming will give poor people the desire to lift themselves out of poverty. Lawyers and doctors make a good living and they have to obtain an education to be in their fields, and poor people must be inspired to continue their education after high school. Good parenting, an education, inspiration, and skills can lead poor people to a better life.[23]

Portis completed trucking school after this interview and became an over-the-road truck driver; he died in 2008 from heart complications in a hospital in Memphis, Tennessee. He did not have health insurance.

Carl Easley, a financial advisor in Flowood, Mississippi, asserted that have-nots should go after more education and seek gainful employment in order to pull themselves from the have-not into the have status. Easley, who comes from a sharecropper family, proclaimed, "There is no reason why any one cannot pull himself or herself up in America."[24]

Ivey Stokes, CEO of MyEcon, said: "The number one thing for people to understand in America is that we live in a capitalist society. A capitalist society is like a sporting event; people who know how to play can be successful." However, he assumed that if one does not know how to play, he or she will not succeed. "It is very important that we understand the rules. One rule dictates that everyone is responsible for his own finances," he added.

People have to understand how money works in order to be able to survive in a capitalist society. He recalled hearing President Bush say in his inauguration speech that the government is not to provide people with wealth but to build an environment where people have the opportunity to build wealth. Ivey contended that:

One of the problems with the president's statement is that America does not create an environment where everyone can learn how to create wealth. The public school system does not show students how to survive in our capitalist society. They are not taught about credit, debt, investing, and risk management during their primary school years.

On the other hand, it is a fallacy for people to assume the government should help people obtain wealth. Some people believe the government should divide up wealth and distribute it to American citizens. However, the government promised to provide her citizenry with a 12th grade education, student loans for college, and the rest is left up to us.

Fifty years ago, we were master farmers, and as such we became successful economically by mastering farming rules. A good farmer would replant his watermelon seed crop. A good cattle herdsman would never kill his bull, because the bull is needed to produce more cattle.

If people do not have enough money to produce or replace money, then they have killed their bull. This dilemma exists among the middle-class group, in particular, because many of them spend a lot and save little. If families invest half of the money they spend on Christmas, materialism, cigarettes, beer, and alcohol over a 20-year period, they would have a nice nest egg.[25]

Stokes noted that he has met dozens of people who acquire lump sums of money from the lottery and from lawsuits, but he contended that one must have financial savvy in order to hold on to their winnings. He said he and his associates often ask financial-training participants, "What would you do if you had $1 million?" He recalled, "Some people express that they would buy family members cars and houses, but such spending would land them in the poor house in ten or twelve years." He concluded:

However, some people note that they would create business entities and invest their money, which could allow them to live off their money for a life time, if they make wise investments. People need to learn how to make sound business investments in order to create wealth. Once people are equipped with the tools to survive in a capitalist society they will be able to create a nest egg of savings, make sound business investments, accumulate assets, and increase their net worth.[26]

Rev. Brian Robinson was the interim pastor of Shiloh Baptist Church in Buffalo, New York, at the time of this interview. He asserted that the disintegration of the black community hindered its economic growth. He does not think Dr. Martin Luther King Jr. wanted the black community to disintegrate, which is what happened after integration. "Before integration we had striving black owned businesses in our communities; we patronized the black owned barbershops, hotels, clothing stores, furniture stores, and restaurants in our community," he added. It is his perception that money flipped over in the black community approximately seven times before integration, but today money turns over once and the rest is spent with the majority community.

He asserted that the black community needs drum majors in it like Dr. King. Next, community residents need to make demands on their school system. "We should not accept our children being passed on to the next grade if they don't satisfy the requirements," he proposed. He added:

Our school systems should not produce students who cannot read or write when they graduate from high school. We need to hold parents and the school system accountable. Parents should meet their children's teachers and be a part of their children's educational development. Our children should be taught the primary colors and how to count at home before they get to kindergarten. All of our children are capable of doing well in school. If they can memorize a rap song, they can learn their time tables and how to read and write.[27]

He admitted that churches have gained a bad reputation of not supporting the community since the roaring civil rights movement. "Churches should lead the way to take care of the poor and needy in the community," he contended. Rev. Robinson reported:

Around seven inner-city black churches in Buffalo formed the Jeremiah Project; the group has remodeled an abandoned shopping plaza, which is now leased out to six black-owned businesses. In addition, St. John Fruit Belt Community Development Corporation, a faith-based group, secured funds to rehabilitate 350 homes over a five-year period in the Fruit Belt, which includes Peach Street, Orange Street, etc.

St. John Baptist Church started St. John United Federal Credit Union over 30 years ago. Community-owned banks are important to the progress of the community. The credit union will grow considerable when the community provides greater support. It will reach greater heights as a bank and as a lender for the community when it is used by more people. I pray the credit union will be successful in attracting tens of thousands of new members from the community.[28]

Rev. Robinson concluded, "The conditions for have-nots will improve when churches restore the community, when money begins to turn over and stay in the community like it did before the 1970s, when we make more demands on our school system, when drum majors come forth, and when the community unites." He is presently the pastor of Fillmore Community Church in Buffalo.[29]

Percy Trimont, a native of New Orleans and a former resident of the Ninth Ward asserted that one of the worst problems that poor people in New Orleans had to contend with was high taxes and high unemployment. He asserted:

> Money is tight for adults who have to settle for burger jobs, and college graduates who end up settling for low-wage jobs. People who can barely make ends meet are unhappy and needy, and the result of unhappy, needy people is crime.
>
> For 20 years, New Orleans led the country with murder statistics. During the rise of the crack cocaine problem, an average of 420 people were murdered each year and the murder rate passed 700 in 1994, making New Orleans the murder capital of the world.[30] Many people who were unemployed created criminal jobs, which increased crime. A lot of the city's murders were related to turf [territory] issues. Black men in the 16 to 25 age group are being eliminated by each other. Funeral homes have high business success rates with over 100 funeral homes citywide.
>
> White business owners have always owned most of the businesses in the community; when they left the city and headed to the suburbs they took the jobs with them. Crime increased when job opportunities decreased, and New Orleans 9 percent tax rate constantly drained the limited funds of poor city residents. People in the suburbs have the city's best jobs, but they spend their dollars in the suburbs, which drained the city's infrastructure and education tax funds.[31]

It is Trimont's perception that limited jobs, the lack of respect residents have for each either, and poor parenting negatively affect have-nots. He noted:

> Parents should respect their children and children should respect their parents and other people. When a child is hugged and sent to school, he is more likely to have a good day at school, but a child who is cursed out before he goes to school is more likely to have a bad day at school. People who are unhappy or who have alcohol or drug problems sometimes have abusive tendencies. People who have little self-respect often have little respect for others. There is a lot of disrespect when a group of people prey off of each other to make ends meet.[32]

He concluded, "Lower taxes, good parenting, more jobs, and more inner city businesses will improve life for have-nots." Before Hurricane Katrina the Trimonts were home owners and their mortgage was paid off. Their home was well maintained and in good repair. They were renting a home in Jackson, Mississippi, when this story was written. Since the interview, the Trimonts' home in New Orleans was demolished; they have relocated to Houston, Texas, and became propertyless.[33]

Eddie Cotton, a Mississippi blues singer, asserted that one of the first steps that anyone can do to create wealth is to become a home owner. "One of the first rules for home ownership is having a safety nest set aside for repairs," he said. Cotton added:

No one should buy a home if they don't have money saved because home repairs are expensive, but since you have to pay rent, you might as well buy. Acquiring skills or an education will increase one's ability to earn money, but it is just as important for people to pay bills on time so that they can have good credit, because high interest is expensive.

When you go to a bank to apply for a loan to buy a home or to start a business, program officers evaluate an applicant's income and credit, and if one of those factors is short, the bank will take into consideration the amount of collateral a person owns. Ownership of assets is important. We need to put our money in places that build wealth [stock ownership, homes, businesses], instead of things that depreciate. We should stop buying things that make us look wealthy because there is a difference between looking wealthy, wearing luxurious things, and owning wealth.

Back in the day, a lot of people had rent parties and fish fries to supplement their incomes. People in the community supported each other's fish fries and yard sales, and bartered with each other, which was a means of turning over money in the community. People at the bottom of the economic arena have to go against the grain and make the system work for us. Before segregation, black businesses prospered and employed community residents.

I once visited Chicago and was impressed with Chinatown, which is like a small city. The streets have Chinese names and anything a Chinese desires is in Chinatown. They buy and sell to each other, and money turns over in their community instead of leaving their community.[34]

It is Cotton's belief that the black community needs to have its own business districts. "All communities need business districts around them to sustain them; we need to support each other like we did back in the day!" he added. In summary, Cotton concluded that, "The have-nots need good credit, income, skills, more jobs, an education, collateral, and successful business districts in order to employ community residents, which will close the wealth gap."[35]

Nettie Stowers, a member of Women for Progress who lives in Jackson, Mississippi, reasoned that a good nuclear family is the foundation upon which wealth is created. She asserted:

> Families should provide a basic education to their children from birth to six years of age at home, and help their children obtain a good formal education afterward. Advance degrees and trades will provide individuals with better incomes and will give them access to a sufficient amount of disposable income. Regardless of race or national origin, the two-parent family structure is important; for children who are raised by two parents are often more successful than children raised by single parents. Strong family units, school preparation at home, and a quality distribution of income will help close the wealth gap.[36]

Richard Williams, who lives in Atlanta, Georgia, gave his views on how the U.S. economic gap can be closed. He stated:

> Making business loans available to low-income people will help close the gap, because business ownership can increase the income of ordinary Americans. I once saw a show on PBS that showed how five people borrowed money together. The advantage of them being coborrowers is that if one person was not able to make his payment on any given month, the others could pitch in and made the payment. The group had a vested interest in repaying the loan, which reduced their chances of forbearing on the loan.
>
> I read in a *Jet* magazine while I was at the doctor's office that the average black and Hispanic family has a net worth of $6,000, while white families have an average net worth of $90,000. Low-income people should be taught how money works and how to manage money. The average person does not know what they are worth, but it is important for people to understand the cycle of money in a capitalist society. Consumers put money in the economy, while private businesses earn profits off consumer spending, but consumers increase their net worth by investing in retirement accounts and acquiring assets.
>
> Nothing is more important than having cash, because cash is needed to buy every necessity that a family needs. The amount of money a family earns has nothing to do with their ability to save.

Therefore a family earning $40,000 a year can save as much money over a life time as a family earning $100,000 a year. People have to consistently set aside a portion of their income every month in order to build savings. A couple can save $35 per week for one year and have $1,820 at the end of the year. In six years, that $35 per week would turn into $10,920. It is not what you make, but it is what you do with your money that really counts.

Discriminatory policies hurt poor people too. For example, insurance regulations allow insurance companies to charge poor people higher insurance rates. High car and home insurance and taxes shrink a family's income. People spend about 30 percent of their income in taxes, which helps widen the economic gap.[37]

He assumed that there must be a better connection between the community and elected officers. "When bills are proposed and enacted by the Georgia State Assembly, legislators should hold community meetings to spread news to the public" he proposed. He affirmed that the same laws and regulations that widen the economic gap can be changed to help close the gap. He believes, "The government should level the playing field by giving poor people the same tax breaks that wealthy people receive." He concluded, "Families should save a portion of their income for rainy days so they can pay cash for car repairs, appliances, and other household goods as opposed to getting into debt."

In conclusion, multiracial interview respondents have made a number of suggestions concerning their perceptions on how the wide economic gap in America can be closed today. While there are no "quick fix" solutions to closing the wealth gap in America, have-nots may be the best group of people to become voices to tackle this problem. Although, billions of dollars have been contributed to charities over the past five decades and funneled into social organizations and faith-based initiatives, charity has not put a dent in poverty.

As interviewees noted, parents need to start going to Parent Teachers Association meetings and school board meetings, and residents need to attend city/town hall meetings. Churches and organizations can turn vacant lots into business ventures. Vacant lots can be converted into community gardens, which are a means of supplementing food needs. Plus gardening requires physical exercise and can help people lose weight, and fresh food is healthier than can goods. Inmate literacy activities, halfway house facilities, job training, and inmate job opportunities can help reduce repeat-offender rates.

Maybe as Richard Williams suggested, elected officials ought to bring government to their constituents by holding meetings in their wards or districts to spread political news, and it may just be practical for low-income families to tuck away $35 per month every month to create savings. As Jimmie Stokes noted, poor people must become the producers of goods and services, which increases their earning power and can allow them to rise economically.

James Meredith, Representative Alyce Clarke, Dr. Leslie McLemore, Brad "Kamikaze" Franklin, and Sean Devlin all noted that a quality education will balance the economic playing field for have-nots. School preparation at home is also essential. Representative Clarke noted that constituents ought to make regular contact with their elected officials, because officeholders foster and create ordinances and laws that affect the lives of citizens. During the Second Reconstruction, white-owned businesses located in majority-black communities would not hire blacks; now other ethnic groups own businesses in black communities and hire mainly members of their race, stunting job opportunities for residents and preventing the flow of money from reentering the community.

James Meredith's home state remains at the bottom in terms of poverty, due in part to persistent poverty. The lack of financial support absent parents provide for children contributes to poverty. According to the Mississippi Commission of the Status of Women, child support payments in Mississippi average less than $60 per month, which is less than the cost of child care for one week. Perhaps future policies will require absent parents to provide more support for their biological children. The report noted,

> The recession had increased the number of persons living in poverty, and the percentage of female-headed households with children living in poverty climbed to 59% in 2010.[38]

Communities must be represented by business districts that provide jobs to residents. If the rules of supply and demand dictate business growth, and there are three times as many convenience stores as they are dollar stores in some communities, then liberal spending creates others problems for families. Shopping regularly at convenience stores is just simply expensive, as Cressie Nelson Hopkins noted. If individuals are broke before payday, he or she may want to evaluate their spending habits, by collecting receipts and determining what they have purchased and at what price.

Poor people must become conservative consumers, who are financially savvy, and the business class must master entrepreneurial skills in order to obtain a larger share of the consumer market. James Meredith noted to local vendors during a Black History Expo at Farish Street Baptist Church in Jackson, Mississippi, that in a capitalist environment, vendors must market to everyone. "I hear a lot of talk about us blacks supporting black-owned business, but in a capitalist environment, black vendors must market to whites and all Americans," he said.[39]

Businesses need to consider the preferences of consumers in order to operate competitive business entities. Small businesses must market their products and services to people of all races and from all walks of life in order to succeed. Today, consumers have a broad range of values. Some want the bells and whistles. They want to see shiny glass windows, manicured lawns, and glossy or textured marketing material. Consumers are impressed with employees who offer assistance, greet them when they enter, and are friendly. Consumers want first-class dining experiences and top-notch services. Feedback from consumers is very important. We should seek feedback from consumers by asking questions such as "Did you find what you needed?" and "Are there other services or products that we can offer to accommodate your needs?"

Personal finance courses would help public school students become more financially savvy, but as Hollis Watkins noted the haves will not provide the tools to make the have-nots competitive with them. Therefore it is incumbent upon have-nots to learn how to survive in a capitalist society. During this century, Americans witnessed governmental bailouts and a massive deficit that revealed the economic failure of capitalism, which dictates that consumers need to spend less and save more money in order to hold on to their assets. Cash is, indeed, king, and individuals need emergency funds that are not attached to the stock market—at least $3,000 in one's 30s and $6,000 in one's 40s.

We have to applaud the community improvements made over the past half century, but at the same time we must continue to advance, by tackling unresolved issues. During the Second Reconstruction, many brave souls made sacrifices to improve life for black Americans. In 1957, Little Rock Arkansas High School was integrated by seven black high school students, and in 1962 James Meredith integrated the University of Mississippi. A ripple effect occurred afterward. The University of Alabama was integrated in 1963, college sports in the South gradually became integrated, and a larger percentage of southern blacks became lawyers and obtained advanced degrees.

At age 75, Meredith used his voice for 27 days during his 2009 Walk for the Poor to encourage parents to train their children for school at home, to encourage residents to walk at least one mile a day, and to highlight the plight of the poor; he walked from door to door in apartment buildings passing out bookmarks and talking to citizens, hoping to promote a message of school preparedness; he also met with elected officers, clergy, and talked one-on-one with citizens. During the Walk, Meredith met a 26-year-old black male who had finished high school but could not read, a man whose car was his home, and preschool children who could barely count 10. He saw the bondage of drug infested communities.

"Today, the average black high school student in the state makes a 15 when a 17 is required to get accepted into state colleges, making them only eligible to attend junior colleges after graduating from high school," James Meredith noted repeatedly to audiences during his Walk for the Poor. "We've gone backward. They [the media] need to stop talking about what I did at Ole Miss; if I can't do anything today, I may as well not be here," he added.[40]

The election of America's first president of African and Caucasian descent with prominent African features in November of 2008 was monumental. He was proof, although a rare case, that a black male who could climb to the very top of American society. Senator Barack Obama's presidential election is an indication that a segment of white America has buried the ideology of white supremacy. His rivals, Senators John McCain and Hillary Clinton, had hardly conceived that he would beat them at a game that had been dominated by white males for 232 years.

Mr. Obama was a history maker before he ran for president. He was the first black to be elected to the U.S. Senate in the twentieth-first century, and the first black president of the Harvard Law Review. Edward Broke (Senate term 1966–79) and Carol Moseley Braun (Senate term 1992–98) were the only black senators in the twentieth century, while Hiram Rhodes Revell (Senate term 1870–71) and Blanche K. Bunche (Senate term 1875–81) were the only black senators in the nineteenth century.

In the 1960s, a black candidate's presidential bid would not have been announced on the six o'clock news. "The media is another arm of government," Meredith proclaimed.[41] Clennon King Jr., who attempted to integrate Ole Miss in 1958, was the first black man to run for president in 1960. King was labeled "crazy" by the media, and the majority of the people in his racial group accepted this classification of him, but 1,500 voters embraced his presidential bid. King's vision for America was ahead of his time, but he broke the ice. Others stood on his shoulders and garnered more votes than he did; then, voters finally gave the world—Obama.

Hickory, Mississippi, native and BET founder Robert ("Bob") Johnson climbed to the top of American society by developing a niche in the television market. He became the first black billionaire when he sold BET to Viacom. BET was the first black-owned company listed on the New York

Stock Exchange. Johnson accumulated a diverse list of holdings. In 2002, Johnson became the first black to purchase a major sports franchise—the NBA's Charlotte Bobcats. He also owns RLJ Development, a real estate investment company; Three Keys Music, a recording studio; and Posh, a restaurant. His divorce in 2004 to his ex-wife Sheila reduced his holdings and he forfeited his billionaire status. In late 2006 at the age of 60, Johnson regained his billionaire status, after purchasing 100 hotels.

Incidentally, education is the foundation upon which Oprah Winfrey and James Meredith accumulated wealth. Today, Meredith owns his father's farmland, and she owns her grandfather's farmland in rural Attala County, Mississippi. Perhaps in the future, their land will be turned into tourist attractions.

As Rev. Robinson noted, today we need drum majors for justice to use their voices to improve the conditions of minority communities. Native Americans face the same problems on reservations that others face in trailer parks and in urban districts around this great nation. When poor people open the doors of dialogue, create a united front, and develop a plan for the future, we will be able to break the chains of poverty.

History has shown us from the slaves on the sugar plantations to the poor in American ghettos that people must be strong to rise economically in society. "Strong" has multiple meanings including training, skills, unity, hope, planning, vision, mobilization, freedom, political clout, power, and wealth. Have-nots have to keep on walking, and keep on moving out of the pits of poverty into the bliss of financial security by developing an underpinning of savings, forming alliances, uniting, and building a threshold of assets. As Sly Stone (funk and rock icon) sang decades ago, "We can make it if we try."[42] Have-nots can become haves if we try. Try!

Appendix

FAMILY TREE OF JAMES HOWARD MEREDITH

Paternal Great, Great Grandfather:
Edward Meredith, a Canadian Trader

Paternal Great, Great Grandmother,
unknown, Choctaw female of African descent

Edward Meredith—unknown Choctaw female
Child: Alberta Meredith

Paternal Great, Great Grandfather:
Josiah Campbell, a Scottish Irish immigrant

Paternal Great, Great Grandmother:
Abigail Blair Patterson, a Scottish Irish immigrant

Robert Bond Campbell—Mary Ada Patterson
Child: Josiah Abigail Patterson Campbell

Maternal Great, Great Grandfather,
William Patterson, a Scottish Irish immigrant

Maternal Great, Great Grandmother:
Caroline Patterson, slave

Maternal Great Grandfather:
Columbus Patterson

Maternal Great Grandmother:
Mariah Patterson

Columbus Patterson—Mariah Patterson
Child: William Patterson

Chief Sam Cobb—Alberta Meredith
Child: Ned Meredith

Josiah A. P. Campbell—Millie Brown, slave
Child: Francis Brown

Grandfather: Ned Meredith 1849–1922	Spouse: Ellen Franklin 1855–80 Children of Ned and Ellen: James Cleveland Child: name unknown
Grandfather: Ned Meredith	Grandmother: Francis Brown 1865–1903 Children of Ned and Francis: Alberta Meredith Leroy Meredith Moses Arthur "Cap" Meredith Eddie Meredith Jessie Meredith Gene Meredith Willie Lou Meredith Eugene "Plunder" Meredith Elyses "Plain" Meredith Clifton "Cliff" Meredith
Grandfather: Ned Meredith	Spouse: Julie Holton Winters Child of Ned and Julie: Betty Meredith
Grandfather: Ned Meredith	Spouse: Sarah Lewis Dodd Children of Ned and Sarah: Hattie Meredith Daniel Meredith John Meredith

Father: Moses Meredith 1891–1965   Spouse: Barbara Nash 1893–1929

Children of Moses and Barbara:

Emmett Meredith

Leroy Meredith

Delma (Sister) Meredith

Thelma Meredith

Mary Meredith

Miriam Meredith

Maternal Great Grandfather: Grandmother's Father:
Columbus Patterson   Judge Harvey Davis

Maternal Great, Great Grandmother: Grandmother's Mother:
Mariah   Arteal Hickman

Mother's Father: William Patterson   Maternal Grandmother:
Roxie Lee Hickman

Children of William and Roxie:

William (Buddy)

Alma

Caroline

Columbus (Lum)

Solomon (Sol)

Esau

Henderson

Roxie (Sis)

Hattie

Mary (Mae)

Katie

Harvey

Arthur

Benjamin (Bennie)

Father: Moses Meredith 1891–1965   Mother: Roxie Mariah Patterson
1903–86

Children of Moses and Roxie:

(*continued*)

	J. H. (J-Boy) Meredith

	Clifton (Cliff) Meredith
	Everett Herman Meredith
	Hazel Janell (Nell) Meredith
	Arthur Claudell Meredith
	Willie Lou Meredith
	Devilla Meredith
J. H. Meredith (James Howard Meredith)	Spouse: Mary June Wiggins 1938–79
	Children of James and Mary June:
	John Howard Meredith
	James Henry Meredith
	Joseph Howard Meredith
James H. Meredith	Spouse: Judy Alsobrooks 1949–
	Children of James and Judy:
	Kemp Naylor
	Jessica Howard Meredith

Notes

CHAPTER 1

1. "History of Mississippi," *Monkeyshines on America*, June 2001.

2. Jennifer Peterson, "Let's Take a Look at Mississippi," *About Mississippi*, 2010.

3. Robert Behre, "Why Cotton Got to Be King," *America's Civil War* 22, no. 6 (2010): 40.

4. "Francois Rene Chateaubriand, vicomte de," *Columbia Electronic Encyclopedia*, 2011.

5. Brian C. Baur, "American Field Trip: Thaddeus Kosciusko Statute," *U.S. Stamp News*, 2008, 16.

6. James Meredith, *J.H. Is Born* (Jackson, MS: Meredith, 1995), 3.

7. Ibid., 8.

8. Isiah Edwards Jr., "The Battle of New Orleans," *Footsteps* 5, no. 4 (September–October 2003): 3.

9. Meredith, *J.H. Is Born*, 5.

10. K. H. Carleton, "A Brief History of the Mississippi Band of Choctaw Indians," Tribal Historic Preservation, Mississippi Band of Choctaw, 2002.

11. Ibid.

12. Meredith, *J.H. Is Born*, 12.

13. Ibid.

14. Michael F. Doran, "Negro Slaves of the Five Civilized Tribes," *Annals of the American Association of Geographers* 65, no. 3 (1978): 338, 340.

15. Meredith, *J.H. Is Born.*

16. Judge Campbell, "Autobiography of Judge J.A.P. Campbell," *Daily Clarion-Ledger* (Jackson, MS), October 22, 1914.

17. Ibid.

18. David Sansing, "John Marshall Stone: Thirty-First and Thirty-Third Governor of Mississippi: 1876–1882; 1890–1896," *Mississippi Department of Archives and History*, 2003, 1.

19. Meredith, *J.H. Is Born*, 3.

20. Judge Campbell, "Letter to the Editor," *New York Times*, November 30, 1895.

21. Campbell, "Autobiography."

22. Joyce Williams Sanders, *Brief History of Communities of Attala County* (Kosciusko, MS: Attala Historical Society, 1970).

23. Meredith, *J.H. Is Born*, 45.

24. Ibid., 3.

25. David Barton Smith, "The Politics of Racial Disparities: Desegregating the Hospitals in Jackson, Mississippi," *The Milbank Quarterly* 83 (2005): 248.

26. Ibid.

CHAPTER 2

1. John B. Judis, "Doom!" *New Republic* 242, no. 14 (2011): 3.

2. James Meredith, *J.H. Is Born* (Jackson, MS: Meredith, 1995), 3.

3. Hazel J. Meredith, *My Brother J-Boy*, 4th ed. (Jackson, MS: Amerikan Press), 11.

4. Ibid.

5. Lerone Bennett Jr., *Ebony Pictorial History of Black America*, 2 vols. (Nashville, TN: Southwestern, 1971), 107.

6. Interview with Alexander Conner, Jr., December 4, 2012.

7. Southern Poverty Law Center "Civil Rights Martys," www.splceter.org/civil-rights-memorial/civil-rights-martys (accessed December 4, 2012).

8. "Blood Flows in the Street of Belzoni," *Ebony*, no. 10 (10): 70.

9. Ibid.

10. Interview with Alexander Conner, Jr., December 4, 2012.

11. MPB, "Timeline: The Murder of Emmett Till," PBS, http://www.pbs.org/wgbh/amex/till/timeline2.html (accessed October 30, 2012).

12. Brian Ward, "Civil Rights and Rock and Roll: Revisiting the Nat King Cole Attack of 1956," *OAH Magazine of History*, 2010, 21.

CHAPTER 3

1. Leslie E. Laud, "Moral Education in America: 1600s–1800s," *Journal of Education* 176, no. 2 (2001): 2.

2. Ibid.

3. Harvard University, "The Early History of Harvard University," http://www.news.harvard.edu/guide/intro/index.html (accessed August 21, 2005).

4. "William and Mary in Virginia, College of," *Columbia Electronic Encyclopedia* (New York: Columbia University Press, 2011).

5. Spartacus Educational Schoolnet, "USA History: Education of Slaves," http://www.spartacus.schoolnet.co.uk//USASeducation.htm (accessed August 21, 2005), 2.

6. Ibid., 1.

7. Brian C. Baur, "American Field Trip: Thaddeus Kosciusko Statue," *U.S. Stamp News*, 2008, 16.

8. John Boman, "Thaddeus Kosciusko (Tadeusz Andrzej Bonawentura) 1746–1817," in *Cambridge Dictionary of American Biography* (Cambridge, UK: Cambridge University Press, 2001).

9. Spartacus Educational Schoolnet, "USA History," 2.

10. Gariot P. Louima, "Antioch Alumna Edythe Scott Bagley Has Died," Antioch College, http://antiochcollege.org/news/archive/edythec-scottc-barley.html (accessed April 5, 2012).

11. Joyce Kuo, "Excluded, Segregated, and Forgotten," *Chinese America: History & Perspectives*, 2000, 1–34.

12. Ibid.

13. Ibid.

14. Ibid.

15. P. Robbins, "Choctaw Gold: New Enterprises on a Mississippi Reservation," *World & I* 10, no. 10 (1995): 214–26.

16. Marge Scherer, "Once upon a Time before *Brown*: A Conversation with Clifton L. Taulbert," *Educational Leadership*, May 2004, 20–25.

17. James H. Meredith, "Big Changes Are Coming," *The Saturday Evening Post*, August 13, 1966, 23–27.

18. Interview with James Meredith, November 10, 2005.

CHAPTER 4

1. Leon L. Bram and Norma H. Dickey, "Blacks in the Americas," in *Funk & Wagnalls New Encyclopedia*, Vol. 4 (Pan-American Republican and USA, Funk & Wagnalls, Inc., 2005).

2. Ibid.

3. Vinise Weeks, "HBCU Law Schools," January 13, 2011, http://www.ehow.com/list_6535665_hbcu-law-schools.html.

4. Ebony Magazine, "Reconstruction to Supreme Court Decision 1954," in *Ebony Pictorial History of Black America* (Nashville: Southwestern, 1971).

5. Isobel V. Morin, "Constance Baker Motley Civil Rights Lawyer and Judge," *Women Chosen for Public Office*, 1995, 104–19.

6. Ebony Magazine, "Reconstruction."

7. John Bartlow Martin, "The Deep South Says 'Never,'" *The Saturday Evening Post*, June 29, 1957, 23.

8. Jennifer L. Peters, "The Case That Rocked Education: *Brown v. Board of Education*," *Current Scene* 53, no. 13 (2004): 28–31.

9. Earnest McBride, "Racism in Mississippi: The Secret History," *The Jackson Advocate*, September 11–17, 2003, 8A.

10. Interview with Dolores Smith, November 6, 2006.

11. James Meredith, *Three Years in Mississippi* (Jackson, MS: Meredith, 1966), 48.

12. Ibid.

13. Ibid.

14. Ibid.

15. Ibid., 55.

16. Charles W. Eagles, *The Price of Defiance: James Meredith and the Integration of Ole Miss* (Chapel Hill: University of North Carolina Press, 2009).

17. John R. Lynch, *The Facts of Reconstruction* (Indianapolis and New York: The Bobbs-Merrill Company, Inc., 1970).

18. Eagles, *The Price of Defiance*.

19. Ibid., 106.

20. Ibid.

21. Ibid.

22. "Kennard, Miss. School Victim, Dies of Cancer," *Jet*, July 18, 1963, 21.

23. James M. McPherson, "Parchman's Plantation," *New York Times Book Review*, April 28, 1996.

24. Jerry Mitchell, "Judge Rights Wrong," *Clarion-Ledger*, May 18, 2006, 8A.

25. Interview with James Meredith, November 15, 2006.

26. Meredith, *Three Years in Mississippi*, 57, 58.

27. Ibid.

CHAPTER 5

1. James Meredith, *Three Years in Mississippi* (Jackson, MS: Meredith, 1966), 83.

2. Ibid.

3. Ibid., 79.

4. Personal interview with James Meredith, November 12, 2007.

5. Meredith, *Three Years*, 87–90.

6. Interview with George Harmon, November 12, 2007.

7. Interview with Rudolph Jackson, November 19, 2007.

8. Interview with Katherine H. Nelson, August 3, 2007.

9. Meredith, *Three Years*.

10. Interview with Dorothy ("Dot") Benford, February 1, 2012.

11. Personal interview, James Meredith, November 22, 2007.

12. Meredith, *Three Years*.

13. Isobel V. Morin, "Constance Baker Motley Civil Rights Lawyer and Judge," *Women Chosen for Public Office*, 1995, 104–19.

14. Charles W. Eagles, *The Price of Defiance: James Meredith and the Integration of Ole Miss* (Chapel Hill: University of North Carolina Press, 2009).

15. James Meredith, *Three Years in Mississippi* (Jackson, MS: Meredith, 1966), 88–89.

16. Ibid., 107–8.

17. Ibid., 143–62.

CHAPTER 6

1. Tiffany Brown, "White Resistance," Brown-Tougaloo Project, http://wwwstg.brown.edu/projects/FreedomNow/themes/resist/ (accessed September 16, 2005).

2. John F. Kennedy, "Address by John F. Kennedy," *The Public Papers of the President*, June 11, 1963, 237, 468.

3. James Meredith, *Three Years in Mississippi* (Jackson, MS: Meredith, 1966), 176.

4. Ibid.

5. James Meredith, "I'll Know Victory or Defeat," *The Saturday Evening Post*, November 10, 1962, 14.

6. Ibid., 16.

7. Meredith, *Three Years*, 207–8.

8. Herb Boyd, *We Shall Overcome* (Naperville, IL: Sourcebooks Media Fusion, 2004), 119.

9. Personal interview with Dorothy Burton Henderson, July 10, 2009.

10. Personal interview with Leroy W., July 29, 2009.

11. William Doyle, *An American Insurrection: James Meredith and the Battle of Oxford, Mississippi, 1962* (New York: Anchor Books, 2001).

12. Ibid., 278.

13. Meredith, *Three Years*, 212.

14. Ibid., 213.

15. Meredith, "I'll Know Victory," 15.

16. Personal interview with Rudolph Jackson, July 9, 2007.

17. Larry Still, "Man Behind the Headlines: On-the-Scene Reporter Tells What James Meredith, Mississippi Hero, Is Really Like," *Ebony*, December 1962, 32.

18. James Meredith, "I Can't Fight Alone," *Look*, April 19, 1963, 70.

19. Personal interview with James Meredith, November 28, 2006.

20. Meredith, "I Can't Fight Alone," 70.

21. Meredith, "I'll Know Victory," 15.

22. Boyd, *We Shall Overcome*, 122.

23. Meredith, *Three Years*, 214.

24. Personal interview with James Meredith, November 28, 2006.

25. Personal interview with Stanley Whitcomb, June 5, 2009.

26. Interview with James Meredith, November 24, 2006.

27. Personal interview with Fannie Alice Webb, July 15, 2009.

28. Personal interview with Dorothy Burton Henderson, July 6, 2009.

CHAPTER 7

1. Herb Boyd, *We Shall Overcome* (Naperville, IL: Sourcebooks Media Fusion, 2004).

2. Interview with Robert Terrell, September 4, 2006.

3. Interview with Jimmie Robinson, November 11, 2006.

4. Interview with James Meredith, November 28, 2006.

5. Interview the Charles Sherrod, July 8, 2006.

6. Howard Zinn, *A People's History of the United States: 1492–Present* (New York: HarperCollins, 2005), 455.

7. Interview with Charles Sherrod, July 23, 2006.

8. Lerone Bennett Jr., *Ebony Pictorial History of Black America*, 2 vols. (Nashville, TN: Southwestern, 1971).

9. George E. Sewell and Margaret L. Dwight, *Mississippi Black History Makers* (Jackson: University of Mississippi Press, 1984), 126.

10. Ibid., 127.

11. Phyl Garland, "Builders of a New South," *Ebony*, August 1966, 28.

12. Ralph J. Bunche, "A Message to the Negro," *Negro Digest*, January 1963, 3–5.

13. Charles Evers and Andrew Szanton, *Have No Fear: The Charles Evers Story* (Hoboken, NJ: Wiley, 1996).

14. Interview with Jimmie Robinson, August 30, 2006.

15. Interview with Floreada Harmon, September 10, 2006.

16. Interview with Beulah Thomas, July 10, 2005.

17. Interview with Rosie Clay McGee, November 28, 2005.

18. Interview with Leon ("Dr. Dirt") Goldsberry, March 17, 2012.

19. Interview with Dorothy ("Dot") Benford, February 1, 2012.

20. "I Have a Dream," in *Ebony*, May 1968, 133.

21. "Atlanta Arrest of Jamil Abdullah Al-Amin," *New York Times*, August 10, 1995, 2.

22. Interview with Clint Alexander, June 6, 2009.

23. Interview with Catherine Coleman, November 19, 2005.

24. Betty Shabazz, *Malcolm X: By Any Means Necessary* (New York: Pathfinder, 1970), 82–83.

25. P. A. Bullins, "All for the Cause: The Demonstrator," *Negro Digest*, November 1963, 28–29.

26. M. Golden Cooper, "Race and the South," *U.S. News & World Report* 109, no. 4 (July 1990): 23–24.

27. Ibid.

28. Frank R. Parker, *Black Votes Count* (Chapel Hill: University of North Carolina Press, 1990), 31.

29. Interview with Glennie Alston Kirkland, October 16, 2005.

30. Suzanne McCade, "Is This America?: Story of Fannie Lou Hamer," *Junior Scholastic*, March 2005, 18.

31. Vern Smith, "We Didn't Come All This Way for No Two Seats!: Fannie Lou Hamer at the 1964 Democratic National Convention," *The Crisis*, July/August 2004, 34.

32. Interview with Rev. Davis Singleton, September 15, 2005.

CHAPTER 8

1. Interview with Bea Ellis Jenkins, September 21, 2005.

2. Ibid.

3. Interview with Unita Blackwell, September 2, 2005.

4. Frank Parker, *Black Votes Count: Political Empowerment in Mississippi after 1965* (Chapel Hill: University of North Carolina Press, 1990), 72.

5. Ibid.

6. "What We Said About: 1966," Editorial, *Times* (United Kingdom), June 8, 2009, 1.

7. Interview with Afeni Shakur, March 16, 2007.

8. Interview with Robert Terrell, February 6, 2006.

9. Interview with James Meredith, November 1, 2005.

10. Ibid.

11. James H. Meredith, "Big Changes Are Coming," *The Saturday Evening Post*, August 13, 1966, 24.

12. Ibid.

13. Ibid.

14. Ibid.

15. Ibid., 25.

16. Interview with James Meredith, November 1, 2005.

17. Meredith, "Big Changes," 26.

18. Lerone Bennett Jr., *Before the Mayflower: A History of Black America*, 6th ed. (New York: Penguin Books, 1993), 419.

19. Denise Henry, "Message Behind the Music," *Scholastic*, October 9, 2006, 19.

20. Interview with Charles Sherrod, November 15, 2005.

21. Meredith, "Big Changes," 26.

22. R. Williams et al., eds., *The Black American and the Press* (Los Angeles: Ward Ritchie Press, 1968).

23. Ibid.

24. Phyl Garland, "Builders of the New South," *Ebony*, August 1966, 36.

25. Interview with Percy W. Bufkin, April 11, 2012.

26. Interview with Tyrone Davis, August 20, 2005.

27. E. L. Malvaney, "Abandoned Mississippi: Southern Christian Institute," Preservation in Mississippi, December 1, 2010, http://www.misspreservation.com/2010/12/01/abandoned-mississippi-southern-christian-institute/.

28. Interview with Tyrone Davis, August 20, 2005.

29. Interview with Catherine Horhn Nelson, August 16, 2005.

30. Joanna Pitman, "The Shooting of a Civil Rights Activist," *Time*, August 2006, 6.

31. Bennett Jr., *Before the Mayflower*, 578.

32. Martin Luther King Jr., *A Testament of Hope: The Essential Writings and Speeches of Martin Luther King, Jr.* (New York: HarperOne, 1990), 393.

33. Meredith, "Big Changes," 27.

34. Bennett Jr., *Before the Mayflower*, 422.

35. Ibid.

36. Interview with Big Bob, February 6, 2006.

37. Quintard Taylor et al., "Report of the National Advisory Commission on Civil Disorders," BlackPast.org. http://www.blackpast.org/?q=primary/national-advisory-commission-civil-disorders-kerner-report-1967 (accessed April 26, 2012).

38. Ibid.

39. Nathan Ward, "The Time Machine: 1965: Twenty-Five Years Ago," *American Heritage* 41, no. 8 (December 1990): 45.

40. Abraham H. Miller, "The Los Angeles Riots: A Study in Crisis Paralysis." *Journal of Contingencies and Crisis Management* 9, no. 4 (December 2001): 192.

41. Taylor et al., "Report of the National Advisory Commission."

42. Howard Zinn, *A People's of the United States: 1492–Present* (New York: HarperCollins, 2003), 459.

43. Interview with Albert Gibbs, August 28, 2005.

44. Interview with Albert Gibbs Jr., May 1, 2012.

45. Mississippi Department of Archives, SCR ID # 9-31-8-48-1-1-1, Jackson, MS, July 30, 1968.

46. Mississippi Department of Archives, SCR ID # 9-31-10-114-1-1-1, Jackson, MS, February 7, 1973.

47. Mississippi Department of Archives, SCR ID # 13-25-4-61-2-1-1, Jackson, MS, February 7, 1973.

48. Interview with Leon ("Dr. Dirt") Goldsberry, March 17, 2012.

49. U.S. Department of Justice, Civil Rights Division, Voting Section, "The Effect of the Voting Rights Act," http://www.usdoj.gov/crt/voting/intro/intro.c.htm (accessed October 3, 2005).

50. Peniel E. Joseph, "The Black Power Movement: A State of the Field," *The Journal of American History* 96, no. 3 (December 2009): 751–76.

51. Ibid., 754.

52. Ibid.

53. Ibid., 755.

54. Ibid.

55. Ibid., 751.

56. Ibid.

CHAPTER 9

1. See James Meredith's Featured Books, http://www.jamesmeredithbooks.com (accessed April 27, 2012), 1.

2. Larry Still, "Man Behind the Headlines: On-the-Scene Reporter Tells What James Meredith, Mississippi Hero, Is Really Like," *Ebony*, December 1962, 15–35.

3. Interview with James Meredith, February 23, 2005.

4. Robert Fay, "Meredith, James H.," in *Africana: The Encyclopedia of the African and African American Experience*, ed. Kwame Anthony Appiah and Henry Louis Gates Jr. (New York: Perseus Books, 1999), 1290.

5. Interview with James Henry Meredith, April 8, 2012.

6. James Meredith, "Black Defendant Only 16 Goes to Prison for 25 Years: Howard Didn't Get Fair Shake," *Outlook Magazine*, September 1974, 1–2.

7. Interview with Louis Armstrong, May 15, 2012.

8. Interview with Dr. Judy A. Meredith, April 28, 2012.

9. Ibid.

10. Ibid.

11. "Mrs. Roxie Weatherly, 83, Mother of Activist," *Clarion-Ledger*, July 29, 1986, 2B.

12. Interview with Hazel Meredith Hall, August 28, 2005.

13. Meredith Coleman, "Historical Black University in Jackson, Miss. to Present Television Programming to Local Area," *Jackson Advocate*, March 17–23, 1994, 3A.

14. Wilson Boyd, "Meredith's Message: Conquer 3 Rs to Succeed," *Vicksburg Post*, February 21, 2005, A1.

15. "Biography of James H. Meredith," in *Encyclopedia of World Biography*, http://www.bookrags.com/printfriendly/?bios&u=james-h-meredith (accessed April 29, 2012).

16. Mandy Jones, "Meredith Returns to Ole Miss Today," *Daily Mississippian*, March 21, 1997, 6.

17. Marc Perrusquia, "Meredith Is Walking Delta for Espy Seat," *Commercial Appeal*, March 2, 1993, B2.

18. Ali Shamsid Deen, "Civil Rights Legend on Divine Mission," *Jackson Advocate*, June 19–July 3, 1997, 1A–4C.

19. "Hundreds Attend Dedication of U.S. Civil Rights Monument," *Herald Tribune*, October 1, 2006.

20. "Ole Miss Marks Integration Anniversary," *Washington Post*, October 1, 2006.

21. Meredith C. McGee, "James Meredith's Biography," http://www.meredithetc.biz/jamesmeredithbiography.html (accessed April 28, 2012), 1–2.

22. James Meredith, *My Son, Joseph Howard Meredith: A Celebration of Life* (Jackson, MS: Meredith, 2008), 1–2.

23. Meredith C. McGee, "Civil Right Icon's Vision for the Future," http://www.meredithetc.biz (accessed May 9, 2012).

24. Meredith C. McGee, "200 Miles for the Poor and Powerless," *The Mississippi Link*, May 29, 2009.

25. James Meredith presentation in Yazoo City, Mississippi, City Hall, June 11, 2009.

26. "About Us," Justin.tv, http://www.walkagainstfear2012.com/index.html (accessed May 1, 2012), 1.

27. Monica Land, "Famed Civil Rights Leader Organizes 'Walk for the Poor,'" *The Mississippi Link*, May 28–June 4, 2009, 1, 3.

28. Interview with James Meredith, February 23, 2005.

29. "Helms Hires 1960s Civil Rights Figure as Adviser," *New York Times*, September 27, 1989.

30. James Meredith, "Message For Our Time," *Jackson Free Press*, August 12–16, 2010, 10.

31. Interview with James Meredith, April 26, 2012.

32. Interview with Dr. Judy A. Meredith, April 28, 2012.

33. Interview with Jasmine Meredith, April 28, 2012.

34. Interview with Leon ("Dr. Dirt") Goldsberry, March 17, 2012.

CHAPTER 10

1. Vernellia R. Randall, "Widening Gap between Rich and Poor," in *Report on U.S. Human Rights Record in 2000*, 1–2, Information Office of China's State Council, 2000.

2. David R. Jones, "For America's Poor, Life on the Edge," *New Amsterdam News*, October 6–12, 2005, 5.

3. Paul Krugman, "The Great Wealth Transfer," *Rolling Stone*, December 22, 2006, 2.

4. Interview with James Meredith, April 3, 2006.

5. Interview with James Meredith, May 26, 2009.

6. Randall, "Widening Gap between Rich and Poor," 4.

CHAPTER 11

1. Paul Krugman, "The Great Wealth Transfer," *Rolling Stone*, December 14, 2006, 1015.

2. Interview with James Meredith, November 3, 2005.

3. Speech by James Meredith at Tchula, Mississippi, City Hall, June 15, 2009.

4. Interview with James Meredith, November 3, 2005.

5. Interview with Representative Alyce G. Clarke, October 8, 2006.

6. Interview with Beulah Greer, October 11, 2005.

7. Interview with Charles Tisdale, December 2, 2006.

8. Interview with Jimmie L. Stokes, October 28, 2006.

9. Ibid.

10. Krugman, "The Great Wealth Transfer," 46.

11. Interview with Dr. Leslie McLemore, August 21, 2006.

12. Ibid.

13. Interview with Sean Devlin, July 14, 2007.

14. Interview with Marcia Weaver, August 6, 2007.

15. Interview with Frank Taylor, June 9, 2007.

16. Interview with Lakeshia Walters, July 15, 2007

17. Interview with Bettie Mason, October 29, 2006

18. Interview with Cressie Nelson Hopkins, July 9, 2007.

19. Interview with Brad Franklin, March 9, 2007.

20. David Blackwell, "Center of Attention: Powderly Auditorium Opens Tonight," *Messenger Inquirer*, 1, November 30, 2007.

21. Interview with Hollis Watkins, February 9, 2006.

22. Interview with Arthur Meredith, November 9, 2006.

23. Interview with Kendrick Portis, October 6, 2005.

24. Interview with Carl Easley, October 13, 2005.

25. Interview with Ivey Stokes, September 28, 2005.

26. Ibid.

27. Interview with Rev. Brian Robinson, June 17, 2007.

28. Ibid.

29. Ibid.

30. Allen Johnson Jr., "Rise and Decline: A Decade Ago the City Seemed to Have Gotten Better at Fighting Crime," *New Orleans Magazine*, April 2007, 69.

31. Interview with Percy Trimont, February 6, 2006.

32. Ibid.

33. Ibid.

34. Interview with Eddie Cotton, April 12, 2006.

35. Ibid.

36. Interview with Nettie Stowers, May 5, 2006.

37. Interview with Richard Williams, April 15, 2006.

38. Mississippi Commission on the Status of Women, "Women: Key to Mississippi's Future," Annual Report, FY2011, Jackson, MS, 3.

39. Presentation by James Meredith, February 18, 2006.

40. Presentation by James Meredith, June 15, 2009.

41. Presentation by James Meredith, June 21, 2009.

42. Corey Ward, "Celebrate Woodstock with KXCI: Local Acts Will Cover Bands That Played Famed Festival," Arizona, August 13, 2009, *Daily Star*, 2.

Selected Bibliography

"About Us." Justin.tv. http://www.walkagainstfear2012.com/index.html (accessed May 1, 2012).

Appiah, Kwame A., and Henry L. Gates Jr., eds. *Africana: The Encyclopedia of the African and African American Experience*. New York: Basic Civitas Books, 1999.

Asinof, Lynn, Jonathan Clements, Karen Damato, Tom Herman, Georgette Jasen, Deborah Lohse, and Ellen E. Schultz. *The Wall Street Journal Lifetime Guide to Money: Everything You Need to Know about Managing Your Finances—for Every State in Life*. 1st ed. New York: Hyperion, 1997.

Baur, Brian C. "American Field Trip: Thaddeus Kosciusko Statute." *U.S. Stamp News*, 2008, 16–18.

"Beckwith, Assassin of Medgar Evers, Dies Serving Life Term." *Washington Post*, January 22, 2001. http://rickross.com/reference/supremacists/supremacists40.html (accessed September 30, 2005).

Behre, Robert. "Why Cotton Got to Be King." *America's Civil War* 22, no. 6 (2010): 34–41.

Bennett, Lerone, Jr. *Before the Mayflower: A History of Black America*. New York: Penguin Books, 1993.

Bennett, Lerone, Jr. *Ebony Pictorial History of Black America*. 2 vols. Nashville, TN: Southwestern, 1971.

Bergeron, Paul H. "Andrew Johnson: The Issues of Voting Rights." *Humanities*, 1997, 18, 29.

"Biography of James H. Meredith." In *Encyclopedia of World Biography*. http://www.bookrags.com/printfriendly/?bios&u=james-h-meredith (accessed April 29, 2012).

Black Americans in Congress—Charles Coles Diggs, Jr., Representative from Michigan. "Charles Coles Diggs, Jr. Representative, 1955–1980, Democrat from Michigan." http://baic.house.gov/member-profile.html/intID=29 (accessed December 4, 2012).

Boman, John. "Thaddeus Kosciusko (Tadeusz Andrzej Bonawentura) 1746–1817." In *Cambridge Dictionary of American Biography*. New York: Cambridge University Press, 2001.

Bositis, David A. *Black Elected Officials: A Statistical Summary 2001*. Washington, DC: Joint Center for Political and Economic Studies, 2001.

Boyd, Herb. *We Shall Overcome*. Naperville, IL: Sourcebooks Media Fusion, 2004.

Boyd, Wilson. "Meredith's Message: Conquer 3 Rs to Succeed." *Vicksburg Post*, 2005, A1.

Bram, Leon L., and Norma H. Dickey. "Blacks in the Americas." In *Funk & Wagnalls New Encyclopedia*, Vol. 4, 119–39. Pan-American Republics and the United States, 2005.

Brown, Tiffany. "White Resistance." Brown-Tougaloo Project. http://www.stg.brown.edu/projects/FreedomNow/themes/resist/ (accessed September 16, 2005).

Bullins, P. A. "All for the Cause: The Demonstrator." *Negro Digest*, November 1963, 28–29.

Bunche, Ralph J. "A Message to the Negro." *Negro Digest*, January 1963, 3–6.

Campbell, JAP. "Autobiography of Judge J.A.P. Campbell." *Daily Clarion-Ledger* (Jackson, MS), October 22, 1914.

Campbell, Judge (JAP). Letter to the Editor. *New York Times*, November 30, 1895.

Carleton, K. H. "A Brief History of the Mississippi Band of Choctaw Indians." Tribal Historic Preservation. Mississippi Band of Choctaw. 2002.

City of Kosciuko. City of Kosciusko: Beehive of the Hills. 2010. http://www.cityofkosciusko.com/history.html.

Clapp, James E. *Dictionary of Law*. New York: Random House, 2000.

Clark, Eric. *Mississippi Official and Statistical Register, 2004–2008, Mississippi Blue Book*. Jackson: State of Mississippi, 2001.

Coleman, Meredith. "Historical Black University in Jackson, Miss. to Present Television Programming to Local Area." *Jackson Advocate*, March 17–23, 1994, 3A.

Cooper, M. Golden. "Race and the South." *U.S. News & World Report* 109, no. 4 (July 1990): 23–24.

Cozzens, Lisa. *Civil Rights Movement 1955–1965: Mississippi Freedom Summer.* 1998. http://www.watson.org/~lisa/blackhistory/civilrights-55-65/missippi.htm (accessed August 30, 2005).

Deen, Ali Shamsid. "Civil Rights Legend on Divine Mission." *Jackson Advocate*, July 17–24, 1997, 1A–4C.

DeNavas-Walt, Carmen, Bernadette D. Proctor, and Cheryl H. Lee. *Income, Poverty, Health Insurance Coverage in the United States: 2004.* U.S. Census Bureau, Current Population Reports: Consumer Income, 60–229. Washington, DC: U.S. Government Printing Office, 2005.

DeNavas-Walt, Carmen, Bernadette D. Proctor, and Cheryl H. Lee. *Income, Poverty, and Health Insurance Coverage in the United States: 2005.* U.S. Census Bureau, Current Population Reports, 60–231. Washington, DC: U.S. Government Printing Office, 2006.

DeNavas-Walt, Carmen, Bernadette D. Proctor, and Cheryl H. Lee. *Income, Poverty, and Health Insurance Coverage in the United States: 2006.* U.S. Census Bureau, Current Population Reports, 60–233. Washington, DC: U.S. Government Printing Office, 2007.

Doran, Michael F. "Negro Slaves of the Five Civilized Tribes." *Annals of the American Association of Geographers* 65, no. 3 (1978): 335–50.

Doyle, William. *An American Insurrection: James Meredith and the Battle of Oxford, Mississippi, 1962.* New York: Anchor Books, 2001.

Eagles, Charles W. *The Price of Defiance: James Meredith and the Integration of Ole Miss.* Chapel Hill: University of North Carolina Press, 2009.

Ebony Magazine. "Blood Flows on Streets of Belzoni." 10, no. 10 (August 1955): 70–74.

Ebony Magazine. "Reconstruction to Supreme Court Decision 1954." In *Ebony Pictorial History of Black America*, 03–311. Nashville, TN: Southwestern, 1971.

Edwards, Isiah, Jr. "The Battle of New Orleans." *Footsteps* 5, no. 4 (September–October 2003): 1–3.

Evers, Charles, and Andrew Szanton. *Have No Fear: The Charles Evers Story.* New York: Wiley, 1996.

"Francois Rene Chateaubriand, vicomte de." In *Columbia Electronic Encyclopedia*. New York: Columbia University Press, 2011.

Freemon, Joe. "The 1966 Macon County Alabama Campaign." http://jofreeman.com/photos/macon.html (accessed September 24, 2005).

"Free to Succeed or Fail." *The Economist*, August 8, 2005, 20–23.

Garland, Phyl. "Builders of a New South." *Ebony*, August 1966, 27–37.

Grofman, Bernard, Lisa Handley, and Richard G. Niemi. *Minority Representation and the Quest for Voting Equality.* New York: Cambridge University Press, 1992.

Haley, Alex. *The Autobiography of Malcolm X.* New York: Ballantine Books, 1965.

Harvard University. "The Early History of Harvard University." http://www .news.harvard.edu/guide/intro/index.html (accessed August 21, 2005).

Haughney, Christine. "Bloomberg Has Added Jobs, and Lost Some, Too." *New York Times*, October 14, 2009, A21.

"Helms Hires 1960s Civil Rights Figure as Adviser." *New York Times*, September 27, 1989.

Henry, Denise. "Message Behind the Music." *Scholastic*, October 9, 2006, 19.

Hipp, L. "Airport to Bear Medgar Evers' Name." *Clarion-Ledger*, December 22, 2004.

"History of Mississippi." *Monkeyshines on America*. June 2001.

Hit, J. "Original Spin." *Washington Monthly* 25, no. 3 (March 1993): 25–27.

Holmes, Robert A. *New Georgia Encyclopedia: Georgia Legislative Black Caucus.* http://www.georgiaencyclopedia.org/nge/Article.jsp? id=h-1373 (accessed March 19, 2011).

"Hundreds Attend Dedication of U.S. Civil Rights Monument." *Herald Tribune*, October 1, 2006.

Hutchinson, Earl O. "The Real Reasons New Orleans Is So Poor." *Jackson Free Press*, September 29–October 5, 2005, 14.

"In Search of Decent Boundaries." *The Economist*, June 22, 1996, 30–32.

Interview by Edwin Newman. *Meet the Press.* NBC. August 21, 1966.

Johnson, T. "White Resistance." Mississippi Freedom Movement. http:// www.stg.brown.projects/FreedomNow/themes/resist/ (accessed September 16, 2005).

Jones, David R. "For America's Poor, Life on the Edge." *New York Amsterdam News*, October 6–12, 2005, 5.

Jones, Mandy. "Meredith Returns to Ole Miss Today." *Daily Mississippian*, March 21, 1997, 1A, 6A.

Joseph, Peniel E. "The Black Power Movement: A State of the Field." *The Journal of American History* 96, no. 3 (December 2009): 751–776.

Joseph, Tiffany. "White Resistance." Mississippi—Tougaloo Project. http://www.stg.brown.edu/projects/FreedomNow/scans/ SP0008.jpg (accessed August 16, 2005).

Judis, John B. "Doom!" *New Republic* 242, no. 14 (2011): 1–9.

Just the Beginning Foundation. "Constance Baker Motley, United States District Court for the Southern District of New York, New York." 2005. http://www.jtbf.org/five_firsts/Motley_C.htm (accessed August 15, 2005).

"Kennard, Miss. School Victim Dies of Cancer." *Jet*, July 18, 1963, 21.

Kennedy, John F. "Address by John F. Kennedy." In *The Public Papers of the Presidents*, 237, 468. Washington DC, June 11, 1963.

Kennedy, John F. "The Meredith Crisis 1962." http://americandradioworks .pubicradio.org/features/pretakes/kennedyspeech.html (accessed September 16, 2005).

King, Martin Luther, Jr. *A Testament of Hope: The Essential Writings and Speeches of Martin Luther King, Jr.* New York: HarperOne, 1990.

Kingwood College Library. *American Cultural History 1930–1939.* http:// kclibrary.nhmccd.edu/decade30.htm (accessed January 8, 2005).

Knabb, Ken, trans. "The Decline and Fall of the Spectacle-Commodity Economy." *Situationist International Anthology.* 1992. http:// bopsecrets.org/SI/10.htm (accessed September 17, 2005).

Kosova, Weston, and Holly Bailey. "A Clean Count?" *Newsweek,* November 1, 2004, 30–39.

Kroll, Luisa, and Allison Fass. "Wild Wealth." *Forbes,* March 2007, 104–36.

Kroll, Luisa, and Allison Fass. "The World's Billionaires." *Forbes,* March 27, 2006, 111–60.

Krugman, Paul. "The Great Wealth Transfer." *Rolling Stone,* December 14, 2006, 45.

Kuo, Joyce. "Excluded, Segregated, and Forgotten." *Chinese America: History & Perspectives,* 2000, 1–34.

Land, Monica. "Famed Civil Rights Leader Organizes 'Walk For The Poor.'" *The Mississippi Link,* May 28–June 4, 2009, 1, 3.

Laud, Leslie E. "Moral Education in America: 1600s–1800s." *Journal of Education* 176, no. 2 (1997): 1–9.

Louima, Gariot P. "Antioch Alumna Edythe Scott Bagley Has Died." Antioch College. http://antiochcollege.org/news/archive/edythec -scottc-barley.html (accessed April 5, 2012).

Lynch, John R. *The Facts of Reconstruction.* Indianapolis and New York: The Bobbs-Merrill Company, Inc, 1970.

Malvaney, E. L. "Abandoned Mississippi: Southern Christian Institute." Preservation in Mississippi. December 1, 2010. http://www .misspreservation.com/2010/12/01/abandoned-mississippi-southern -christian-institute/.

Mansbridge, Peter. "Forty Years after JFK." *Maclean's,* November 24, 2003, 1–2.

Martin, John Bartlow. "The Deep South Says 'Never.'" *The Saturday Evening Post,* June 29, 1957, 23.

McBride, Earnest. "Racism in Mississippi: The Secret History." *Jackson Advocate,* September 11–17, 2003, 8A.

McBride, Earnest. "What Follows Departure of Mason at JSU?" *Jackson Advocate,* May 6–12, 2010, 1A.

McCade, Suzanne. "Is This America?: Story of Fannie Lou Hamer." *Junior Scholastic,* March 2005, 16–19.

McGee, Meredith C. "Civil Right Icon's Vision for the Poor." Downloadable PDF. http://www.meredithetc.biz (accessed April 30, 2012).

McGee, Meredith C. "200 Miles for the Poor and Powerless." *The Mississippi Link*, May 29, 2009.

McPherson, James M. "Parchman's Plantation." *New York Times Book Review*, April 28, 1996.

Meredith, Hazel J. *My Brother J-Boy.* 4th ed. Jackson, MS: Amerikan Press, 2011.

Meredith, James H. "Big Changes Are Coming." *The Saturday Evening Post*, August 13, 1966, 23–27.

Meredith, James. "Black Defendant Only 16 Goes to Prison for 25 Years: Howard Didn't Get Fair Shake." *Outlook Magazine*, September 1974, 1–2.

Meredith, James. *The Choctaw Nation: 1540–1830.* Jackson, MS: Meredith, 1995.

Meredith, James. *Dancing Rabbit: The Destruction of the Choctaw Nation.* Jackson, MS: Meredith, 1995.

Meredith, James. *The Father of White Supremacy.* Jackson, MS: Meredith, 1995.

Meredith, James. "I Can't Fight Alone: James Meredith Calls on All Blacks to Participate in the Struggle for Racial Equality." *Look*, April 19, 1963, 70–78.

Meredith, James. "I Know Victory or Defeat." *The Saturday Evening Post*, November 1962, 14–16.

Meredith, James. *J.H. Is Born.* Jackson, MS: Meredith, 1995.

Meredith, James. *My Son, Joseph Howard Meredith: A Celebration of Life.* Jackson, MS: Meredith, 2008.

Meredith, James. *Three Years in Mississippi.* Bloomington: Indiana University Press, 1966.

Meredith, James. "Who and What Is Charles Evers?" *Outlook Magazine*, October 1983, 1–13.

Miller, Abraham H. "The Los Angeles Riots: A Study in Crisis Paralysis." *Journal of Contingencies and Crisis Management* 9, no. 4 (December 2001): 189–99.

Mitchell, Jerry. "Judge Rights Wrong." *Clarion-Ledger*, May 18, 2006, 8A.

Mitchell, Jerry. "Mississippi's Best Hope." *Clarion-Ledger*, June 12, 2005, 9A.

Morin, Isobel V. "Constance Baker Motley Civil Rights Lawyer and Judge." *Women Chosen for Public Office*, 1995, 104–19.

"Mrs. Roxie Weatherly, 83, Mother of Activist." *Clarion-Ledger*, July 29, 1986, 2B.

Mullane, Deirdre. *Crossing the Danger Water.* New York: Anchor Books, 1993.

Park, K., ed. *World Almanac and Book of Facts*. New York: World Almanac Books, 2005.

Parker, Frank. *Black Votes Count*. Chapel Hill: University of North Carolina Press, 1990.

Perrusquia, Marc. "Meredith Is Walking Delta for Espy Seat." *The Commercial Appeal*, March 2, 1993, B2.

Peters, Jennifer L. "The Case that Rocked Education: *Brown v. Board of Education*." *Current Scene* 53, no. 13 (2004): 28–31.

Peterson, Jennifer. "Let's Take a Look at Mississippi." *About Mississippi*. 2010. http://www.ebscohost.com

Pitman, Joanna. "The Shooting of a Civil Rights Activist." *Time*, August 2006, 6.

Powell, Mitchell. "Banks Accused of Pushing Mortgage Deals on Blacks." *New York Times*, June 7, 2009, A16.

Purnell, Deborah. "Society of Professional Journalists Honors Paul Guihard with Memorial." http://.news.olemiss.edu (accessed September 1, 2009).

Quarles, Benjamin. *The Negro in the Making of America*. New York: Collier Books, 1970.

The Race and Public Policy Program. Historical Timeline of Public Education in the U.S. http://www.arc.org/j_timeline.htm (accessed August 7, 2005).

Randall, Vernellia R. "Widening Gap between Rich and Poor." In *Report on U.S. Human Rights Record in 2000*. Information Office of China's State Council, 2001.

"Richard M. Nixon." The History Channel. http://www.history.com/topics/richard-m-nixon (accessed January 31, 2011).

Robbins, P. "Choctaw Gold: New Enterprises on a Mississippi Reservation." *World & I* 10, no. 10 (1995): 214–26.

Sanders, Joyce Williams. "Brief History of Communities of Attala County." Kosciusko, MS: Attala Historical Society, 1970.

Sansing, David. "John Marshall Stone: Thirty-First and Thirty-Third Governor of Mississippi: 1876–1882; 1890–1896." Mississippi Department of Archives and History. 2003.

Scherer, Marge. "Once upon a Time Before *Brown*: A Conversation with Clifton L. Taulbert." *Educational Leadership*, May 2004, 20–25.

Scott, Matthew S. "Robert L. Johnson: The Captain of Capitalism." *Black Enterprise*, November 1, 2005, 34.

Seubold, Linda. U.S. Marshals History Symposium. *Entertainment Fort Smith* 8, no. 3 (October 2007): 8–9.

Sewell, George E., and Margaret L. Dwight. *Mississippi Black History Makers*. Jackson: University of Mississippi Press, 1984.

Shabazz, Betty. *Malcolm X: By Any Means Necessary*. New York: Pathfinder, 1970.

Smith, David Barton. "The Politics of Racial Disparities: Desegregating the Hospitals in Jackson, Mississippi." *The Milbank Quarterly* 83 (2005): 247–69.

Smith, Vern. "We Didn't Come All This Way for No Two Seats!: Fannie Lou Hamer at the 1964 Democratic National Convention." *The Crisis*, July/August 2004, 34.

Spartacus Educational Schoolnet. "USA History: Education of Slaves." http://www.spartacus.schoolnet.co.uk//USASeducation.htm (accessed August 21, 2005).

Stein, L. "Top of the Week." *U.S. News & World Report*, June 3, 2002, 20–23.

Still, Larry. "Man Behind the Headlines: On-the-Scene Reporter Tells What James Meredith, Mississippi Hero, Is Really Like." *Ebony*, December 1962, 25–35.

Sullivan, Bartholomew. "FBI Building to Carry Civil Rights Workers' Names." *The Commercial Appeal*, June 18, 2010.

Taylor, Quintard, et al. "National Advisory Commission of Civil Disorders (the Kerner Report), 1967." http://www.blaskpast.org/?q-primary/national-advisory-commission-civil-disorders-kerner-report-1967 (accessed April 26, 2012).

U.S. Census Bureau. Historical Poverty Tables—Poverty by Definition of Income (R&D). http://www.census.gov/hhes/www/poverty/histpve/rdp01a.html (accessed December 9, 2005).

U.S. Department of Education. *The Nation's Report Card: Mathematics 2007*. Jessup, MD: U.S. Department of Education, 2007.

U.S. Department of Education. *The Nation's Report Card: Reading 2007*. Jessup, MD: U.S. Department of Education, 2007.

U.S. Department of Justice, Civil Rights Division, Voting Section. "The Effect of the Voting Rights Act." http://www.usdoj.gov/crt/voting/intro/intro.c.htm (accessed October 3, 2005).

Wal-Mart Kraft. *Strong Traditions & Soaring Dreams* [Brochure]. 2004.

Ward, Brian. "Civil Rights and Rock and Roll: Revisiting the Nat King Cole Attack of 1956." *OAH Magazine of History*, April 2010, 21–24.

Ward, Nathan. "The Time Machine: 1965: Twenty-Five Years Ago." *American Heritage* 41, no. 8 (December 1990): 45.

Weeks, Vinise. "HBCU Law Schools." January 13, 2011. http://www.ehow.com/list_6535665_hbcu-law-schools.html.

"William and Mary in Virginia, College of." *Columbia Electronic Encyclopedia*. New York: Columbia University Press, 2011.

Williams, R., Charles Evers, A. S. Pride, G. Myrdal, J. Caughey, R. McGill, K. Fleming, J. Jones et al., eds. *The Black American and the Press*. Los Angeles: Ward Ritchie Press, 1968.

Zimbelman, Karen, E. Kim Coontz, and Audrey Malan. *Steps to Starting a Marketing Co-op*. Davis: Regents of the University of California, 1996.

Index

About the Author

MEREDITH COLEMAN MCGEE is the coauthor of *Married to Sin*, a published poet, and a contributing writer for *The Jackson Advocate*. She founded Heirs United Investment Club, which received the Booker T. Washington Economic Summit 2010 award, and is a partner of the Coalition for a Prosperous Mississippi. She is a niece of civil rights icon James Howard Meredith. McGee previously served as a community organizer for Southern Echo, as a business developer for the Mississippi Association of Cooperatives, as an assistant director of development for Voice of Calvary Ministries, as an account executive for *The Mississippi Link*, and as owner of Sunrise Foods # II (TS & M Super Stop). She is a rural fellow and a Billie Jean Young Scholar through the Rural Development Leadership Network. McGee holds a bachelor's degree in legal administration from University of West Florida and a master of arts in rural community development and public policy from Antioch University McGregor (now Antioch University Midwest). Her next book, *Odyssey* (a collection of poems and other writings), will be released in the spring of 2013.